D0021401

THE FRUGAL GOURMET COOKS · WITH · WINE

JEFF SMITH
Illustrations by Gary Jacobsen
With articles on tasting
and selecting wine
by Father Corbet Clark

William Morrow and Company, Inc.
New York

Also by Jeff Smith

The Frugal Gourmet (1984)

Permission to reprint has been kindly granted as follows:

Recipe for "Vegetables North Beach" from *Flavor of North Beach,* Chronicle Books, San Francisco.

Recipe for "Little Joe's Vinaigrette" from *Little Joe's Italian Cookbook,* Chronicle Books, San Francisco.

Recipe for "Prawns Sauté" from Scott's Seafood Grill & Bar of San Francisco.

Recipe for "Braised Beef Bouqueterre" from the California Culinary Academy of San Francisco.

Recipe for "Eggplant Salad, Sammy's Style" from Sammy's Famous Roumanian Steak House, New York.

Recipe for "Spicy Italian Pork Sausage" reprinted from *Home Sausage Making* by Charles Reavis ($7.95, Garden Way Publishing, Schoolhouse Road, Pownal, Vermont).

Recipe for "Loin of Pork with Grapes" from *The Encyclopedia of French Cooking* courtesy of Octopus Books Limited, London.

Recipe for "Baked Onions Au Gratin" copyright © The Frugal Gourmet, originally appeared in *Redbook* magazine.

Recipes for "Green Rice" and "Risi e Bisi" reprinted with permission of Macmillan Publishing Company from *The Pleasures of Italian Cooking* by Romeo Salta. Copyright © Romeo Salta, 1962.

Recipe for "Al Cribari's Barbeque Pot Roast" courtesy of Albert Cribari, Wine Master, Cribari & Sons Winery, Fresno, California.

Recipe for "Hooker's Pasta" from *Pasta, Cooking It, Loving It* copyright © by Carlo Middione. Reprinted by permission of Harper & Row, Publishers, Inc.

Recipe for "Vegetable and Champagne Soup" reprinted by permission from *California Wine Lover's Cookbook,* The Wine Appreciation Guild, San Francisco.

Library of Congress Cataloging-in-Publication Data

Smith, Jeff.
The frugal gourmet cooks with wine.

Includes index.
1. Cookery (Wine) 2. Wine and wine making.
I. Title.
TX726.S64 1986 641.6′22 86-12679
ISBN 0-688-05852-3

Printed in the United States of America

5 6 7 8 9 10

BOOK DESIGN BY GINGER LEGATO

To my kind and supportive friends
in Chicago . . .

all three million of them.

• Acknowledgments •

Wine has the wonderful ability to remember its past and the many factors that colored its flavor. One taste and the wine tells everything. All of the powerful factors that gave age and flavor to this book are people. So, a toast . . . and with a very large glass!

To Lester Baskin, who first brought me to an appreciation of the vine.

"To absent friends—though out of sight we recognize them with our glasses."

To those who have trimmed the vine of my own life, so that it might bear more fruit. To Sara Little, Leroy Ostransky, Fr. Corbet Clark, Al Cribari, and Brian St. Pierre.

"Friendship is the wine of life. Let's drink of it and to it!"

To those who have offered such support to this effort. To Maria Guarnaschelli, my editor, who calls me brazen, my agent, Bill Adler, who calls me with the countdown, to Gary Jacobsen, our gracious illustrator, and to Vinita Pattison, who can type night and day.

"Here's how!"

To the four toughies who quietly support . . . Dory, Ivana, Sue, and Karen.

"Bottoms up!"

To WTTW in Chicago. Frank Liebert, who dared me to do this, to Tim Ward, who helped me do this, and to my crew, who did this. To Ralph, Chris, Michael, Tim, and David. To Bosco, Fonzie, Herbie, Betsey, Bruce, Marvin, Rick, Kim, Ray, and maid Marion.

"Salute!"

To Black & Decker Small Kitchen Appliances and to Elkay Sinks, who helped bring me to your home.

"Prosit!"

To the Fields, Harriet, Ronald, Rachel, and Hanna, who helped test and taste, and whose criticism ran from "interesting and yummy" to "double yuk."

"Eat, drink, and be merry!"

To my family, who tasted and cleaned and begged me to stop creating so many leftovers.

"May our feast days be many and our fast days be few!"

And, to the people of the city of Chicago. I have dedicated this book to you because you have changed my life . . . and you seem to be enjoying it as well.

"May you live all the days of your lives!"

And to those who have helped but feel forgotten. Forgive me for I am not as good at remembering as is an old bottle of wine.

"Bless you!"

• Contents •

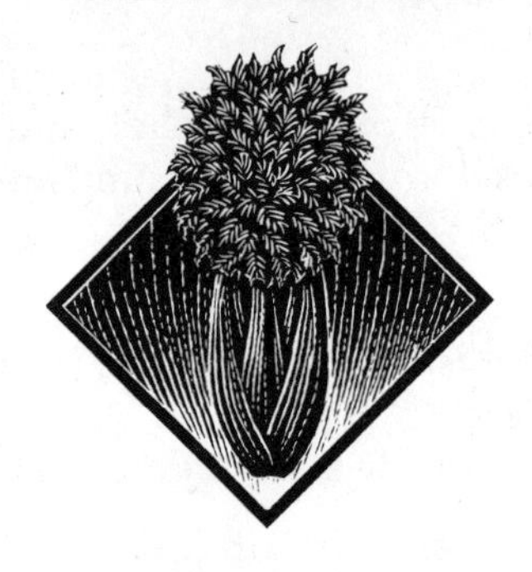

INTRODUCTION

Good wine is a necessity of life.

—Thomas Jefferson

Wine is a food, and it is to be treated as a food, not a romanticized beverage to be drunk only on special events. It will help you be more creative in your cooking, cut down on your desire for salt, raise the normal meal to that of an occasion, and it will help your appetite. All of this occurs without leaving any alcohol in the food, since the alcohol evaporates when cooking. All that is left is flavor, health, and class.

That is what this book is all about.

The roots for this project are varied. It was my executive producer and friend, Frank Liebert, at WTTW, Chicago, who first suggested such a theme. He knew of my love for wine and was eager that I explain how it could be used creatively in cooking. We have tried to do that very thing with my television series out of the Windy City. You will find the shows and recipes for each in the Glossary. The special section on "The Background" will give you an affectionate description of Dr. Lester Baskin, a man whose influence I continue to feel each day, long after his death. He was the man who first helped me understand . . . no, he demanded that I understand . . . the connection between wine and health. Al Cribari, a third-generation Italian wine maker from California, has caused me to think about wine and body chemistry, particularly as it pertains to our addiction to salt. His insights and friendship have been most helpful to me.

Then there is Leroy. It is hard to explain his place in all of this. It is always hard to explain Dr. Leroy Ostransky. He is not a particularly devoted wine connoisseur, but he loves good wine. His gift to me has been his constant refusal to endure the "put-on." For Leroy the phony attitude, in any camp, is just totally objectionable, and he will tell you so. I had become aware of this part of Dr. Ostransky when I was a student in his music literature classes at the University of Puget Sound, in Tacoma. He is one of the truly fine teachers under whom I have been honored to learn. But he is murder on phony music trends or cheap composition. And he is murder on wine phonies.

A wine phony is simply a person who wants to use wine for the sake of snobbery and pretension. No, wine is to be enjoyed. Leroy once interrupted a very formal wine tasting at my old shop in Tacoma. Several well-known wine experts were seated about a private table tasting wine in small but loud slurps, and then giving the wine points for color, bouquet, finish, legs, all of that wine taster type talk. Leroy became so bored and upset with the scientific approach, the utter ostentatiousness of the event, that he howled, "There is a big difference between what you guys are doing and what I am doing. You are tasting wine. I am drinking it!" He was right, of course. Wine is to be savored the way food is. In order to bring us to our appreciative senses he continued, "The question is not how many points a wine gets for color or body, the real question is: Is it spaghetti wine or isn't it spaghetti wine!" The last wine we drank that day was my pride and joy: a fine Chateau LaTour. We were all so busy tasting this noble bordeaux that no one spoke. That wine tasted like a blessed classic. Leroy growled, "Now, that's spaghetti wine!"

I am hurt and insulted by advertising campaigns that perpetuate the kind of wine-as-snob-food attitude that Leroy so dislikes. In advertising, wine is presented as something you need to make you feel important and wealthy. Ads feature gorgeous women in white furs standing in courtyards alongside fancy black limos. Of course, a glass of wine is in their hands. Wine is a gift of God and it is a food. We need not romanticize it or we will wind up with people who drink wine for the wrong reason, just as high school kids take up smoking in order to feel important. Nonsense!

As a result, many people are intimidated by the whole wine mystique. There should be no threat to enjoying wine. After all, there are no real rules that must be followed. Drinking wine is not like playing golf. You can enjoy wine any way you wish. The fancy wine tasting words, the "in" words, have now changed from "fruity, bold, finesse, body, bouquet," to such descriptive terms as "wet dog, mustard, old socks, blackberries, and chocolate." So it seems to me that the enjoyment of wine is up for grabs. Enjoy it on your own terms.

There are also people who are going to be a bit uneasy over the fact that a United Methodist minister is urging them to cook with wine. I am sure that it has something to do with our Puritan upbringings. I really believe that wine must not be thought of as a demon in its own right. While it is true that some people overindulge in wine drinking, it is not true that the way to prevent your children from such overindulging is to tell them to avoid wine altogether. The Yale Alcohol Studies of some years ago indicated that those groups who enjoy wine at the table produce college offspring with fewer alcohol problems than groups that abstain. To put it bluntly, the Roman Catholic and Jewish students (whose cultures treat wine as a food) have fewer alcohol problems than the Baptists and old camp Methodists. I think that is still somewhat true, even on today's campuses. Don't make a big deal of wine in your home and your children in turn won't make a big deal of it when they go off to college seeking freedom and independence. Wine is a food. Regard it very matter-of-factly. Avoiding something as wonderful as wine because some people misuse it just doesn't make sense to me. Saint John Chrysostom saw the same problem in the early church. "If you say, 'Would there be no wine' because of the drunkards, then you must say, going on by degrees, 'Would there be no steel,' because of the murderers, 'Would there be no night,' because of the thieves, 'Would there be no light,' because of the informers, and 'Would there be no women,' because of adultery." He makes an interesting point. And he made his point in the fourth century.

Wine and food celebrate each other. With a little planning you can match foods to wines and produce wonderful results, for both the wine and the food. Some wines make certain foods taste better than they actually do, and some foods make some wines better than they ever could be without the support of the food. In cooking, wine is simply an essential, a basic.

I remember my first glass of wine. Our next-door neighbor, in Seattle, was a lovely man from Italy. He designed and made fine accordions in his basement, and he made wine down there, too. While I was visiting him one day with my mother, Mr. Petosa came into the front room to offer wine to his wife and his guest, my mother. I was twelve years old and very surprised to see that there were four glasses on the tray. He offered me a glass of his wonderful sweet wine as if it was a very normal thing to do. For Mr. Petosa it was normal. But I watched my mother's eyes as she stared at me. I reached for the glass and thanked him. My mother played it cool and said nothing, though I knew she was uncomfortable. She has always seemed to have confidence in my ability to make sound decisions. I have tried to do the same with my own boys, and as they were growing up they tasted wine often at our table, from little glasses, true, but they have always seen wine as a matter-of-fact food.

I have arranged this book in such a way so as to coax you to read the articles first. That way the recipes and uses of wine in cooking that follow will make more sense to you. The sections at the back of the book on entertaining with wine, a Frugal Gourmet wine cellar, wine tastings, etc., are contributions by my dear friend, Fr. Corbet Clark. He is both an Episcopalian priest and wine authority, and the two go together well in him. You will love his insights. Together we have provided wine suggestions for each main course, but feel free to choose whatever you wish, and don't be afraid to use whatever you may have on hand. On page 42 you will find a list of the most used wines in my cooking.

In short, this book is about enjoyment. So I offer it with a great deal of affection for you, my reader. We shall have a good time together in the kitchen, and at the table. And after reading the sections on wine as history, medicine, and theology, you will better understand what it is that I am about.

I bid you peace.

—JEFF SMITH

Lent, 1986

GLOSSARY

PRACTICAL HINTS • KITCHEN EQUIPMENT • COOKING TERMS • INGREDIENTS AND FOOD DEFINITIONS • HERBS AND SPICES • THE TELEVISION SHOWS AND RECIPES FOR EACH • HINTS ON ENTERTAINING •

• Practical Hints •

• KITCHEN EQUIPMENT •

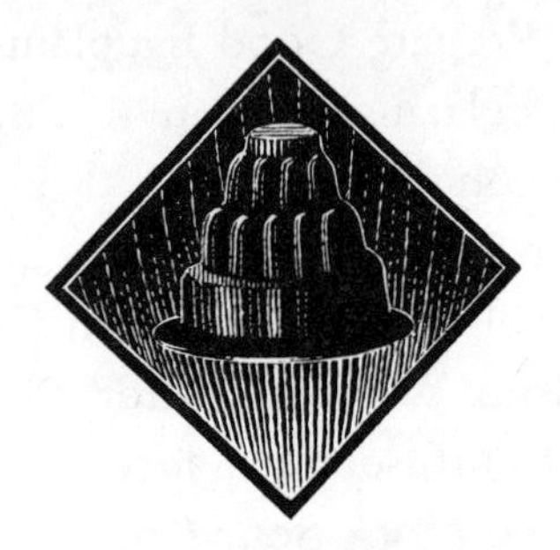

I suppose that if you were to walk into my kitchen you would question the meaning of frugal. I have more equipment than I can possibly use, because I love the stuff. My wife, Patty, used to threaten me with divorce each time I brought home some new dishes or pans, or perhaps a new corkscrew. Now she just avoids the kitchen.

I may have too much equipment, but the real issue in kitchen equipment is a matter of quality. There is no point in buying cheap equipment since you will just have to replace it over and over again. Frugal means that you don't waste anything, and that certainly goes for money. Buy good equipment to start with and you will be happy with it for years. That is a much more frugal attitude.

Find a good restaurant-supply house and do some shopping there. You will be surprised at the good things you will find at fair prices. Don't forget to check in their back room where they keep all the used equipment. They sell it at low prices and most of it is in good shape.

KNIVES

Be careful of the knife that looks modern or contemporary but simply doesn't cut properly. I am conservative when it comes to knives because they are your most important kitchen tools. I choose the old standard French-style knives. When you purchase knives be sure to choose those that fit your hand and can be sharpened easily. The stainless steel knives that you buy in the dime store or department store are generally difficult to work with because they are made to go into dishwashers. They are not made for cooks. Buy good knives that are made of high carbon steel, and then keep them sharp with a sharpening steel. Most will not stain.

I use the following constantly:

10-inch chef's knife
Boning knife
Paring knife
Long slicing knife (thin)
Sharpening steel

Keep your knives very sharp. A dull knife will force you to work too hard, and it will slip and cut you. Better to have a very sharp knife that will work for you with little effort. Use your sharpening steel often, and carefully.

I am particularly fond of Henkel's knives from Germany. They are expensive, but I have never had to replace one. You will also be happy with Elephant Brand Sabatier Knives from France. They are good quality and not quite so costly.

Chinese Cleaver: I could not cook without my Chinese cleaver. They are not expensive and once you learn to use one you will find yourself depending upon it for many kitchen jobs. There are two basic styles. The thinner one is for vegetables and the thicker for meats and light bone cutting or "hacking." Either will cost between $10 and $15. Do not buy stainless steel cleavers. Go to a Chinese or Oriental market, where you'll find a cleaver of carbon steel.

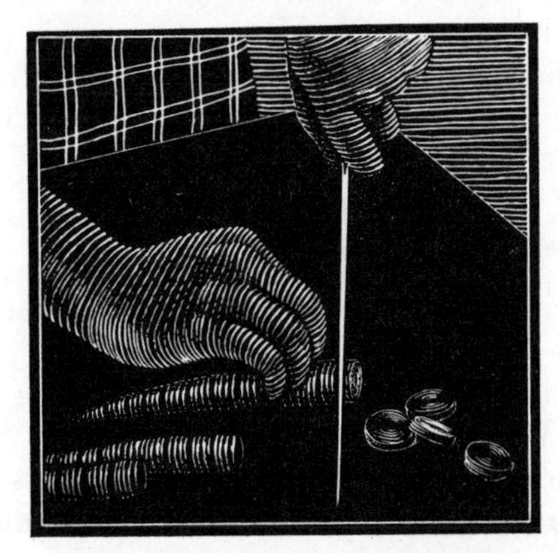

HINT: Hold Your Knife Properly When Cutting
I find that the easiest and most efficient way to handle a knife is also the safest. Hold the knife as shown in the illustration, and hold the food with the opposite hand, *with your fingers bent under.* Let your knuckles be your guide to where your knife is cutting. If you stick your fingers out, you will cut yourself. Keep them bent under.

HINT: To Clean Your Knives
If your knife is sharp and you wish to scrub it with a green scrubbing cloth in order to remove stains, please remember that you will dull the edge of the knife and probably cut yourself as well unless you lay the knife down flat on a countertop. Scrub the knife on one side and then turn it over.

POTS AND PANS

Good pans will make good cooking easy. Pans that are thin and flimsy can offer only burning, sticking, and lumps. Buy good equipment that is heavy. You will not be sorry.

I have made only a few changes in my opinions about pots and pans since the last book. You may, however, detect those few.

Tips for Buying Good Equipment

1. Don't buy pots and pans with wooden or plastic handles. You can't put them in the oven or under a broiler.
2. Buy pans that fit your life-style, that are appropriate for the way you cook. They should be able to perform a variety of purposes in the kitchen, and avoid pans that can be used only for one dish or one particular style of cooking. I am thinking of such things as upside-down crepe pans. What for? They have no other use and are therefore not a frugal investment.
3. Choosing the material for pans

Aluminum is fine for cooking. Buy heavy restaurant-quality from a restaurant-supply house. Wearever and Leyse are both good brands. Keep it clean with a 3M green scrubbing cloth and do not store food in it. The old scare about getting aluminum poisoning from such pans need not concern you. As long as you are cleaning your pans and you do not cook foods high in acid (such as tomatoes or lemon juice) in the pans you will have a good time with them. As a matter of fact, I store no food in aluminum. Many now come coated with Silverstone and are a joy to use.

I am not particularly fond of anodized, or blackened, aluminum pans. The advantages are few and the cost is almost doubled.

Copper pans are a joy. The heat always stays even during cooking and the pans look great on your wall. Buy good heavy weight with tin lining, as thin decorative pans are not functional. Don't worry if it is not French. Chile and Korea are now making good pans, and my favorite copper pieces come from Brooklyn.

The brand is Waldo Copper and more reasonable than European brands.

Stainless Steel pans used to have no place in my kitchen because they have been so cheaply made and are so thin. Plastic handles, the works. You know the brands. Several companies, however, are now making heavy stainless wear with metal handles and an aluminum core sandwiched inside the bottom. These are great. Plan to spend some money, but you will probably be giving them to your grandchildren someday. Restaurant-supply houses carry several brands. I am fond of a product called Centurion. You should be able to find this in both restaurant-supply houses and large department stores. Be ready for a big bill for very good equipment.

Cast Iron with Porcelain Enamel pans are heavy but wonderfully versatile. You can cook in them, serve in them, and they are easy to keep clean. I have a whole collection of the stuff. Le Creuset is probably the best-known brand. French made, it is of high-durable quality.

4. The pots and pans I use the most:

 20-quart aluminum stockpot, with lid
 12-quart aluminum stockpot, with lid
 4-quart aluminum sauteuse, with lid
 10-inch aluminum omelet and crepe pan, lined with Silverstone
 12-inch aluminum frying pan, lined with Silverstone, with lid
 Several cast-iron casseroles, with lids; varying sizes (I like Le Creuset)
 Copper baking pans and saucepans; varying sizes

HINT: Pans for Cooking With Wine
Do not use black iron or aluminum pots when stewing or cooking with wine. These pans are fine if you are simply browning something and then deglazing the pan with wine. When simmering a food in a wine sauce, however, it is best to use porcelain-covered cast iron, stainless steel, or ceramic pans.

CASSEROLES AND BAKING PANS

I have a good selection of porcelain casseroles with lids. They are easy to clean, very attractive, and useful. I both cook and serve in them. You can find many from France, but Hall China, here in America, is now offering wonderful porcelain casseroles and bowls of all sizes and of heavy construction.

Glass casseroles are also attractive and work well. Corning is bringing in a great selection from France.

MOLDS

I have had the most wonderful time lately using molded foods for buffet suppers. (See the section on Molded Dishes.) You can find food molds in many shapes and of many materials. Some of my favorites are simply old glass molds that I have found in English antique stores. Tin, copper, porcelain, and aluminum molds also work well.

MACHINES AND APPLIANCES

Please do not fill your kitchen with appliances that you rarely use. I do not have a deep-fryer nor a crock pot nor an electric hamburger fryer nor an electric egg cooker nor . . . well, you get the point. I would rather spend my money on good equipment that I can use in many different ways.

I do regularly use the following:

Food Mixer: Choose a heavy machine, one that will sit in one spot and make bread dough, grind meat, cake batters, etc.

Food Processor: I use my food processor less than my mixer, but a processor is great for special chopping and mincing jobs. It is also a must for a good pâté.

Food Blender: There are many good ones on the market. Just remember to find a brand that you trust, from a company that will stand behind what it sells.

Electric Coffee Grinder: This small German gadget is great for grinding spices and herbs. I rarely use mine for coffee.

HINT: To Cure or Season Your Pans
Remember the rule: *Hot pan, cold oil, foods won't stick.* That means that you never put the oil in the pan and then heat the pan. You heat the pan first; add the oil and then, immediately, the food. You will have much less sticking that way.

An aluminum frying pan is cured, or seasoned, by this simple method. First, wash the pan with soap and water, using a cloth or sponge, never a steel soap pad or steel wool pad. Rinse the pan, and dry it. Never put soap in your frying pan again! Heat the pan on a burner until quite hot, and then add 2 or 3 tablespoons of peanut oil. Gently swirl the oil about the pan, and allow the pan to cool. Heat the pan again, add more oil, cool, and repeat once more. Your pan is now ready for use. If foods should stick or if you have trouble getting the pan clean, do not resort to soap. Instead rub the pan with a green scouring cloth, or try a bit of peanut oil and salt; rub with a paper towel to clean.

Stainless steel frying pans cannot be cured. Everything will stick. For this reason I urge you never to buy stainless steel frying pans.

Chinese woks are cured according to the directions on page 322.

SilverStone frying pan: This excellent product from Du Pont is easy to care for. Wash once with soapy water, and cure just as you cure aluminum frying pans (see above). Care for the pan in precisely the same way.

Black iron pans are cured as you would a wok (see page 322).

Toaster Oven/Broiler: This is one of those things that you do not invest in because you already have an oven. But for smaller jobs such as baking potatoes and heating rolls, it is not frugal to heat your whole oven. We use ours at least twice a day. Buy one that mounts under your cabinets, off the counter. Ours is a Black & Decker so I know it will last.

Microwave Oven: Yes, I do use mine. I love it for heating leftovers, thawing frozen vegetables, melting butter, or for assisting when I am in the midst of a big meal. It is a very frugal device since it helps you use your leftovers.

Cordless Appliances: The most wonderful thing has taken place in American kitchen design. Since we need space for several members of the family to cook at once, why not use cordless appliances that allow a person to work anywhere in the kitchen. My favorite is the Portable Handy Mixer from Black & Decker. You have seen me use it on the show and I have two in my own kitchen. They also make a portable mixer for larger jobs. No cord means that you have greater use of your kitchen.

Boiling Water Faucet: I would never have believed that this device, which attaches to your sink, could be so useful. You always have boiling water for soups, tea, instant things, blanching—anything. Find one of good quality so that you don't have to worry about it. Elkay makes fine equipment.

SPECIAL ITEMS

Wok: I use my Chinese wok constantly. It is an ingenious device that is actually much larger than it appears because of its shape. Buy a plain steel wok. Aluminum woks heat too evenly, and the advantage of a Chinese wok is a "hot spot" in the center of the pan where juices and liquids can evaporate; an aluminum wok does not have the necessary hot spot. A copper wok will have the same problem. A stainless steel wok cannot be seasoned properly, and food will always stick. Finally, an electric wok generally heats too slowly and cooks too slowly, so the advantage of the wok—quick heat and rapid cooking—is lost.

Bamboo Steamers from China: These stackable steamers, usually three or four in a set, allow you to steam several dishes at once. The advantage that these have over metal steamers stems from the fact that bamboo will not cause moisture to condense and drip on your food. Metal steamers drip, always. I use bamboo steamers for Chinese cooking and for warming up leftover dishes. Find them in Oriental markets or in any good gourmet shop.

SPECIAL GADGETS

Flavor Injector: This is a strange-looking plastic and metal device that resembles a hypodermic needle. Used for injecting flavors and juices into meats. You can find them in any gourmet shop.

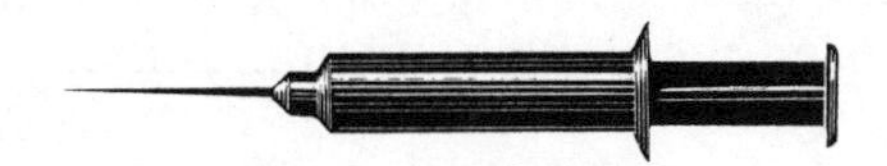

HINT: Clear Off Your Countertops!
Most kitchens have little space in which to work because the counters are covered with electric appliances. Put away everything that is not absolutely necessary so you have space to work and spread out. You'll be much more comfortable. Or consider purchasing appliances that will mount underneath your kitchen cabinets, rather than sitting on the kitchen counter. You'll get your counters back!

Garlic Press: I cannot abide garlic in any form except the form that the Creator intended. Buy a Susi garlic press, also labeled Zyliss. Looks expensive to start with, but it remains the best on the market.

Lemon Reamer, Wooden: Any good gourmet shop should have one of these for you. Works better than any other lemon juicer I have ever seen. You can now find them in plastic and they work well.

Heat Diffuser or Tamer: This is an inexpensive gadget that you place on your burners to even out and reduce the heat. It will save you from a lot of burned sauces. Any gourmet shop or hardware store should have this item.

Wooden Spoons and Spatulas: I never put metal spoons or gadgets into my frying pans or saucepans. Metal will scratch the surface, causing food to stick. Buy wooden gadgets, and avoid that problem. Yes, they will be clean if you wash them in soap and water and allow them to dry before putting them away. Never soak your wooden cooking gear.

Pepper Mill: I love freshly ground black pepper. You cannot get that kind of flavor in something preground. I have three good mills: one for the dining room table, one for the kitchen stove, and one for my traveling cooking kit. Buy pepper mills made in France; they last much longer than the Japanese versions.

Flour Dredger: Looks like a big salt shaker. Fill it with flour and have it ready to help you flour things with much less waste and time.

Meat Pounder: A heavy disk of metal with a handle that will help you prepare thin slices of meat for dishes such as Chicken Marsala (page 170). You can also use a short length of two-by-four wood.

Plastic Sheeting: Very helpful when you are pounding meat thin or when you need another piping bag. Inexpensive and available at most large lumber yards. Ask for clear vinyl sheeting, 8 millimeters thick.

Fire Extinguisher: A must for your kitchen. Buy one that will work on electrical fires as well as stove fires. Talk to the salesperson. You will sleep better at night.

Marble Pastry Board: This can be purchased in many sizes. I could not make bread or pastry without one.

Wine Bottles: Save old ones for oils, soy sauce, vinegars, and of course, wine.

Oil Can: I keep near the stove, a tiny spouted little can filled with peanut oil. The little spout means that I use less oil in my cooking. Found at any gourmet shop.

Kitchen Scale: Buy something that is fairly accurate. It will be helpful in baking perfect French bread and in judging the size of meats. You will be able to buy things in bulk and save some money.

Sausage Stuffer: If you intend to get serious about sausage then you must have a sausage stuffer. Some electric mixers offer these as optional equipment. Or you can find a "sausage funnel" in your gourmet shop.

Stainless Steel Steamer Basket: This is a great help. It will fit any size pan and is readily available and very cheap.

Ice Cream Maker: The section on sherbets and ice cream will be a place of particular value to you if you purchase a Donvier Ice

Cream machine. It is inexpensive and foolproof, and can be found in any department store or gourmet shop.

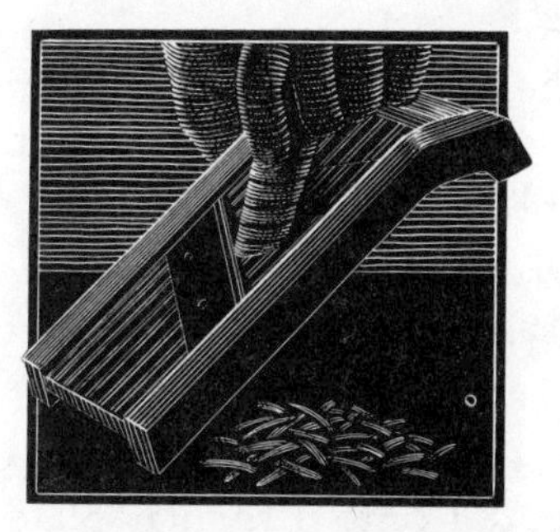

Mandoline: This is a most wonderful device for cutting vegetables into thin slices or into julienne-style matchstick cuts. The French model is very expensive, but the Zyliss people have brought one in from Germany that is plastic with steel cutters. It works better than any I have seen on the market. The brand name is Moha.

Cold Water Coffee Maker: The Toddy Coffee Maker is a great device, if you are still drinking coffee. It makes a coffee extract from cold water, thus cutting down on the acid and oils in the coffee. You can find this device in any fancy coffee shop or good gourmet shop. It is not expensive.

THINGS I LOVE BUT COULD PROBABLY DO WITHOUT

When I buy a new piece of cooking equipment I must always ask myself, "Do you really need this to be creative?" Often the answer is no, but I buy it anyway. I have few electric gadgets like hot dog cookers or electric egg poachers or upside-down chicken cookers. These I can do without. But the following items are in my kitchen because I love them:

Glass Plates, Dessert Size: These are cheap, and I use them for salads, pastas, and desserts. They make the food look attractive.

Big Dinner Plates: I hate eating a nice dinner that has been squeezed onto a regular plate. Buy big ones, 12 inches in diameter. You may have to go to a restaurant-supply house.

Good Wineglasses: I do not enjoy drinking wine from a glass with a lip or heavy rim. Shop carefully and you will find good wineglasses without lips, and they are not expensive. I own several dozen big ones, glasses big enough to make even a medium-class wine look and taste fine. You can get carried away with wineglasses because there are many different kinds for several different wines. Start with a 10-ounce clear tulip glass; it will do fine for any wine. Your collection can grow as your wine cellar grows.

Big Serving Platters: I find these in antique stores and junk shops—serving platters from a time gone by. It is great fun to put an entire main course on a gigantic platter and bring it to your friends and family.

Big Wooden Salad Bowls: I don't really believe that you can make a good salad in glass or metal. Metal is harsh in its appearance, and glass is too fragile for a proper mixing or tossing of the salad. A wooden bowl can be seasoned with a clove of fresh garlic and thus impart a most delicate flavor to your greens.

Pitchers and Serving Jugs: My sons never put a container of milk on the table, and every liquid is served in a pitcher of some sort. It makes the event of the meal seem a little more important to all of us.

Piping Bags and Tips: These will help you add some class to your efforts in the kitchen. I use three sizes the most—10, 12, and 14 inches. Choose several tips that will be helpful in cake icing, in piping cheese, mayonnaise, or potatoes.

HINT: Plan a Second Sink

A second sink will be helpful in dinner preparations. If you can possibly afford it, consider adding a second sink (preferably stainless steel, they're terrific) at the other end of the kitchen next time you remodel. It will mean the person who is preparing the salad, baking bread, or even making dessert will stay out of the way of the regular cook.

HINT: Three Kitchen Stations

Encourage your children, or your mate, for that matter, to help in preparation of the evening meal. In order to do this you must prepare stations for each member of the family. There should be at least three cooking stations, each with a cutting board, in your kitchen. This can be done by clearing the counters of any excess appliances.

• Cooking Terms •

AL DENTE

This is a wonderful Italian term that means to cook "to the teeth." It means nobody wants soggy pasta. Cook pasta to the teeth, or until it is barely tender, still a bit firm. It is much better that way . . . and the way Italians intended same to be eaten.

BLANCHING

Plunging food into boiling water for a very few minutes (the time varies and will be explained in each recipe). The food is then removed and generally placed in cold water to stop the cooking process. The purpose is to loosen the skin of a vegetable or fruit, to set the color of a vegetable, or to cook a food partially in preparation for later completion of the dish.

BROWNING MEAT

When preparing stews and cassoulets, I usually do not flour the meat. You then end up with browned flour instead of browning the natural sugars that are in the meat itself. Use a hot pan, and do not crowd the meat or cook it slowly. The meat should be seared or browned very rapidly, thus giving color to the stew and sealing the meat cubes.

CHOW (STIR-FRY)

A basic cooking method in the Chinese kitchen. Generally a wok is used, but you can also do this in a frying pan. The food is tossed about in a hot pan with very little oil, in a process not unlike sautéing.

DASH

Generally means "to taste." Start with less than 1/16 teaspoon.

DEGLAZING A PAN

After meats or vegetables have been browned, wine or stock is added to the pan over high heat, and the rich coloring that remains in the pan is gently scraped with a wooden spoon and combined with the wine or stock. If there is excess fat in the pan, you may wish to pour it out before deglazing.

DREDGING IN FLOUR

Meats or fish, generally sliced thin, are rolled about in flour in preparation for frying or sautéing. The flour is usually seasoned.

HACK

When cutting up chickens or thin boned meats, one "hacks" with a cleaver, thus cutting the meat into large bite-size pieces and retaining the bone. The presence of the bone will help keep the meat moist during cooking. Do this hacking carefully.

MARINATING

Meats or vegetables are soaked for a time in a flavoring liquid, such as soy sauce, wine, oil, or vinegar. The time of the marinating varies with the recipe.

MATCHSTICK OR JULIENNE CUT

Cut vegetable into thin slices, stack the slices, and then cut the slices into thin sticks, like matchsticks.

MIREPOIX

A blend of vegetables and herbs sautéed and used to flavor other dishes.

PINCH OF HERBS OR SPICES

Usually means "to taste." Start with less than 1/16 teaspoon, and then increase if you wish.

POACHING

Gently cooking fish, meat, or eggs in stock or water at just below a simmer. The liquid should just barely move during the poaching process. When fish or eggs are poached, a little vinegar or lemon juice is added to the liquid to help keep the food firm.

REDUCING

Boiling a sauce or liquid over high heat until it is reduced in volume, generally by half. The result is a very rich concentration of flavors.

ROUX

A blend of oil or butter and flour used to thicken sauces and gravies. The fat and flour are mixed together in equal amounts over heat. If a white roux is desired, the melting and blending are done over low heat for a few minutes. If a brown roux is desired, the flour is cooked in the fat until it is lightly browned.

SAUTÉ

This term comes from a French word that means "to jump." In cooking, sauté means to place food in a very hot pan with a bit of butter or oil and to shake the pan during the cooking process so that the food jumps about. Thus one can cook very quickly over high heat without burning the food. Not unlike Chinese chowing, or stir-frying.

SHOT

A liquid measurement that amounts to very little, or to taste. A shot of wine is about an ounce, but a shot of Tabasco is less than 1/16 teaspoon.

STIR-FRY

See Chow.

TERRINE

A dish used for the cooking and molding of coarse-ground meat loaves or pâtés. Also the meat itself. The dishes can be found in many styles and materials.

• Ingredients and Food Definitions •

ANCHO CHILIES

Find in any Mexican market or large delicatessen. Remove seeds and soak before using.

ANCHOVIES (flat, canned)

Used for salads and Italian and French cooking. Buy in cans from Portugal or Spain. Very salty.

BALSAMIC VINEGAR

Italian wine vinegar that has been aged for years. This is wonderful and no other vinegar can quite compare. From Modena, Italy. Find in any Italian market. The fancy food shops will charge you much too much money for this item.

BEAN CURD

Cheeselike product made from soybean milk. Buy fresh in cakes at Oriental markets or in produce sections of most supermarkets. It can also be purchased in cans, but the flavor is far inferior. Fresh bean curd looks very much like a 5-inch rectangular block of soft but firmly shaped white cheese.

BEAN SPROUTS

You will find these fresh in most produce sections. The canned variety is so tasteless that you should omit them if you cannot find fresh ones.

BÉCHAMEL SAUCE

Basic white sauce made of milk or stock and thickened with a roux of flour and butter also known as cream sauce. See page 287 for recipe.

BEEF STOCK

Please make your own. Canned consommé or bouillon is little more than salt. Real beef stock is rich in flavor and inexpensive to make from fresh bones. See page 100 for recipe.

BOK CHOY

A vegetable resembling Swiss chard in shape, but much lighter in color and flavor. A member of the mustard family, it can be found fresh in most supermarket produce sections and in Oriental markets.

BRINE-CURED OLIVES

Sometimes called Greek olives or Calamata olives. Imported. Find in Italian markets or good delicatessens. California black olives are a very poor substitute.

BULGUR WHEAT

Processed wheat for Middle Eastern dishes. Three grinds: fine, medium, and coarse. Find in Middle Eastern stores or in fancy supermarkets or gourmet stores.

CALAMATA OLIVES

See Brine-Cured Olives.

CAPERS

Pickled buds used in salads and dressing. Found in any good supermarket.

CELLOPHANE NOODLES

Noodles from China made from the mung bean, the same bean from which bean sprouts grow. Find in Oriental stores and in some supermarkets. Also called glass noodles, sai fun, or bean threads.

CHEESE

This list is offered simply because I use all these in my recipes, though I rarely have them all on hand at once. Buy fresh cheeses, and grind or grate your own. Find a good delicatessen or cheese store, and you should find each of the following:

Parmesan (imported, aged Italian, if you can afford it)
Romano
Swiss (Wisconsin fine for baking; imported for snacking)
Monterey Jack
Kasseri (Greek)
Asiago (my favorite Italian pasta cheese for grating)
Bleu (imported Danish excellent for cooking)
Feta (Greek)
Mizithra (dried ricotta in hard ball)
Ricotta
Brie

CHILI SAUCE

Bottled product found in the catsup section of market.

CHINESE INGREDIENTS

Please look under individual headings for each of the following items:

Bean Curd
Bean Sprouts
Bok Choy
Cellophane Noodles
Dow See
Fermented Black Beans
Five-Spice Powder
Glass Noodles
Hoisin Sauce
Hot Bean Sauce
Hot Pepper Oil
Mein See
Mushrooms, Chinese
Napa
Oyster Sauce
Red Chili and Garlic Paste
Rice Wine Vinegar
Sai Fun Noodles

Sesame Oil
Soybean Condiment or Jam
Soy Sauce
    Light, Dark
Sweet Bean Sauce
Szechuan Peppercorns
Turnip Ball

COCONUT MILK

Canned or frozen in Oriental markets or fancy supermarkets.

CREAM

When the term is used in this book, I mean half-and-half or whipping cream. Either may be used, or you may dilute whipping cream with milk.

CREAM SAUCE

See Béchamel Sauce. Same item, only made with cream instead of milk; very rich.

DIJON MUSTARD

A style of mustard from France. A good American brand is Grey Poupon.

DOW SEE

See Fermented Black Beans.

FERMENTED BLACK BEANS

Fermented black beans are a classic condiment in Chinese cuisine. Buy in Oriental markets, and then keep in tightly sealed glass jars. No need to refrigerate.

FILBERTS

Sometimes called hazelnuts, these are delicious in many ways in the kitchen. If you use them a lot, buy in bulk from food co-ops or from health food stores. They are cheaper that way.

FILLO DOUGH (PHYLLO)

Thin sheets of dough for Middle Eastern baking. Can be found in most delicatessens. Also spelled phyllo dough.

FIVE-SPICE POWDER

A Chinese blend of spices. Find in any Oriental market, or blend equal amounts of powdered cinnamon, ginger, anise, fennel, and clove. Some blends contain a bit of black pepper.

GLASS NOODLES

See Cellophane Noodles.

GRAPE LEAVES

Treasures from Greece; can be found in Middle Eastern markets in glass jars, packed in brine. Drain and use.

HAZELNUTS

See Filberts.

HERBS AND SPICES

See pages 43 to 48.

HOISIN SAUCE

A soybean and pepper sauce common to Chinese recipes. Find in some supermarkets and in any Oriental market.

HOT BEAN SAUCE

Found canned or in jars in Oriental markets. It is mein see with hot pepper oil. That blend would be a good substitute.

HOT PEPPER OIL

May be purchased in Oriental markets.

HOT SAUCE

Tabasco or Trappey's Red Devil will do well. Found in any supermarket.

IMITATION MAYONNAISE

Low-fat mayonnaise and called imitation simply because it does not have all the fat of ordinary mayo. Good for low-fat diets.

JAPANESE INGREDIENTS

Please look under individual headings for each of the following items:

- Bean Curd
- Bean Sprouts
- Bok Choy
- Mirin
- Miso, Light or Dark (red)
- Mochiko
- Mushrooms, Chinese
- Napa
- Panko
- Rice Wine Vinegar
- Sake
- Sesame Oil
- Short-Grain Rice
- Soy Sauce
    - Light, Dark, Japanese
- Tenkatsu-sosu

KASHA

Buckwheat groats common in Middle Eastern dishes. Find in any large supermarket or Jewish market. This is delicious stuff!

LEEKS

These look like very large green onions in the produce section. Wash carefully because they are usually full of mud.

LIQUID SMOKE

For use in barbecue sauce. Find in the condiment section of the supermarket. I like Wright's.

LOW-FAT MAYONNAISE

See Imitation Mayonnaise.

MEIN SEE

The remains of the process of making soy sauce. Very rich soybean jam used in many Chinese dishes. Can be found in Oriental markets under this name or soybean jam or condiment. Refrigerate after opening.

MIRIN

Sweet rice wine vinegar. Find in some supermarkets and in any Japanese market or add a bit of sugar to regular rice wine vinegar.

MISO, LIGHT OR DARK (red)

Fermented soybean paste used as a basic ingredient in many Japanese dishes. Find in any Japanese market.

MOCHIKO

Sweet rice flour. Find in any Japanese market. No substitute.

MOCK SOUR CREAM

Made from cottage cheese in order to eliminate fat. Easy to prepare. See recipe on page 289.

MUSHROOMS, CHINESE

Find in Oriental markets. Soak for 1 hour in water before cooking. Trim the stems and save for chicken soup.

MUSHROOMS, DRIED EUROPEAN

Cepe, boletus, or porcini. These are delicious, but if they come from Europe they will be terribly expensive. Find an Italian market that brings them in from South America, and you will pay only somewhere between $10 and $14 a pound. The real Italian dried mushrooms will cost you a fortune! You may also find some that are domestic. In any case, keep them in a tightly sealed jar at the back of your refrigerator, where they will keep for a year.

NAPA

Sometimes called Chinese celery cabbage, it can be found in many supermarket produce sections and in Oriental markets.

OILS

Butter
Olive Oil
Peanut Oil
Sesame Oil

These are the common oils that I use in my kitchen. I use little butter, but I enjoy the flavor and dislike margarine. See page 128 for a discussion of olive oil.

ORZO PASTA

Pasta shaped like rice. Great for pilaf. Find in Middle Eastern or Italian shops or in a good delicatessen.

OYSTER SAUCE

Classic cooking sauce from China. While actually made from oysters, it has no fishy taste. Found in Oriental markets. Refrigerate after opening.

PANKO

Japanese bread crumbs. These are special and can be found in any Japanese market. You might substitute fresh white bread crumbs, oven dried.

PASILLA CHILIES

Find in any Mexican market or large delicatessen. Remove seeds and soak before using.

PESTO

A sauce of northern Italian origin, made from fresh basil, olive oil, garlic, cheese, and pine nuts. Great on pasta or in soups and on vegetable dishes. Best to make your own. For recipe, see page 126. You can purchase this frozen or in glass jars at Italian markets.

PICKLING SALT

Used in pickled meat dishes. Find in any supermarket.

PINE NUTS

Expensive little treasures that actually do come from the large pinecone of Italy. Find in Italian markets, or substitute slivered almonds.

POLENTA

Coarse cornmeal used in Italy. You can find this in any Italian market, or use ordinary cornmeal.

PROSCIUTTO

A very firm and salty ham from Italy. The imported version is illegal in America but you can find fine domestic versions in Italian markets. Buy very little at a time, as it is very rich. Have the butcher slice it very thin. You may substitute sliced Virginia ham or, in some recipes, a fully cured uncooked ham will do.

RED CHILI AND GARLIC PASTE

Very hot Chinese sauce made of red peppers and garlic. Find in Oriental markets, or substitute garlic and Tabasco. It is worth the effort to find this delicious sauce.

RED CHILI PASTE WITH GARLIC

See above. Same product.

RICE WINE VINEGAR

Delicious vinegar used in Oriental cooking. Find it in Oriental markets.

ROASTED SWEET PEPPERS

Find in jars in any Spanish or Italian market. These are not regular pimientos.

SAI FUN NOODLES

See Cellophane Noodles.

SAKE

Japanese rice wine. Necessary to good Japanese cooking. Find in Japanese markets or liquor stores.

SALTPETER

A common kitchen chemical used in preserving meat or preparing corned beef or pork. May be purchased at a drugstore.

SEMOLINA

A very coarse ground flour made from hard durum wheat. Buy in an Italian grocery. Wonderful for gnocchi, and flavor is far superior to farina, which may be used as a substitute in a pinch.

SESAME OIL

Used as a flavoring in Oriental cooking but not a cooking oil. Find this at an Oriental market. Used for flavoring a dish at the last minute. The health food store version is not made from toasted sesame seeds, so the flavor will be very bland.

SESAME SEEDS

Buy in bulk, and then roast them by stirring them in a hot frying pan until lightly browned.

SHALLOTS

A cross between garlic and onion. Classic ingredient in French cuisine. Find in the produce section or substitute a blend of onion and garlic.

SHORT-GRAIN RICE

This is a Japanese variety grown in this country. Used in Italian dishes as well as Japanese dishes, it should be readily available.

SOYBEAN CONDIMENT OR JAM

See Mein See.

SOY SAUCE

Light, Chinese: To be used when you do not wish to color a dish with caramel coloring, which is what dark soy contains. Find by this name in Oriental markets.
Dark, Chinese: Used in dishes in which you wish to color the meat and sweeten the flavor with caramel sugar. Most common soy sauce.

Japanese: Chinese soy is very different from Japanese. Japanese soys contain much more wheat flour and sugar. I like Kikkoman. Buy in larger quantities at a Japanese market. It is cheaper that way and will keep for years.

SWEET BEAN SAUCE

Find canned in any Chinese market. Use mein see with a bit of sugar for a substitute.

SZECHUAN PEPPERS

A wild peppercorn from China, sometimes called fagara. Not hot but very flavorful. No substitute. Find in any Chinese market.

TAHINI

A light paste made of toasted sesame seeds and sesame oil—almost like a peanut butter. Used in many Middle Eastern dishes, it is to be found in Middle Eastern delicatessens or fancy supermarkets.

TENKATSU-SOSU

A wonderful sauce for pork tenkatsu. Find in any Japanese market. It is much like sweet English steak sauce.

VINEGARS

These are the vinegars that I use most in my cooking. They are all readily obtainable in most markets.

Red Wine Vinegar
White Wine Vinegar
Plain White Cider Vinegar
Tarragon Wine Vinegar
Rice Wine Vinegar

WHITE SAUCE

See Béchamel Sauce.

WINES FOR COOKING

All of these wines are readily obtainable, with the exception of the Chinese rice wine. That you can find in any Chinatown. Please do not buy wines that have salt added; they are labeled "cooking wine" but really should not be used at all. My rule is simple: If you can't drink it, don't cook with it.

The wines are arranged in the order of their importance in my kitchen.

Dry Red Wine
Dry White Wine
Dry Cocktail Sherry
Dry Marsala
Sweet Marsala
Madeira
Dry Vermouth
Sweet Vermouth
Brandy
Tawny Port
Ruby Port
Champagne
Chinese Rice Wine
Sake

• Herbs and Spices •

HINT: Buying, Storing, and Grinding Herbs and Spices

Herbs and spices are some of the most important ingredients in your kitchen. Try to keep them as fresh as possible, so don't buy them in large amounts. Keep them in tightly sealed jars. Try to buy most herbs and spices whole or in whole leaf form; they have much more flavor that way. Crush the leaf forms as you add them to the pot. Or use a wooden or porcelain mortar and pestle. For seeds that are hard to grind, I use a small German electric coffee grinder. I have one that I use just for spices; it works very well.

Try to buy the herbs and spices that you use most frequently in bulk, and then put them in your own spice bottles. The saving realized here is about 70 percent. Hard to believe, but it is true. Find a market that has big jars of spices, and you will also be amazed at the difference in flavor.

ALLSPICE

Not a blend of spices at all, but a single one. Basic to the kitchen. Buy it ground because it is hard to grind.

BASIL

Common in French and Italian cooking. Grow it fresh or buy it dried, whole.

BAY LEAVES

Basic to the kitchen for good soups, stews, etc. Buy whole, dried, or if your area is not too cold, grow a bay laurel tree. I have one in Tacoma.

BOUQUET GARNI

A bouquet of fresh herbs, generally tied in a bundle or in a cheesecloth sack. Usual ingredients include parsley, thyme, and bay leaves. You can use all these dried.

CARAWAY

Whole seed, dried.

CARDAMOM

Common in Scandinavian and Middle Eastern dishes. Rather sweet flavor. Expensive. Buy whole seed, and grind as you need it.

CAYENNE PEPPER

Fine-ground red pepper, very hot.

CHERVIL

Mild French herb that resembles parsley in flavor. Buy dried, whole. Use in soups and sauces.

CHILI POWDER

Actually a blend of chili peppers. Buy in the can, ground. Usually I use the hot blend.

CINNAMON

Hard to grind your own. Buy it powdered.

CLOVES

I use both the powdered and the whole.

CORIANDER

The dry, whole seed is common in Mediterranean cooking. The fresh plant, which looks like parsley, is common in Chinese, Indian, and Mexican cuisines. You may see the fresh form in your supermarket listed as cilantro or Chinese parsley.

CUMIN

Used in Mexican, Middle Eastern, and Indian cooking a great deal. Buy powdered in the can, or buy the whole seed and grind it. The flavor is much brighter with the whole seed.

CURRY POWDER

An English blend of many spices. Many brands are on the market, so choose one that seems to fit your family. I like Sun from India. Or a much more powerful one may be made at home. Find a recipe in any good Indian cookbook or see page 227.

DILLWEED

Dried, whole. Great for salad dressings and dips. Common in Middle Eastern cuisine.

FENNEL

A seed that resembles anise or licorice in flavor. Produces that special flavor in Italian sausage. Buy it whole, and grind it as you need it.

FILÉ

Ground sassafras leaves, along with a bit of thyme. Essential in New Orleans cooking. Also called gumbo filé.

FINES HERBES

A blend of parsley, chervil, tarragon, and chives. Very mild and very French. Used in everything from salads to soups and stews.

GARLIC

The bulb, of course. Use only fresh. And buy a good garlic press!

GINGER, FRESH

Very common in Chinese dishes. Buy by the "hand," or whole stem, at the supermarket. Keep in the refrigerator, uncovered and unwrapped. Grate when needed.

GREEN PEPPERCORNS

These delicious peppercorns are literally green and come packed in water in a tin. Find them in any gourmet shop or good delicatessen.

JUNIPER BERRIES

These are to be found dried in good spice shops. They will remind you of the flavor of English gin. There is no substitute.

MACE

The outer covering of the nutmeg. Not as strong as nutmeg, but rich in flavor. Buy ground. Common in early American cooking.

MARJORAM

Common kitchen herb, light in flavor. Buy whole, dried.

MINT, DRIED

Common in Middle Eastern dishes. Buy whole. Also makes a great tea.

MINT, FRESH

Grow this in the backyard if you can. Great for salads, mint juleps, Middle Eastern dishes.

MUSTARD, DRY

Absolute necessity if you love salad dressings. I buy Colman's, from Britain.

NUTMEG

Basic to the kitchen. Buy it in bulk, and grate your own with an old-fashioned nutmeg grater.

ORANGE PEEL, DRIED

Great for Italian tomato sauces for pasta. Dry your own by saving the peelings and letting them sit on the top of the refrigerator.

OREGANO

Basic to the kitchen. Salads, meats, sauces, etc. You can grow your own, but the best comes from Greece. Buy whole, dried.

PAPRIKA

Light, lovely flavor and color. Buy ground, imported from Hungary.

PARSLEY, DRIED

I use this rarely because fresh is better. But in salad dressings or anything that is to be kept for a few days the dried lasts much better. Buy whole.

PARSLEY, FRESH

Buy in the supermarket produce section, or grow your own. I like the Italian variety, which has flat leaves and a bright flavor.

PEPPERCORNS, BLACK

Buy whole, and always grind fresh. See page 24.

RED PEPPER FLAKES, HOT, CRUSHED

Also labeled "crushed red pepper flakes." Buy in bulk, and use sparingly. The seeds make this a very hot product.

RED PEPPERS, HOT, DRIED

Buy whole. Necessary for many Chinese dishes and in southern cooking.

ROSEMARY

Basic to the cooking of Italy and southern France. Grow your own, or buy whole, dried.

SAFFRON

Real saffron is from Spain and is the dried stamens from the saffron crocus . . . and costs $2,000 a pound. Buy it by the pinch or use Mexican saffron, which includes the whole flower and is very cheap. Works well; just remember to use much more.

SAGE

Basic kitchen herb. Grow your own, or buy it whole, dried.

SAVORY

Close to thyme in flavor. Common in French cooking. Buy it whole, dried.

THYME

Necessary to good French cooking—soups to stews to meat dishes. Buy it whole, dried, or grow your own.

TURMERIC

Bitter orange-colored spice that gives the flavor and color to pilafs, curry powders, and Indian braised dishes. Buy it ground. Cheaper in Middle Eastern and Indian stores.

• *The Television Shows and Recipes for Each* •

SHOW 201

The Tapas Buffet

SHOW 202

The Molded Meal

SHOW 203

The Sandwich Buffet

SHOW 204

Whole Meal Soups

SHOW 205

Cheese for the Meal

SHOW 206

Coffee for Entertaining

SHOW 207

The Stand-Up Buffet

SHOW 208

The Pasta Buffet
Pasta Bagna Cauda 149
Tortellini and Green Pea Salad 139
Pan-Fried Ravioli with Bleu Cheese Dressing 152
Pasta with Olives 148
Stuffed Shells 150

SHOW 209

The Sit-Down Buffet
Crown Roast of Pork 219
Panties for Decoration 220
Cold Brussels Sprouts Salad 133
Turkey with Salsa Mole Poblano 192
Rice with Chilies and Cheese 159
Chicken with Olives 178

SHOW 210

Casseroles for the Buffet
Lamb with Fennel Sausage and Eggplant 304
Duck, Pork, and Sausage 305
Philippine Chicken and Pork 307

SHOW 211

Tabletop Cooking
Hoko Pot 310
Sukiyaki 354
Korean Barbecue Steak Strips 312
Onion Rings with Herb and Egg 313

SHOW 212

Entertaining 2, Just 2
Baby Shrimp with Butter Lettuce Salad 137
Whitefish with Filbert and Lemon Sauce 120
Scallops in Pesto 125
Chicken Under a Brick 179

SHOW 213

Sherbets and Ice Creams

Lemon Ice Champagne 397
Peach Sherbet 397
Raspberry Ice 398
Watermelon Ice 398
Ginger Ice Cream 399

SHOW 214

Beef in Wine

Pot Roast with Port and Mushrooms 202
Beef with Bleu Cheese 205
Quick-Fried Beef Venetian Style 208
Beef in Wine on Skewers 210

SHOW 215

Chicken in Wine

Chicken Marsala 170
Chicken and Ham Rolls 172
Chicken with Tomatoes, Shallots, and Vermouth 173
Garlic Chicken with Garlic, Garlic! 174
Chicken Stuffed in the Front 176

SHOW 216

Cooking with Champagne

Oysters in Champagne Sauce 123
Vegetable and Champagne Soup 112
Fish in Champagne Sauce 121
Carrots in Champagne and Dill 265
Champagne Cream 393

SHOW 217

The Italian Kitchen

Real Garlic Toast 341
Italian Gravy 341
Italian Sausages in Gravy 343
Spareribs in Italian Gravy 344
Chicken Gizzards with Marsala 344
Dried Codfish in Cream Sauce 347

SHOW 218

Vegetables in Wine?

SHOW 219

Confit!

SHOW 220

Duck in Wine

SHOW 221

Eggplant!

SHOW 222

First Courses and Wine

SHOW 223

The Chinese Kitchen

SHOW 224

The French Kitchen

SHOW 225

The Japanese Kitchen

SHOW 226

Lamb in Wine

SHOW 227

Meat Marinades

SHOW 228

Pork in Wine

Pork in Wine and Vinegar Sauce 213
Grilled Pork New Orleans 216
Piggies Tied Up 215
Pickled Pork Ribs with Lentils 217

SHOW 229

Pasta and Wine

Green Onion Pasta 144
Pasta with Anchovy and Onion 147
Semolina Dumplings with Ham 161
Baked Polenta 160
German Dumplings 162
Fried Rice Balls 163

SHOW 230

Rabbit in Wine

Rabbit in Red Wine 230
Rabbit in Mustard Sauce 231
Rabbit in Vermouth 232
Plain Fried Rabbit 233
Rabbit in Green Peppercorns and Wine Sauce 234

SHOW 231

Salads—Wine or No?

White Wine Vinaigrette 128
Garlic Dressing 129
Burgundy and Herb Dressing 129
Pesto Vinaigrette 130
Mayonnaise 131
Eggs and Mayonnaise 132
Pasta and Green Onion Salad 134
Egg in Tomato Salad 135
Cauliflower Salad 136
Tuna and Potato Salad 136

SHOW 232

Sauces from Wine

SHOW 233

Sausages and Wine

SHOW 234

Seafood and Wine

SHOW 235

Soup and Wine

SHOW 236

The Spanish Kitchen

SHOW 237

Wine Specialties

SHOW 238

Wine Vinegars

SHOW 239

Dessert

Hints on Entertaining

All people should eat and drink, and enjoy the good of all their labor; it is the gift of God.
—Ecclesiastes 3:13

The point behind entertaining is simple: Everyone is to have a good time, and that includes the host or hostess, and the cook. In times past that meant that you brought in help and they took care of preparations and serving so that you could spend time with your guests. Who can afford such a practice now? Certainly I cannot, so I suggest that you learn to take good advantage of the buffet or sideboard.

Prior to common use of the table, everyone lay down on a couch and the food was brought before you. In biblical times one ate all formal meals in this manner, thus pointing out a major historical error in Leonardo da Vinci's wonderful painting, "The Last Supper." They are all at table! And no buffet or sideboard in sight.

The background of the sideboard is simple. The servants put the food there and then served the dining table from the sideboard. Thomas Jefferson, one of our great cooks and fine entertainers, was very upset over the fact that the servants would get in the way of the conversation when they were presenting the food. And they never seemed to stop interrupting! Since Tom was also one of our greatest American inventors and architects, he set about to solve the problem by keeping the servants out of the dining room.

He invented the lazy Susan, and he placed one in a doorway between the kitchen and the dining room. The rotating table was built to fill the door and have two sections, or sides, separated by a middle board, or wall. The kitchen staff would load the cooked dishes on their side of the board and turn it so that the food appeared in the dining room. The handsome Mr. Jefferson, dressed in his red velvet coat, with a head of red hair to set everything off, would instruct his guests to help themselves and sit down. When a course was finished the staff would turn the device again, bringing the empty dishes and leftover food into the kitchen. This marvelous invention was then restocked with the next course and turned again to the dining room. The guests were fed well and their dinner conversation never interrupted.

The American custom of using the buffet has its roots in President Jefferson's lazy Susan. Rather than expect a staff to feed us we urge our guests help themselves to the buffet table and be seated. The advantages of this method are many, the most important one being the comfort of the host or hostess. I believe that the comfort of the head of the house comforts the guests. Buffet tables work for stand-up parties as well as for sit-down dinners.

But our culture always seems to go too far with a good idea. Rather than just celebrating a self-service buffet for a formal sit-down dinner, we had to invent fast-food stops. I suppose it has something to do with our Puritan background and the belief that the only real value in our culture was to be found in work, not in satisfying any one of the passions. To this day many of us feel guilt when "dawdling about the table." That is time wasted. Work, for the night is coming, and the enjoyment of one's food under such circumstances is simply self-indulgence. Could we possibly want to fall into two of the seven deadly sins, sloth and gluttony? And the pioneer attitude did not help the enjoyment of the table one bit. The belief that the tough life was good for you resulted in our thinking that we should not be choosy about our food and that we should eat what is put in front of us. And in a hurry! Europeans still cannot understand why we eat so fast.

The first fast-food bar opened in this country, of course. It was in New York City in 1895 and was called The Exchange Buffet. Businessmen, anxious to fulfill the Puritan work ethic, ran in and chose their food from a long buffet. They waited upon themselves and ate standing up. You can't get more American than that. The fast-food business was born.

You can avoid the pains of the fast-food buffet by following a few simple rules that will help you enjoy your guests and the meal, and they will better enjoy you. Brillat-Savarin, the great French food and dining philosopher of the eighteenth century, said, "You are responsible for the entire comfort of your guests all of the time that they are under your roof." Nothing makes a guest more uncomfortable than the knowledge that the hostess is about to go crazy trying to get food on the table. Use the buffet and calm down.

Some hints for the comfortable use of the buffet:

1. Don't cook over your head. Cook dishes you feel comfortable making and which you do not have to be cooking at the last minute.
2. Choose dishes that will stand up well on the buffet while people mill about waiting to see who is going to be the first to violate the Puritan ethic and admit that he or she is hungry. Good casseroles and heavy vegetable salads are great on the buffet. And molded courses always add some character and class.
3. Avoid putting things on the buffet that need to be cut. It is always a hassle. Have everything prepared so that people can easily dish up a fine meal. The Chinese do not understand our practice of expecting our guests to work at the buffet, or even the table, and do the work that the cook should have done. That is why they find a knife and fork ungracious. The chopsticks indicate that the cook is complimenting you by having everything ready to go into your mouth. No butchering at the table. There is a profound lesson for entertainers in this somewhere.
4. Nothing that is covered with a thin and runny sauce should be on the buffet. You know someone is going to spill it on your new carpet and the guest will feel terrible.
5. Have the silverware already on the dining table and the plates at the buffet. If you must have the silverware and napkins on the buffet for a stand-up gathering, remember to place the silverware at the end of the line, not at the beginning with the plates. I have never learned to balance a plate, hold a napkin, and juggle a setting of silverware while trying to dish up my own plate. Yet that is the way most people set up the buffet.
6. Rehearse the meal. Put the plates on which you are serving the main courses on the buffet, empty, of course, perhaps the day ahead. Then go through the line yourself and decide if it will work. Anticipate problems that your guests might encounter due to a misplaced dish or the wrong order of things.
7. Cook everything ahead of time. Be ready to set the buffet with very little work on your part.
8. Pour a glass of sherry for yourself, very dry, and relax with your guests. Everything is ready and you deserve a good time, too. Your friends will think that you are the most organized person they have ever seen, and you will know that it is true!

THE BACKGROUND

A glass a day keeps the doctor . . .

I want to tell you how I came to understand wine as food, as a joy, as a cooking component in my kitchen.

There are some events in your life that cause you to wonder what you would be or be doing had that event not happened. Such is the event of my meeting with Dr. Lester Sidney Baskin.

Pearle—Mrs. Baskin—and I were involved in a course in aesthetics at the University of Puget Sound. I was all of twenty, but I had a student supply parish in a nearby farming community for which my bishop had made me responsible. I felt I was far beyond the years marked twenty. Mrs. Baskin and I took to one another immediately. This older woman had come to a class in the appreciation of the arts. We gossiped during class. We chatted after class I thought this woman had some class! On the day that she invited a couple of us to her home for lunch, I could not help but say yes. We climbed into her Jaguar, the only one in Tacoma at the time, and set off for lunch. I was far beyond the years marked twenty.

The arrival at the home brought on a request from the hostess. Would we be so kind as to put a case of wine in the cellar? The wine was to be found in the trunk. While unloading the wine in the cellar I decided I had to meet this man, this Dr. Baskin. He had a wine cellar! My Methodist background told me that he must be some kind of an extravagant man to have such a thing. And old wines. Some of them going back decades!

Our meeting came about soon enough. After a symphony concert, a brief introduction on the stairs, the usual remark about joining them for dinner sometime . . . the usual. When the call came the next day, the call about the dinner, I was shocked. Why should a man as famous and as respected as this surgeon invite a college sophomore to his table? The evening was off to a great start until I said no to a glass of wine. I was a Methodist pre-theological student. The evening was grand, the food superb, and the other guests, people from all styles of life in the arts and medicine, fascinating. The next day came the call that has brought forth this article, this book, my person, my love for the table and for food and theology.

Lester Baskin called me late in the day and asked if I could join him. Upon arrival at his home I found Pearle to be absent. Dr. Baskin brought forth a tray, an old bottle, and two glasses, only two. "Is it true," he asked, "that your bishop does not want you to drink wine?" I said, "Yes." He poured two glasses from the bottle and extended his hand, carefully holding a bit of crystal that was filled with a dark amber liquid. "Drink this!" I did. "Oh, I have never tasted anything so beautiful. What is it?" "It is an 1875 California port, and you will never be the same again." I have not. And I am thankful. He led me from my Puritan upbringings to a true appreciation of wine as a necessity, as a food. He also warned against misuse. In the following years he researched biblical theology so that I could fully understand the biblical position on wine. He researched the writings of John Wesley, the founder of Methodism, and made it very plain that Wesley was a great lover of wine. And he brought me to his table, over and over again for years. He was right. I have never been the same. Nor have many of our bishops. Many of them now enjoy a bit of wine with dinner, so things are certainly looking up!

A lesson in wine from a lesser person probably would not have had such an effect upon me. In this man, however, I saw a warm and earnest concern for the welfare of all people, not just his patients. Pearle and Lester always had some faces or couples at table who were new in town . . . and he wanted them to meet everyone. I don't even know where he found all these people. On one occasion I would be seated next to a highly respected artist. At the next dinner party I sat next to Lester's cabinetmaker, his repairman. I met people at his table who have changed my life . . . drastically. And both he and Pearle knew it. "We love to collect people," Mrs. Baskin once said. "Our art collection is second."

The journey on which he took me is filled with memories and stories, because he was filled with memories and stories. When he heard that my current bishop frowned on wine and thought that anyone who drank wine was automatically a "wino," Baskin wrote out a prescription. It was on his regular prescription pad from Western Clinic, in Tacoma. He was a founding partner of the first socialized medical clinic west of the Mississippi. It is now called The Baskin Clinic. On his clinic prescription pad he had written the following order: "Jeff Smith is to have a glass of red wine each night before retiring. It will calm him down and it is much better for him than any medicine." He gave me a copy for my bishop! He included, along with the prescription, a copy of Salvatore Lucia's wonderful book, *Wine as Food and Medicine.*

He relished stories about the wines that he served at dinner. In the midst of a formal dinner party he would jump to his feet and begin to tell us that we were drinking the very wine that Benvenuto Cellini used to bring to the mother of his girl friend. He and the mother would drink the wine, the mother would fall asleep, and finally, he and the girl could run off. On and on the stories would go.

For the first two or three years of our friendship, Lester would offer the 1875 port to all at the table. Then, as the supply dwindled, he would sneak it only to me. He called one day while I was a student and bid me hurry to his home. A terrible thing had happened. Because I loved him so much I ran as fast as I could, hoping that the news would not be too painful. He sat me down and produced a bottle of the 1875 port. "This is the last one," he said. "We should drink it together!" And we did.

When I returned home from graduate school my second year, a dinner party was held for me by some dear friends, John and Kathryn Magee. In the midst of the party I told them that I thought I had fallen in love with a girl from New York named Patty. All listened as I described her . . . but Lester said nothing. "But, does she like wine?" he asked. I explained that her mother was a bit conservative and a Methodist at that. "Oh," he replied. Nothing more was said until the day that I was to return to the East Coast. He met me just before my departure with a small plastic bottle from his pharmacy. The label read:

> Prescription #1875 From Dr. Bacchus
> For: Jeffrey L. Smith
> Take as often as needed for depression.

The bottle contained some of the old port, of course. He pressed it into my hand as if he were carrying the solution to the problems of the Western world. He instructed me to give Patty a sip of this wine at my first available opportunity. If she did not like it I was to promise him that I would never see this woman again. Don't ask me why, but I agreed. I called Lester at three in the morning to tell him that the bottle was a success. Patty and I were later married.

Following my ordination in 1965, I returned to my room to find a message from the doctor. I called and he asked, "Well, can you do it? Can you change perfectly good wine into, ugh, blood?"

We both laughed with affection and then he offered me a line I have never forgotten. "Jeffrey, listen to me. Always remember that no priest should ever raise the chalice and pronounce the presence of the healing blood of the lamb without being able to turn to the congregation and state the vintage, and state it proudly!" He was right, of course.

His occupation as a traumatic orthopedic surgeon placed him in the midst of many tense and seemingly unsurmountable situations. Another physician who worked with him told me that during one very tense moment in surgery all were leaning forth to see what the brilliant surgeon would do next. Lester looked into the faces of tension and said, "Say, have you ever tasted a 1955 Château La Tour?"

He gave my mother a bottle of La Tour '55 and instructed her to deliver it to Patty and me at our wedding in New York. My mother got off the plane, dressed in white clothing (a loss in New York air), and handed me the bottle. She heaved a sigh of relief and only then did she speak to Patty, a daughter-in-law-to-be whom she had never seen. I do not know what the doctor told her about that wine.

At the Baskin table I was introduced to the most fascinating people. Many of them have remained the dearest of friends. The two Baskins loved to gather an unusual crowd . . . and they loved to shape people's lives. Why else would they have brought a college sophomore to a formal dinner table where artists, medical doctors, musicians, and philosophers, all sat? Oh yes, and Gil, the cabinetmaker. Pearle and Lester wanted me to understand, and from the very beginning, what joys could be shared with wonderful and diverse people at table . . . and over a glass of wine. I felt very special in their presence, but through the years I learned that a good portion of our city felt special in the eyes of the Baskins. The University of Puget Sound, where I had been both a student and the university chaplain, awarded each of them an honorary degree of arts and letters. These two had influenced so many lives together that one degree for either was out of the question. So, we had two Dr. Baskins.

You will better understand the effect this man had on people if you can understand his image of himself as a physician. He was a highly respected surgeon, head of the surgery staff, and sought after by many in difficult cases. One evening he returned to his home from work, almost late for dinner. I asked him how the day had gone and he gleefully told me of a surgical procedure that he had performed that day. He had saved the arm of a child. I remarked that it was wonderful that he was such a great healer. He turned on me and chided me for such a remark, a chiding for which I was not prepared. But now you will understand my fascination with the man. "I am not a healer," he said. "I participate in healing. God heals. I do not. And the fact that some medical procedure that has always worked in the past works in this particular situation always amazes me."

While a young pastor, I called upon Lester when he was recuperating from sickness and surgery. His dear son Michael asked me to walk with the two of them down the hallway. I was carrying the I.V. bottle and the doctor was taking his first uncomfortable walk after surgery. As we went down the hallway, I felt his painful steps . . . and I was miserable. Do you know what he was doing? He was looking into the other rooms and shouting encouragement to his patients on that floor. He saw one who needed something and the Baskin bellow that good nurses loved, and inattentive nurses dreaded, rang down the hall.

Wine was a healing symbol for him. When he raised a glass of his beloved wine, a Protestant such as I was finally made to understand the Kiddush prayer, "Praised art thou, O Lord, our

God, King of the Universe, Creator of the Fruit of the Vine." The table and the glass of wine brought together the goodness of life that we must feel for one another as God's people. The sharing of the feast and the cup were basic to Lester's sense of well-being and happiness. This insight remains his greatest gift to me.

Sometimes his willingness to share got him into mild trouble. Mrs. Baskin told me that during the Depression the very young doctor was an intern. Those were difficult times financially, for Pearle and Les, and what little income appeared was important indeed. When he returned from the hospital Pearle would ask how the day had gone. Lester often had to give a reply something like this: "Well, Mrs. Johnson came in with her six children. I saw them all. You know, Pearle, her husband can't work anymore." And then there would be a pause and he would quietly explain that rather than charge her he had given her twenty dollars.

The last thing that the kind doctor said to me came in response to a tape I had given him. He was dying and he heard the tape, a discussion of the history of wine as medicine. I had been asked to present the lecture for the Washington State Enological Society. He heard the tape and then called me. He told me that I could not understand this yet, but someday I would, when I had sons. "It makes you very proud when one of your sons succeeds." I had been adopted through a glass of wine.

Pearlie has not stopped giving dinner parties. They are still among my most joyous of times, although she often bids me pour the wine and sit in the doctor's chair. The first time this happened I found tears in my wine. They were mine!

Mrs. Baskin asked me to offer the blessing over the wine at his funeral. And I offer the same toast again. It is of unspeakable grief that he is not here to witness the publication of this book on wine as food and necessity. He was my teacher, my doctor, and my friend. L'Chaim, Lester!

THAT SINGLE FLUID

WINE AND HISTORY

How simple and frugal a thing is happiness: a glass of wine, a roast chestnut, a wretched little brazier, the sound of the sea. . . . All that is required to feel that here and now is happiness is a simple, frugal heart.

—*Zorba the Greek*
Nikos Kazantzakis

I can think of no fluid that has changed the course of history more than wine. It is one of our most elegant foods, it is our oldest medicine, it is a profound theological category, and a source of joy and color and peace. Wine has the ability to reduce disasters to small inconveniences. It is a source of truth and beauty, an inspiration to artists and lovers, and a diplomatic blessing bringing together strangers around a common glass and table. It is a symbol of community, since only a pervert would buy a fine wine and not immediately consider the possible persons with whom he might share it. Finally, wine teaches us that we are not in full control of history, for wine is not our invention. It is a gift of the Creator, an unexpected, undeserved gift, and totally beyond our arrogant attempts at driving the meaning of history into the ground. Wine is beyond our death as it is beyond our life. To drink a fine wine is to drink history, history as the Creator intended it to be. (And you thought you were just buying a cookbook!)

Historians argue about the background of what we call civilization. There is good evidence for claiming that wine helped give birth to civilization, and the claim is not as farfetched as it may seem. Alexis Lichine reminds us that civilization grew out of agriculture, for when the first nomads planted seeds and waited for the crop to grow, their wanderings ceased. Since wine takes longer to grow, to develop, for the vine to actually give fruit, longer than any other crop we know, the nomadic tribe would be well settled in one place by time the grapes came about, settled long enough to begin practicing the domestic arts. Since we were all nomads at first, we can understand and appreciate the momentous change brought about in our ancient life-style with the dawn of domesticated grapes, with the beginning of a community that watched the grapes develop, and created artistic and cultural treasures in the meantime.

We do not know who first discovered wine. Surely wine is not to be called an invention as wine comes about on its own. We simply crush a bit here and there and the process of wonderful fermentation takes over, by its own intention. No, the discovery probably came about just as did the discovery of cheese and bread, by accident and necessity. When attempting to save milk in goatskins we discovered cheese. When attempting to save grains and doughs the wind offered wild yeasts which crept into the bowl. So, bread was accidental, too. And wine must have been first. I can see the old tent or cliff dweller munching on wild grapes. What a wonderful treat they were. His intelligence seemed to be increasing and he decided that he would save some of these round treasures for another time. Placing them in a crude stone bowl, off he went to hunt. Days later, upon his return, he discovered that his savings had collapsed and something had gone right! They had turned to wine. He gathered more grapes . . . eventually choosing to stay with the grapes . . . and, well, the first formal dinner party was not far away.

The Hittites used the word "wine" as early as 1500 B.C. We know that wine was popular and common by this period in all of Asia Minor, and it is probably there that wine developed. During the early Bronze age (2500 B.C.) wine was common in Egypt and Syria, though the name was not as we know it now. Homer was very fond of good wine, thus placing wine in classical Greece by 1000 B.C. By 500 B.C. the normal Greek diet consisted of wine, fish, bread, and oil, not far from what it is today.

By the sixth century B.C., Marseille, in southern France, boasted a thriving wine trade, though Rome also offered hundreds of wines to the Mediterranean market. Tacitus, the Roman historian, spends a great deal of time talking about the wonderful wines from the wine regions of France.

The problem of imported wines versus inexpensive local wines offers us a strange bit of history, even as early as the Fall of Rome (A.D. 200–400). The two major qualities of wine wound up in the two major economic groups in Rome, the aristocracy drinking wines imported from Egypt and Phoenicia, and the peasants drinking cheap wine from goatskins. The wine amphoras used for shipping wine were ingenious in their design. The long clay flasks had pointed bottoms so that they could be stuck in the sand that was used as ballast in the hold of old ships, and then unloaded by simply sticking them into the sand on the beach. The only problem is that they were sealed with a ceramic glaze containing a great deal of lead. Since wine is heavy with acids, the wine would dissolve the lead and carry it to the stomach of the drinker. One of the most interesting theories about the Fall of Rome maintains that the educated classes died off from drinking imported wines. We have examined the remains of the ruling classes and have indeed found a lead content in their bones that would be lethal. The peasant bodies examined did not contain this lead poison, although both classes drank from the famous Roman aqueduct, which was lined with lead. No, cold water will not dissolve lead. And the peasant drank from goatskins. It is the imported wine that is accused here.

The wine of those first centuries must have been interesting stuff, though I doubt that we would be charmed by it today. Much of it was flavored with everything from seawater to pitch to flowers. Wine kept in goatskins often tasted of pitch, since the skins were sealed with the resin from trees. To this day Greeks are fond of retsina, a wine to which resin is still added to bring back the flavors of the old days, and old days they were. Germany is still making wine flavored with flowers, May wine seasoned with woodruff blossoms being the most well known.

When the Fall of Rome came upon us the Romans had established wine trade with Spain, France, and Germany. All would have been lost had the Church not been most careful to protect the special fluid that it needed for its services.

Wine was held in high esteem in the early American colonies. The early Americans brought with them cuttings from grapes in Europe, although the New World already had wild grapevines of several varieties. Leif Ericson had called the land Vinland. The grapes produced, however, were tiny and not suitable for making wine, thus the importing of French vines. The early American fathers loved wines from Europe, and Thomas Jefferson spent a fortune each year in the French wine market. His favorite to the day he died was from Château Rusan Segla. I was at the vineyard in France a few months ago and saw carefully preserved order forms baring the signature of this great American designer, architect, statesman, cook, agriculturalist, inventor, and president.

American vines played a most interesting role in wine history. Since we had hardy wild grapevines already growing about in America, it became common practice to simply graft the European varieties of grapes onto American vines. Some of these vines were shipped back to Europe and the result was disaster. The American vines were infected with a root-eating grub called *phylloxera,* although the vines seemed almost immune to the little critter. European vines were not immune, however, and in 1870 almost all of the French vineyards were attacked and nearly wiped out by the parasite. The solution was to ship the hardy native American rootstock to France, upon which the French grapes were then grafted. So, we share with Europe the French grape varieties, and they share with us the American rootstock. Such a wonderful trade to protect such a priceless treasure—wine.

America contributed one other disaster to wine history. It was Prohibition. Originally thought of as a grand way of "legislating voluntary abstinence from alcohol," the whole period turned into a fiasco. You already know of the consequences of such legislation. We were the only nation in the Western world to experience Prohibition, and the most severe problem, as far as I am concerned, was the fact that wine was considered to be in the same category as booze or distilled liquor. Wine is very different from such spirits since wine is natural and it is not distilled. Nevertheless, American wineries, many begun hundreds of years before by Jesuit priests in California, were ordered to shut down. Only a few wineries were allowed to operate, and they were only to sell wine to the Church. So once again the Church protected its own special gift, the blessing of the vine.

In our time wines, good wines, are produced in France, Germany, Spain, Austria, Argentina, Australia, Italy, Hungary, and Israel. And America. We make some of the finest wines in the world, and you do not need to feel bad when serving a fine wine from California, or Washington, for that matter. To say that French wines are better is sheer snobbery, something that The Frugal Gourmet can do without. I have the same feeling about restaurants that print their menus in French . . . in South Tacoma! What for? We have wonderful foods in this country. I believe we eat better, and drink better wines, than just about anybody on the face of the earth.

Enjoy wine and remember the history that splashes into your glass when you pour. It goes back to ancient times, and it has been blessing us as a food, a medicine, and a symbol of joy ever since. All wines are filled with history, even inexpensive jug wines. All have history except wine coolers. The only history they can have is that of a passing fad. And I pray for their passing, soon.

THE SURE PROOF

WINE AND THEOLOGY

Wine is sure proof that God loves us and wants us to be happy!

—Benjamin Franklin

The first thing that Noah planted when the ark finally hit the beach was a grapevine. If you love biblical theology, as do I, then you know why he did this. In the ancient Hebrew world it was impossible to have a celebration of thanksgiving without wine. As far as I am concerned, it still is.

In biblical times, wine functioned as both a food product and a profound theological symbol. Hebrew was, and is, a very concrete language. Since there are so few universals, so few general terms, one had to symbolize or mytholigize in order to speak and be understood. Hebrew was a desert language, and as concrete as the desert. If you could not point to it you could not talk about it . . . without using something else as a symbol. Food and wine became a natural bit of language since you could talk about hunger and yet be speaking about one's longing for fulfillment. Salt, used as a means of preservation in the Old World, becomes a symbol of friendship under this Hebrew method of speaking. Bread, the staff of life, since you ate bread three meals a day. Oil, because it stood for fatness, or fulfillment, or joy. "Blessed is he who drips with fatness," here not meaning something designed to shock the dieting American but rather something that points to the communal nature of our being "fat" or fulfilled together, not as individuals. And wine. Enter blessed wine. Wine is "to gladden the hearts" of the people of God. It was a symbol of the fact that the Creator of the Universe loves us beyond all sense of proportion, beyond all sense of reason. Thus he gave us wine for joy. We could have gotten along without wine, I suppose, but who would want to bother? Ben Sirach, the scriptures of the Apocrypha, says that wine is one of the good things created for good people. Ben Franklin was right . . . and he was simply quoting the biblical message. Wine is proof that God loves us and wants us to be happy.

Surely this proof is still obvious and valid. The cleverness of the King of the Universe shows through in each grape. And looking for the cleverness of the Creator in Creation is precisely how the old Jewish prophets did theology! Fr. Robert Farrar Capon, author of *The Supper of the Lamb,* urges us simply to look at a grape. Yeast on the outside and sugar on the inside is a divine idea, he maintains. All we need do is crush a grape and it goes its God-given course. Indeed, something underhanded, such as pasteurization, must be done to a grape to prevent it from going its God-given course. Capon is right! The process of pasteurization was not used on grape juice in this country until Prohibition, a process put on the market by the Welch family. Up until that time all Methodist churches celebrated the Lord's Supper with wine. They always had. That all went with the marketing of the Welch family product. Is it not odd that one of our major bishops at the time of the ruling out of wine at the Eucharist was a chap named Welch? Yes, same family, same market. No, something underhanded has to be done to wine to prevent it from going its God-given course.

On occasion a well-meaning friend attempts to convince me that Jesus never drank wine. How could that be? They drank grape juice? Impossible! The juice began to turn to wine of its own accord the moment that it was pressed. I will admit that much of the wine consumed in biblical times was the result of little aging, but it was wine nevertheless. It was used as a medicine and as a symbol of joy, as it is still used in the Temple. We know that Jesus received rabbinic training. We know that He celebrated the Jewish holidays with His family. Therefore, we know that He enjoyed wine . . . as a symbol of the kindness of the King of the Universe. To this day every Jewish service opens with the Kiddush. There seems to be an unasked question on the floor of the Temple, a question that need not be asked. Nevertheless the answer is given. The question? "Just how clever is this god that you worship?" The answer? "Blessed art thou, O Lord God, King of the Universe, Creator of the Fruit of the Vine." That settles the discussion! Only the Lord could have come up with something as blessed as wine. Biblically wine was always seen as a sign of the cleverness of the Creator.

Wine was also a sign of commitment. Our image of the table is so private in our time that we have trouble understanding a culture that saw the table as the place for serious agreements, even for pacts. In ancient Israel never was a pact formed, an agreement reached, a wedding celebrated, a feast noted, without the presence of wine. It was there not just as a food but as a sign of the graciousness of the host . . . and of the wisdom of the Creator. Even in ancient Rome we find no word for treaty. The word that was used was "libation." "Let us drink together and form a pact, a libation." The older texts even talk about Moses eating and drinking with the King of the Universe upon receiving the Ten Commandments. Drinking wine with God? Yes, as a sign of intimacy.

Wine eventually became a symbol of adoption. This one is more complicated than those above, but when I finally came to understand this, the use of wine in the Church made eternal sense to me, at last. And it still does.

The image of adoption was connected with the image of blood, a symbol that still causes American Puritans to wince. But see this! In the old shepherding communities, all would have understood this image because all knew the problem of the shepherd. He would check his flock in the morning and find a new lamb . . . but the mother had died during the night. In another portion of his flock he would find a mother, sitting silently beside her child stillborn during the night. The mother would die of a broken heart and the orphan would die from lack of sustenance. All logic would tell you to put the orphan under the care of the childless mother . . . but the two would know they were foreign, and they would not accept each other. The moment of wisdom came when the old shepherd, this old Jewish philosopher and theologian, would see in this event the nature of our relationship to the Godhead. We are so separated from God, he said, that God is dying of a broken heart and we are dying from lack of sustenance. And it seems that nothing can be done. We are foreigners to one another. But one thing can be done. It is still being done by shepherds. If you slit the throat and drain the blood of the dead baby and wash the orphan in the blood of the lamb, the living mama smells her own and moves around so that the orphan can suckle, can come home to the table. This image of the blood of the lamb being the symbol of adoption was common in the early traditions, and it remains common in the Church.

Wine took on the meaning of the blood of adoption. Indeed, during the service most traditions maintain that the wine in the Eucharist actually does become the blood of Jesus as the Lamb, the One who was slain and by whose blood we are brought home for adoption. The presence of the wine in the service of the Lord's Supper has always caused me great excitement. You need not bother with the factual presence. The true presence is the issue, and the wine/blood brings us home. It is the only feast that really matters.

When Jesus blessed the wine in the Upper Room, He was not doing anything new. All Jews would have done the same at such a festival, for it was probably the Feast of Passover. When He proclaimed Himself the source of the healing blood of the lamb, however, and held forth the chalice in order to say, "Drink of this, always, and I will be with you," the wine ceased to be normal wine and participated in the very thing to which the wine points, the presence of God in the world. The Church has celebrated with wine ever since. Wherever the Church went wine had to go, or, like Noah, the Church could not celebrate.

There seems to be no time when the Church did not drink wine. The early Church Fathers and historians discuss wine at length, Pliny, from the first century, listing 150 kinds of wine on the market. Athenaseus knew of 85. During the Fall of Rome, all of this could have gone, but Mother Church needed wine and so it was protected as carefully as were the ancient manuscripts that we now call classics. From the desert, from the home of the Jews, came our three most ancient food products—wine, bread, and cheese. All are gifts of yeast. All point to the fact that we are cared for beyond our greatest hopes, since we did not invent any of these most ancient foods. We simply discovered them, as Manna in the Wilderness.

The Church continued to care for wine in a particular way. During the fifteenth century, Pope Clement so carefully tended his vineyards that we now have a whole region in France called Chateauneuf du Pape (Household of the Pope). The Chateau Pape Clément, a fine wine of the Bordeaux region, remains one of the great wines of the world, and certainly a favorite of mine. I love to drink history, for that is what wine is. It is wonderful history!

The Church's concern for and protection of wine resulted in some interesting discoveries. In ancient times one drank fine wine from flagons, enormous flagons. One had to be very wealthy to afford such vast amounts of wine. The peasants drank wine from goatskins, and obviously it was new wine since you cannot age wine in a goatskin. With the invention of the bottle, whole new possibilities were offered to the common man. But wine would die in the bottle if sealed. Wine is alive and needs just the most minute interchange with the atmosphere or death comes very soon. It was a priest, Dom Perignon, who invented the cork. It would allow just the right interaction between the air and the atmosphere so that the wine could live and breath and grow and age. More important, in terms of theology, the bottle meant that wine had at last become a great social leveler. It meant that a normal workingman could order a bottle of the greatest wines available. He did not have to live on goatskin wines nor did he have to buy a whole barrel or flagon. This is true today.

Perhaps the most popular discovery that good Dom Perignon made was the result of his genius and some accident. When he should have been upstairs in the chapel at prayers with his brothers, he was in the wine cellar playing with his new discoveries, the bottle and the cork. He knew that a still wine, or a wine that had completed fermentation, would continue to age and improve in the bottle. He removed the cork from a few and added a little more yeast and sugar and corked the bottles up again. And then, typical of the life of the Church, he watched. The day he tasted his new creation the brothers were again above him singing hymns in the chapel. Tradition has it that the good priest tasted the now carbonated wine and ran to the bottom of the stairs, yelling and interrupting the service of worship. "Brothers, come quickly," he cried. "I think I am drinking stars!" He had invented champagne.

You see, there are a lot of wonderful things about Church history that you did not know! The caring of wine by the Church is one of those wonderful things.

I do not expect the Church's love affair with wine to cease, ever. Wine is the gift of the Creator, a symbol of joy, and that by which we are brought to the Table of the Feast of our own meaning. There! I bet you'll never let your parish serve cheap wine again!

THE ORIGINAL MEDICINE

WINE AND HEALING

No longer drink only water, but use a little wine for the sake of your stomach and your frequent ailments.

—I Timothy 5:23

Wine is the oldest and safest medicine in the world. It is also one of our most ancient liquid foods, milk being the only drink that could possibly be more ancient.

The use of wine as a medicine goes back so far in history that it is difficult to trace. Egyptian papyri list wine as a major medicine as early as 1900 B.C. In pre-Christian Greece wine was considered basic to diet and necessary to health. Even the book of Ecclesiastes, which was written hundreds of years before Christianity, bids us, "Go thy way, eat thy bread with joy and drink thy wine with a merry heart." Joy and health are obviously connected in the early biblical traditions.

It appears that most of the ancient world saw wine as a symbol of joy, and as a critical medicine. In ancient Greece, during the time of Hippocrates, wine was considered the principal medicine. Different wines were prescribed for different illnesses. France still practices this way. And in ancient India wine was so prized as medicine that it was worshiped as a god.

The Chinese seem to be the ones who first used wine as a means of carrying healing herbs into the body. Wouldn't you know that the Chinese had done it first! They discovered that the body will absorb the herbs much faster if the prescribed ingredients are first dissolved in wine.

In America wine was regularly and commonly used as medicine since the founding of the colonies. It reached its pinnacle as a medicine during the nineteenth century, but with the discovery of the twentieth-century wonder drugs, wine as a medicine was put on the back shelf, a very poor place for storing wine unless the shelf is rather low and somewhat cool. During Prohibition wine became even less used as a medicine and we came up with an entire generation of medical doctors who knew nothing about wine as medicine. They knew and understood only the wonder drugs and believed the only value to be found in wine was in the alcohol.

Following repeal of Prohibition, a whole new series of studies began to appear that gave us insight into the healing properties of wine. There may be hope for the doctors of the Prohibition period. We have found that wine contains at least 300 beneficial ingredients, including vitamins, minerals, tranquilizers, and antibiotics. The nutrients in wine, the amino acids, vitamins, and all thirteen elements considered necessary for human life, are presented to us in a most lovely and palatable form, a gift of the grape. Indeed, alcohol is the minor healer in wine, although it is interesting to note that the alcohol found in wine is three times more antiseptic to the body than the same amount of alcohol mixed with a proportionate amount of water. Something happens when all of these components come together in a natural form. When we analyze these wonderfully healing ingredients and take them apart, they are not anywhere near as effective in your system as when in the natural form of wine.

Wine has long been used as an aid to digestion. A glass of wine with your meal will not only help you to digest your food, but it will help in maintaining your appetite, a serious problem of the elderly in our culture. Several studies indicate that the loss of appetite in the elderly accounts for much of their ill health. How do you keep people eating and enjoying their food when their taste buds have worn a bit and the food offered them in institutions and hospitals is about as exciting as the American television game shows? We have learned to deal with, and have accepted, the meaning of infectious diseases. We have done much with degenerative diseases. The old boys who live to be ninety in the Médoc region of France attribute their longevity to the wonderful deep red wine that they consume with lunch and dinner. It keeps their appetite up and their systems going. There are still doctors in France who prescribe only wines!

Wine will also help you cut down on your addiction to salt. Since wine contains a mixture of acids and natural salts, it will cut the fat and enhance the flavors of your food. Most of us have accepted the fact that we must cut down on sodium chloride—common table salt. Wine, however, contains a good amount of potassium chloride as well as calcium chloride, two ingredients relatively close to the chemical nature of salt. These elements react on your tongue much in the way that salt does, so when the doctor tells you to cut down on salt, remember that he means sodium . . . and thus you can begin cooking with wine and avoid the sodium much more easily. As we get older and our taste buds tend to wear out, we generally react by seeking more flavor, more salt, more alcohol, more fat, more sugar. Since our desire for salt, our addiction to salt, is the toughest to overcome, we can give thanks to wine in cooking. It will help us cut down on the old salt shaker without giving up flavors. This tenet is basic to what I am trying to do in this cookbook.

Current conversations around the medical community are aimed at understanding wine as a natural tranquilizer, thus a great help in relieving the stress and strain that is an everyday part of our culture. For me wine does have the ability to reduce major catastrophes into minor inconveniences, but the studies that maintain wine is good for your heart are probably stretching it a bit. It is too easy to use such an argument as an excuse to misuse wine. That is not the point of this essay. In fact, quite the opposite is the case. While wine is good for us in many ways, we must remember that we are talking about moderate use, two or three glasses a day. We are not talking about drinking in order to avoid a heart attack. No such luck!

Wine helps with our own self-image, our sense of integrity. Several studies have centered on the use of wine in hospitals, particularly in geriatric wards. Some wards have installed wine bars and have announced a marked and obvious increase in the sense of self-worth and integrity of the patients. That is not difficult to understand. Consider your own experience in the hospital, and how degrading the event. She appears at about nine in the evening, carrying her tray of paper cups filled with pills. She gives you a cup containing two blue ones and one orange one. What are they for? She tells you they are to put you to sleep. Sleep? Would it not help your self-esteem, let alone your suspicions about her giving you the wrong pills, if she were to come down the hallway, wineglasses clinking on her cart? Upon entering your room she would greet you and offer you a red or a white. At last. A decision that you could make for yourself. Upon tasting the wine you would realize that the institution is not going to go broke serving wines of this quality, but it is good, nevertheless. And after a day of degrading poking, barium treatments, and visiting relatives who demand that you feel well, the wine is healing. You sit back and relax and realize that you may get out of that hospital in one piece after all. Many hospitals are now doing this very thing, and noting a favorable influence on self-esteem, mood, and sociability of their patients. Of course, this can only be celebrated with the advice of your physician. Certain ailments will not take nicely to wine.

Using wine as medicine will be difficult for some people, I know. Even though Louis Pasteur called wine "the most healthful and hygienic of beverages," and even though there is endless evidence of the healing properties of wine, many still react with a bit of guilt left over from their upbringing. Salvatore Lucia, the doctor who wrote *Wine as Food and Medicine,* tells of an older woman in a nursing home whose doctor told her to cut down on the pills and drink a little port each evening. She thankfully obliged, but she pleaded with the doctor, "Don't tell my children." We all know her and can understand her feelings.

Finally, as we use wine in the kitchen and at table, as we use it as medicine for the merry heart and for health, we must remember that moderation is the key to the rightful use of wine. For every medicine that we have there is both a helpful level and a lethal level. Too much of anything can harm or kill you. This is even true of water. The result of our living and seeking health should be happiness, and nothing less. *In Omnibus Rebus—Media* (In all things—the middle). I love the line from Sir Alexander Fleming, the doctor who discovered penicillin: "Penicillin may cure human beings, but it is wine that makes them happy!" Given moderation in all things, I hope for health and happiness for you.

WINE AS FOOD
ON COOKING WITH WINE

Without bread, without wine, love is nothing.

—French Proverb

Now, if you have finished the preceding articles we can continue on to wine as food.

I am going to stick my neck out and tell you which of the world's cuisines I appreciate the most. In order of my affections the list begins with China. Then Italy, Greece, Old Rome, America, France, and Spain. I refer to all of the many regions in each, of course. But the wonderful thing that these cultures have in common is this: They all use a good deal of wine in their cooking.

Wine cleanses food, supports food, flavors food. And it will help you get rid of your addiction to salt.

Since ancient times wine has been seen as a food. As a matter of fact, we can list our three most ancient food products—wine, bread, and cheese—and see that all three are gifts to us from yeast. But bread and wine seem to be the most basic. "A jug of wine, a loaf of bread—and thou beside me singing in the wilderness." It is true that a whole meal can be made from bread and wine, and we have been doing that since biblical times. Ben Sirach, in the Apocrypha, maintains that a normal daily diet in the Bible days consisted of bread, wine, salt, olives, olive oil, and on special occasions, a bit of fish. Meat was eaten only on festival days, but wine was a part of the daily diet . . . for everyone.

Cooking with wine must be as old as wine itself. We in America were driven away from this habit during Prohibition, and it has taken some doing to return to this sound practice. I think the return is due primarily to our much increased traveling to Europe, where wine has always been in the pot. As our palates became a bit more sophisticated we began to ask for more complex foods and flavors in this country. And it was not long before we all began putting a little sherry in the soup.

Not every recipe in this book uses wine. That is not the point of the book. But every recipe can certainly be enjoyed with wine. So either way we will have a good time.

Please note that I have given you a suggested wine for each of the main courses. Do not feel bound to that. A good-quality jug wine will do.

Finally, enjoy your cooking. The point behind any effort in the kitchen is not simply to survive. You can do that by living out of the supermarket. The point behind the kitchen work that I love is to celebrate our lives together, and to place that celebration squarely where it belongs . . . on the table. So call the family and friends, make the soup stock, buy some wines for your cooking, and enjoy. Wine is meant for food, and the food for you.

THE RECIPES

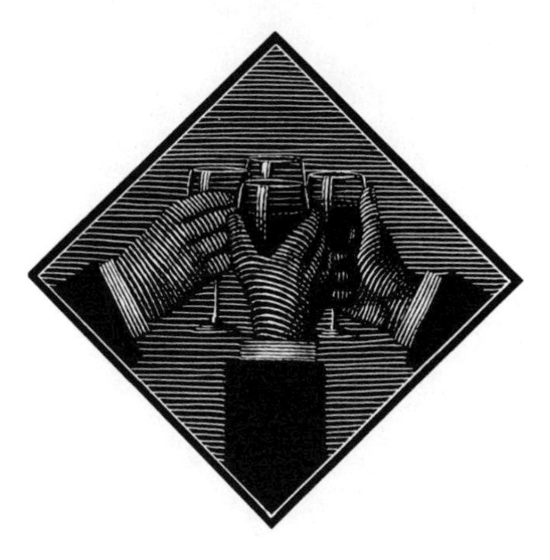

Strange to see how a good dinner and feasting reconciles everybody.

—Samuel Pepys
1633–1703

APPETIZERS

Appetite is the best sauce.

—French Proverb

• The Tapas Buffet •

(Spain)

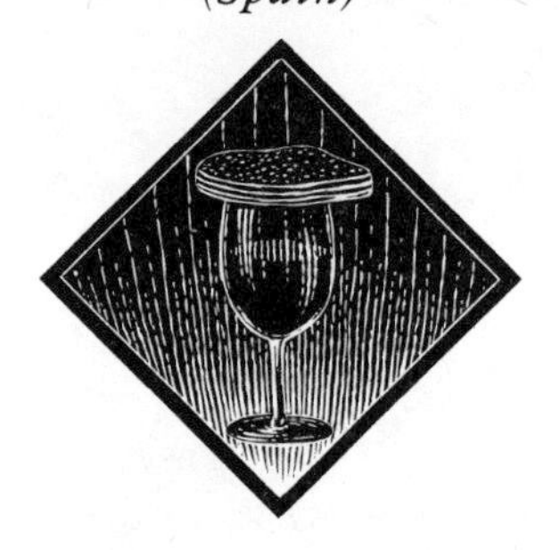

The tapas bar is a custom that Americans do not quite understand. In the evening Spaniards stop by sherry bars that spread out a most wonderful selection of snacks. One buys a glass of dry Spanish sherry and wanders about the tapas bar, eating, talking, drinking, and catching up on the news of the day. It seems to me to be a very civilized way of ending the day. Dinner is eaten very late in the evening, about ten, but then you have had a chance to nibble at the tapas bar for at least an hour.

The snacks are called tapas because in the old days a piece of toast was served, too, so that you might have a "top" on your glass of sherry, a lid that would prevent the flies from getting into the glass.

You can have a wonderful time with a tapas party at your home. People will get enough to eat, if you make enough, and you will be able to sit and talk with your guests. Everything will have been done ahead of time, one of the marks of a truly creative and thoughtful host or hostess.

Dry sherry is served at such an occasion. And the Spanish are very proper and polite. They serve you good food in the tapas bar because it is considered an insult to everyone should you get drunk.

Put as many of these dishes as you wish out on the buffet, or, better yet, in the middle of the dining room table. Your guests can circulate around the table, eat a bit, drink some sherry, talk a bit, and on and on. It is one of the best ways to get a group of newly introduced people to talk. You have to talk with someone when he has just stuck his toothpick in your Spanish shrimp! Good luck!

Shrimp with Garlic and Oil

(Spain)

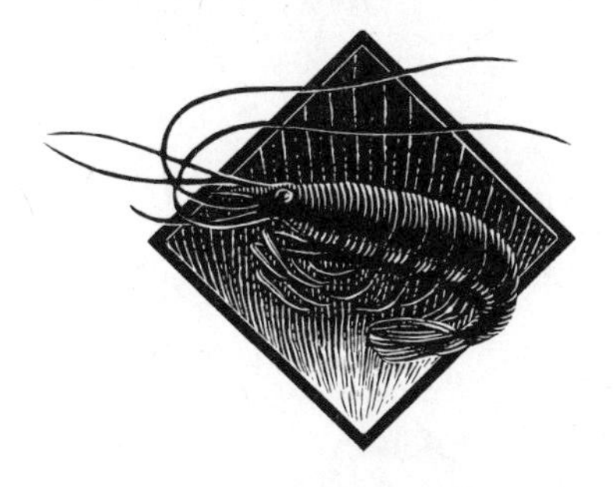

Peel large shrimp and marinate, for 1 hour, in olive oil, garlic, salt, and parsley. Quickly pan-fry and serve. You might try this with a bit of chili powder thrown in.

Toasted Almonds

(Spain)

Use blanched almonds. Toss with a bit of olive oil, salt, ground cumin, and ground coriander. Bake in a 350° oven until light brown.

◆

Sardines in Casserole

(Spain)

- 2 tins sardines
- ½ cup olive oil
- 2 large yellow onions, peeled and chopped
- 1 small can (4 ounces) roasted red sweet peppers, cut in strips*
- Salt, if needed

Rinse sardines under warm water. Drain. Pour half the olive oil into a small casserole and layer in the onions. Cover the onions

*Roasted red peppers can be found in any delicatessen or Italian food shop.

with the sardines and top the sardines with the red peppers. Add just a touch of salt and bake at 350° for 30 minutes. This is served with fresh French bread that one may dip into the oil. Wonderful!

Stuffed Eggs

(Spain)

Prepare deviled eggs, adding an anchovy fillet to each egg yolk used. Mayonnaise, parsley, salt, and pepper. Garnish with pimiento strips and capers.

Meatballs

Albóndigas

(Spain)

- 1 pound hamburger, lean
- 3 garlic cloves, crushed
- 1 tablespoon chopped parsley
- Salt and pepper to taste
- ½ teaspoon ground cumin
- 1 tablespoon olive oil
- ½ cup fine bread crumbs
- 1 egg, beaten
- Olive oil and peanut oil for frying

Mix all the above together. Blend well. Form into ½-inch balls and fry in mixture of olive oil and peanut oil until well browned on all sides. Serve on toothpicks. Should make about 25 meatballs.

Olives

Serve several different kinds. Roll some in oil, lemon juice, and oregano.

Ham Chunks in Hot Sauce

Cut cooked ham into ½-inch cubes. Heat in tomato sauce to which you have added chili powder and garlic. Serve hot with toothpicks.

Squid in Marinara Sauce

Clean the squid and cut into tiny circles (page 123). Cook for a few minutes in your favorite spaghetti sauce. Do not overcook the squid or it will get tough.

Kidney Beans in Oil

Marinate cooked kidney beans in vinaigrette along with parsley, chopped yellow onion, and sweet red pepper.

Mushrooms in Oil

Marinate cooked or canned mushrooms in vinaigrette along with parsley and chopped green onions.

Pickled Beets

Tough job. Open the jar!

Smoked Clams

Serve on toothpicks.

Salami

Thin sliced, make into rolls secured with toothpicks.

Cheese Cubes

Use any good sharp cheese. I love Romano or kasseri.

Fried Red Pepper Strips

These are delicious, but too much work to make from scratch. Simply buy the fried peppers in the glass jar at your Italian or Spanish market. Drain them and cut into thin strips.

Bread

Don't forget to put out a good-quality French or Italian bread, one with a crunchy crust.

• *More Appetizers* •

•

Zucchini Fritters

(Italy)

This simple and lovely little item is from Italy. It is light enough for a first course or flavorful enough to be served as a vegetable dish during the main part of the meal.

- 3 cups coarsely grated zucchini
- 2 eggs, beaten
- ⅛ cup milk
- 2 teaspoons flour
- Salt and black pepper, freshly ground
- Mint, dried or fresh
- Olive oil for pan-frying

Grate the squash and drain in a colander for 1 hour. Mix the eggs, milk, and flour into a smooth batter. Add salt and pepper to taste. Add mint to taste. (I use about 1 teaspoon dried mint in this recipe. If using fresh mint leaf, chop about 1 tablespoon.)

Mix batter with the squash and pan-fry in small fritters in a bit of olive oil. Cook just until golden brown and serve as a first course or a vegetable dish. These can be kept warm in the oven for a bit before dinner. Be sure to cover.

SERVES 6.

Olive Paste

Olivada
(Italy)

My lifelong love affair with food, and with the people who prepare it, was redefined when I was a clerk in the Pike Place Farmer's Market, in Seattle. I was a sophomore in high school and proud of my position behind a counter covered with tubs of fresh cottage cheese, pickles, fresh peanut butter, olives, and pig's feet. It was a wonderful place, and I can still remember the glorious odor that was created by all these foods over which I stood guard. But when I was not working I fled to the basement store, an Italian market run by Pete DeLaurenti. The store is much enlarged now and terribly up to date. But the flavor of the air remains the same, even now. A recipe similar to this is given to customers so that they can enjoy an olive course before dinner. It is easy to prepare and delicious with a very dry sherry.

- **1 pound brine-cured black olives, soaked in 1 quart water for 1 hour, drained and pitted (they use calamatas)**
- **2 garlic cloves, finely chopped**
- **5 anchovy fillets, soaked in ¼ cup milk for ½ hour, drained and coarsely chopped**
- **¼ cup fruity olive oil (extra virgin preferred)**

Combine olives, garlic, and anchovies in a blender or food processor, discarding the milk. Slowly add the oil and blend until the mixture is finely chopped. This should not be a smooth paste as there should be some texture to it.

Ideally, this should be made 24 hours ahead. Remove from the refrigerator and allow it to warm up a bit before serving.

Serving Suggestions:

Serve as a cracker spread.
Use as a canapé spread, too, with a thin slice of mozzarella and put under the broiler until the cheese melts.
Use as a sauce for pasta.
Use as a condiment with steaks, chicken, and fish.

Wine Suggestion: Dry Sherry.

Vegetable-Stuffed Spinach Crepes

I had fun trying to decide where to place this terrific recipe in the book. Was it pasta or vegetable? I decided on placing it in this section of first courses because that is really how the dish functions best. Serve this with a light red wine and enjoy.

SPINACH CREPES:	2	eggs, room temperature
	1¼	cups milk
	¾	cup beer
	¼	teaspoon salt
	1	cup flour
	2	tablespoons peanut oil
	1	package (10 ounce) frozen chopped spinach, defrosted and squeezed absolutely dry of water

Place the eggs, milk and beer in a food blender, and then the salt, flour, and 1 tablespoon of the oil. Blend for 30 seconds, then scrape down the sides of the container, using a rubber spatula. Blend in the spinach. Be sure that you have squeezed the spinach as dry as possible. Cover and refrigerate for 2 hours. You may need to thin the batter with a little more beer.

Fry the crepes in a medium-hot 10-inch pan lubricated with some of the remaining peanut oil. Pour in 2 ounces of batter for each crepe. Tip and turn the pan until the batter covers the bottom. Cook until the top appears dry and the bottom has just begun to brown. Turn with a wooden spatula and brown the other side very lightly; you should have only little specks of brown. Stack with a piece of wax paper between each. You should have about 12 crepes.

VEGETABLE FILLING:

- 2 tablespoons olive oil
- 2 yellow onions, medium size, peeled and sliced
- 2 garlic cloves, crushed
- 1 carrot, coarsely grated
- 1 cup zucchini cut into matchsticks (page 257)
- 1 egg, beaten
- ½ teaspoon marjoram
- 2 tablespoons plus ½ cup Parmesan or Romano, freshly grated
- Salt and black pepper, freshly ground, to taste
- 1 cup Italian Gravy (page 341) or White Cheese Sauce (page 288)
- 2 tablespoons olive oil for oiling the baking dish

Heat a frying pan and add the oil. Sauté the onions, garlic, and carrot just until the onions are clear. Remove from the heat and cool. Place in a bowl and add the zucchini, egg, marjoram, 2 tablespoons cheese, salt, and pepper. Place a portion of the filling on each crepe and roll it up like a blintz or a burrito, leaving the ends open. Place in an oiled baking pan and top with the sauce. Add the ½ cup cheese and bake at 350° for 15 or 20 minutes, until all is hot.

Serve 2 filled crepes per plate. Enjoy as a light first course.

Wine Suggestion: Chardonnay or Macon.

SERVES 6.

Fried Cheese Appetizers

For cheese lovers this is a most enjoyable snack or appetizer. Have everything ready before your guests arrive so that you can throw these together at the last minute. They should be served hot.

Cheese (cheddar, Romano, or kasseri) cut into sticks 1 inch wide and ½ inch thick
Egg
Flour
Bread crumbs
Oil for deep-frying

Bread cheese sticks by dipping in beaten egg and then in a mixture of half flour, half bread crumbs. Deep-fry at 350° until golden brown. Serve with a toothpick.

This may also be done with Montrachet, a mild goat cheese. Pan-fry the sticks in deep olive or vegetable oil.

SOUPS

Troubles go down better with soup!

—Yiddish Proverb

Soups with Wine

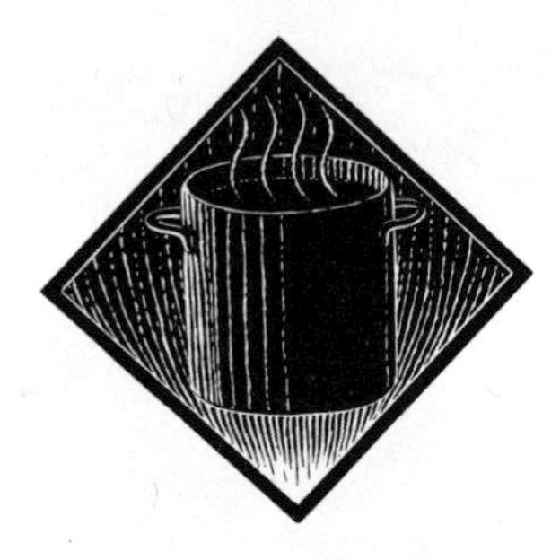

I cannot put into words the comfort that I find in soup. Whether it be a peasant dish of low estate, or an aristocratic dish filled with lobster and truffles . . . it is still soup. Its function is twofold. It is to warm the stomach—and it does so every time—and to warm the soul. For me soup is like wine. It is so basic to our being that we should never eat it by ourselves, but only with other persons. Soup will help us remember that we are dependent upon the great giving forces of the universe . . . the forces of the animal and vegetable kingdom combined . . . and they are best combined in the soup pot.

Basic Brown Soup Stock

This is one of those things that you prepare on your one major cooking day each week. It takes some time to concoct, but this soup stock is just basic to a properly and frugally run kitchen. It is used for soups, sauces, and gravies.

Bare rendering bones, sawed into 2-inch pieces
Carrots, unpeeled and chopped
Yellow onions, unpeeled and chopped
Celery, chopped

Tell your butcher that you need bare rendering bones. They should not have any meat on them at all, so they should be cheap. Have him saw them up into 2-inch pieces.

Roast the bones in an uncovered pan at 400° for 2 hours. Be careful with this, because your oven may be a bit too hot. Watch the bones, which you want to be toasty brown, not black.

Place the roasted bones in a soup pot and add 1 quart water for each pound of bones. For 5 pounds bones, add 1 bunch carrots, 1 head celery, and 3 yellow onions, chopped with peel and all. (The peel will give lovely color to the stock.)

Bring to a simmer, uncovered, and cook, for 12 hours. You may need to add water to keep soup up to same level. Do not salt the stock.

Strain the stock, and store in the refrigerator. Allow the fat to stay on the top of the stock when you refrigerate it; the fat will seal the stock and allow you to keep it for several days.

MAKES 5 QUARTS OF STOCK.

Chicken Soup Stock

Chicken stock, or soup, is used for soups and sauces that have a lighter touch than the heavier beef versions. The stock is not expensive to make nor does it take much time. The result, however, is so far superior to the canned stuff or the salty chicken bouillon cubes that you won't believe it.

- 3 pounds chicken necks and backs
- 4 stalks celery, chopped into large pieces
- 6 carrots, chopped into large pieces
- 2 yellow onions, peeled and chopped into large pieces
- Salt and pepper to taste

Boil the chicken necks and backs in water to cover. Add the celery, carrots, and yellow onions. Add salt and pepper. Simmer for 2 hours. Strain and refrigerate.

MAKES ABOUT 4 QUARTS OF STOCK.

Rich Minestrone

(Italy)

Dr. Angelo Pelligrini is a fine cook and a great lover of wine. His Italian background has given him wonderful insights into the meaning of food. His latest book, *Lean Years, Happy Years,* is a delight. This recipe is very close to his wonderful minestrone soup.

- 1 pound Italian Cheese and Red Wine Sausage (page 245) or Spicy Italian Pork Sausage (page 249)
- 3½ cups white beans, soaked overnight
- 2 quarts water
- 2 tablespoons olive oil
- ¼ pound salt pork, diced
- 1 large yellow onion, peeled and diced
- 3 garlic cloves, crushed
- ¼ cup minced celery leaves
- ¼ cup minced parsley
- 1 can (16 ounce) tomatoes, chopped
- 1 quart chicken broth
- 1 large carrot, diced
- 3 stalks celery, diced
- 1 thin-skinned potato, diced
- 1 cup lightly packed basil leaves or 1 tablespoon dried basil
- 1 large zucchini, thinly sliced
- 1 quart lightly packed, coarsely chopped greens (such as kale, Swiss chard, or cabbage)
- 1 cup dry red wine
- Salt and black pepper, freshly ground, to taste
- 1 cup freshly grated Parmesan cheese

Pierce sausage with a fork and put it in a 4- to 5-quart pan. Drain the beans and add to the sausage, along with water. Bring to a boil, reduce the heat, cover, and simmer for 20 minutes. Remove the sausage and set aside. Continue cooking the beans until they mash readily, about 1 hour total time.

Run the beans through a food processor, along with the water, so that they are coarsely puréed. Return to the pan with all of the water.

In a 6- to 8-quart pan, over medium heat, combine oil, salt pork, onion, garlic, celery leaves, and parsley. Sauté until onion is limp, about 5 minutes. Add beans and cooking water, tomatoes with their liquid, broth, carrot, celery, potato, and basil, if dried. If the basil is fresh, add it later. Bring to a boil, cover, and simmer 15 minutes. Add the zucchini, greens, and red wine. Simmer uncovered until vegetables are tender, about 8 minutes. Add the fresh basil if not using dried, and salt and pepper to taste.

Slice sausage and serve in the soup. Add cheese to taste.

MAKES 4 QUARTS.

Cream of Lentil Soup

You can see from the presence of Tabasco and Worcestershire in this recipe that I tasted it in New Orleans. You will enjoy this, even if you don't make it as hot and spicy as I.

- 2 cups dried lentils
- 1 quart water
- 2 quarts Basic Brown Soup Stock (page 100) or instant beef broth
- 4 slices bacon, diced
- 4 stalks celery, chopped
- 2 yellow onions, peeled and diced
- ½ green sweet bell pepper, diced
- Worcestershire sauce to taste
- Tabasco to taste
- Salt and pepper to taste
- 2 cups cream or half-and-half or Mock Cream (page 289)
- 1 yellow onion, peeled and sliced thin
- 1 tablespoon fresh rosemary or ½ tablespoon dried
- Fresh chives or green onion tops
- Dry sherry to taste

Place the lentils, water, and soup stock in a 6- to 8-quart kettle, with lid, and bring to a simmer. Sauté bacon and chopped vegetables until limp, about 6 minutes. Add to the kettle. Cover and simmer until the lentils mash easily. Purée all of this in a food processor or blender, using small batches. Return to the kettle.

Add the Worcestershire sauce, Tabasco, salt, and pepper to taste. Stir in the cream and allow to simmer while you prepare the onion and rosemary garnish.

Sauté the sliced onion, along with the rosemary and chives, until the onion is tender. Set aside.

Add the sherry to the soup just before serving. Garnish with a little pile of the onion and rosemary placed on top of the bowl of soup.

SERVES 8.

◆

Very Rich Clam Chowder

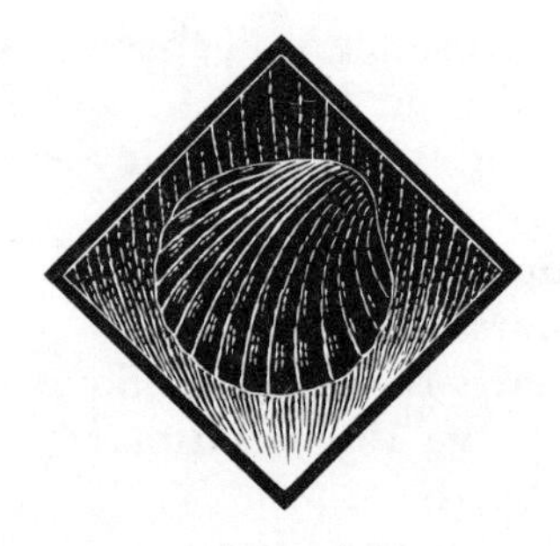

This is not an effort to end the battle over the glories of Manhattan versus New England chowder. It is simply a blend that turns out to be very rich.

- ¼ pound bacon, diced and blanched
- 6 stalks celery, cut thin
- 2 medium onions, peeled and chopped
- 2 tablespoons butter
- 1 quart Chicken Soup Stock (page 101) or use canned if you must
- Black pepper, freshly ground, to taste

½ teaspoon thyme (leaves, not ground)
1½ pounds potatoes
8 tablespoons butter
6 tablespoons flour
1 quart milk
4 very ripe tomatoes, diced
3 cans (6½ ounce) minced clams (I prefer Gorton's. Fresh clams would be even better. Simply steam them first.)
Parsley for garnish

Dice and blanch the bacon in 2 cups boiling water for about 2 minutes. Sauté celery and onions in 2 tablespoons butter for 10 minutes over medium heat. Do not allow to discolor. Add bacon, celery, and onions to the chicken stock. Add the *juice only* from the clams, reserving the meat. Bring to a heavy simmer and add pepper and thyme.

Dice the potatoes *without* peeling. Simply wash well and then dice. The peel has such great flavor. Add to the pot and simmer all until the potatoes are cooked but still firm.

While the potatoes are cooking in the soup, melt the 8 tablespoons butter and blend with the flour. Add the flour mixture (roux) to 1 quart of hot milk, off the heat. Stir and return to the burner. Stir until thickened. Set aside.

When the potatoes are just tender, add the diced tomatoes to the soup. Add the drained clams and the milk sauce (béchamel). Stir and simmer for 10 minutes, no longer. Add salt and pepper, if necessary. Serve with chopped parsley garnish.

MAKES 4½ QUARTS.

Note: You may wish to add more pepper and thyme.

◆

Pepper Sherry for Soup

You may wish to add pepper sherry to your clam chowder. It is delicious!

Simply place 4 or 5 dried long red peppers in a small cruet or oil bottle. Add 2 cups of very dry sherry and allow it to sit, sealed, for 1 month. Shake into soups and stews.

Clam and Corn Chowder

This dish is very American. The Plymouth Bay Colony virtually lived on corn and clams during those first winters. The two foods go together very well.

1 small yellow onion, peeled and diced
2 tablespoons butter
1 can (6½ ounce) minced clams (I prefer Gorton's)
1 can (17 ounce) cream-style corn
Equal amount of milk (17 ounces)
Salt and black pepper freshly ground, to taste
1 teaspoon dried dill weed

Sauté onion in butter until soft. Do not discolor. Combine other ingredients and bring to a simmer. Simmer for 5 minutes and serve. Be sure to add lots of freshly ground black pepper.

MAKES 4 LARGE SERVINGS (5¾ CUPS).

◆

Pumpkin Soup

I told my boys about this soup when they were little and carving jack-o'-lanterns. They doubted my word so I had to develop a recipe. This is easy, and if you clean out a pumpkin and use it for the serving tureen, it is dramatic and fun.

- 2½ pounds fresh pumpkin, cleaned and peeled, or 1 can (29 ounce) *and* 1 can (16 ounce) pumpkin
- 3 celery stalks, chopped
- 1 large yellow onion, chopped
- 2 tablespoons butter
- 2 tablespoons quick-cooking tapioca
- 10 cups Chicken Soup Stock (page 101)
- Nutmeg to taste
- Salt and pepper to taste
- Sugar to taste
- 2 cups half-and-half or Mock Cream (page 289)
- Curry powder (optional)
- Fried toast points for garnish
- Toasted pumpkin seeds for garnish (optional)

Peel the pumpkin and cut into large pieces. Steam until tender, about 45 minutes. Or, you can bake the pieces until tender. If using canned pumpkin, omit this step.

Sauté the celery and onion in the butter until tender.

Simmer the tapioca in 2 cups of the chicken stock until tender, about 8 minutes. Stir this regularly while cooking. Set aside.

If using fresh pumpkin, purée in a food processor using a bit of the chicken stock. Place the pumpkin, either fresh or canned, in a 6-quart soup pot and then purée the sautéed celery and onion with a bit of the chicken stock. Add to the kettle. Add the remaining chicken stock and bring to a simmer. Be careful that you do not burn this soup. Add the tapioca, nutmeg, salt, pepper, and sugar, all to taste. Just a touch of nutmeg, or the soup will be too heavy. Sugar to taste, about 1 tablespoon.

You may wish to add a bit of curry powder to taste. This is also delicious.

When all is hot and you are ready to serve, add the half-and-half and correct the seasoning, that is, taste to be sure you have what you want.

Serve in a pumpkin tureen along with toast points or croutons as a garnish. I bought some fresh pumpkin seeds, hulled, at a bulk food store and fried them a moment. They make a great garnish for this soup.

SERVES 10.

Cuban Black Bean Soup

(Cuba)

I receive many recipes from viewers. Some are delicious. This one was from a viewer who graciously criticized the Cuban Black Bean Soup that I had in the last cookbook. "My Mama didn't do it that way!" So, he has offered this recipe. It is great stuff . . . but don't spend a lot of money on a bottle of good wine. Buy a cheap one as this stuff is going to startle your taste buds a bit.

1 pound dried black beans*
10 cups water
1 teaspoon salt
1 large green bell pepper, cut in half
⅔ cup peanut oil or salad oil
1 large yellow onion, peeled and sliced
4 garlic cloves, minced
1 small green hot pepper, cut in half, seeds removed
3 teaspoons salt or to taste
½ teaspoon freshly ground black pepper
1 bay leaf
¼ teaspoon whole cumin seed
1 teaspoon sugar
2½ tablespoons red wine vinegar
2½ tablespoons olive oil

Rinse black beans and soak overnight in the 10 cups water, with 1 teaspoon salt, and the green bell pepper.

In a large heavy-bottom soup kettle, bring the beans, soaking water, and pepper to a boil. Simmer until tender, about 45 minutes. Remove the green pepper pieces and discard.

Heat the peanut oil in a deep frying pan or heavy saucepan. Sauté the onion, garlic, and green hot pepper until soft. Remove 2½ cups of the bean broth and add it to the frying pan. Simmer this mixture for 10 minutes. Strain the onions, garlic, and green hot pepper from the broth and discard. Add the seasoned broth to the soup pot. Add salt, pepper, bay leaf, cumin, and sugar. Bring to a boil and simmer, covered, for about 1½ hours, or until it thickens. You may have to add more water if too much of the liquid cooks away.

Before serving add the vinegar and olive oil. Mix well.

SERVES 8.

*You will find black beans in any Spanish or Mexican market.

Cabbage Soup

This sounds like some kind of touching story from the Lower East Side of New York during the 1930s. Not so. Cabbage soup will do fine for difficult and pressing times, but it also does well for better times. And let us be thankful you and I are celebrating good times, unless, of course, you found this book on the "Rejects" rack at the Strand Book Store. I would hope that you love cabbage soup during all times . . . good and bad.

- 3 tablespoons olive oil
- ½ pound pork shoulder steak, deboned and diced into ½-inch cubes
- 2 yellow onions, peeled and sliced
- 3 garlic cloves, peeled and crushed
- 1 head of cabbage, about 2 pounds, cored and chopped
- ½ cup flour
- 2 cups dry white wine
- 4 cups Basic Brown Soup Stock (page 100)
- 1 quart water
- 2 tablespoons tomato paste
- 1 tablespoon paprika
- 10 juniper berries
- Salt and black pepper, freshly ground, to taste (use lots of pepper!)
- 1 tablespoon sugar, or to taste
- 1 pound garlic sausage or Polish sausage, sliced

Put a large soup kettle on to heat and add the olive oil. Sauté the pork in the kettle until it begins to brown lightly. Add the yellow onions and garlic and sauté until they are clear. Toss in the chopped cabbage and stir and sauté, covered, until the cabbage wilts. Stir in the flour. Stir very thoroughly. Pour in the wine and stir until it begins to thicken. Add the stock, water, tomato paste, paprika, and juniper berries. Bring to a simmer and cook for 30 minutes. Add salt, pepper, and sugar to taste.

At serving time, add the sausages and cook for 20 minutes.

SERVES 10–12.

Hearty Lima Bean Soup

This one weighs a ton, or *you* will if you eat too much. Actually, soups are generally lower in fat than regular meals, and if you use lots of wine in the pot the soup will not only be satisfying but also lower in salt. This one is a good case in point.

- 1 pound lima beans
- 2 quarts Chicken Soup Stock (page 101) or bouillon (careful of all that salt!)
- 2 quarts water
- ½ pound pork hocks, cut into ½-inch slices (your butcher will do this for you)
- 3 tablespoons olive oil
- 2 yellow onions, peeled and sliced
- 4 garlic cloves, crushed
- 4 celery stalks, sliced thin
- 3 ripe tomatoes, diced
- ¾ pound Italian Cheese and Red Wine Sausage, sliced or bulk (page 245)
- 1 cup dry red wine
- 2 bay leaves, whole
- ½ cup chopped parsley
- Salt and black pepper, freshly ground, to taste
- Parmesan or Romano cheese, freshly grated, for topping

Place the beans in a large pot of water and bring to a boil. Boil for 2 minutes, cover, and let sit for 1 hour. Drain and discard the water.

Return the beans to a large soup kettle and add t… …nd water.

Throw in the pork hocks and bring to a simmer, uncover…

In the meantime, heat a large frying pan and add the olive oil. Sauté the yellow onions and garlic until clear, then add the celery and tomatoes. Sauté for 10 minutes longer. Add the contents of the frying pan to the soup pot.

Pan-fry the bulk Italian sausage or the sliced sausages until the meat begins to separate. Drain the oil and discard. Add the meat to the pot, along with the wine, bay leaves, and parsley.

Bring the pot to a boil and turn to a simmer. Simmer uncovered until all is tender, about 1½ hours total cooking time.

Taste for salt and pepper. Serve with the grated cheese on top.

SERVES 8–10.

◆

Cream of Brie Soup

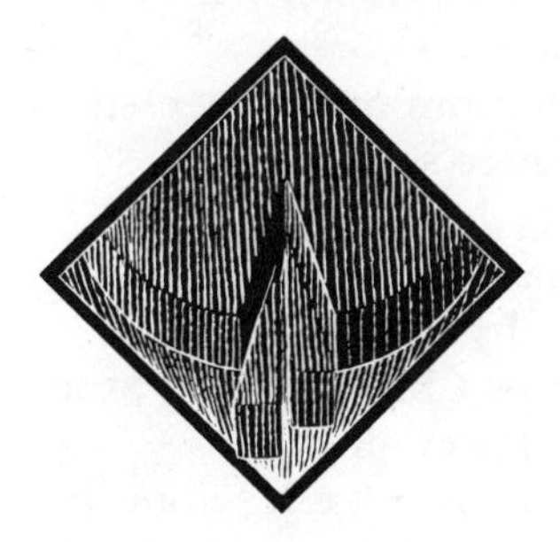

Yes, this is rich indeed. It is a wonderful beginning for a meal and you need very little for each serving.

- ½ cup peeled and chopped yellow onion
- ½ cup thinly sliced celery
- 4 tablespoons butter
- ¼ cup flour
- 2 cups milk
- 2 cups chicken broth
- ¾ pound Brie cheese, cubed
- Salt and pepper to taste
- Chives, chopped, for garnish

In a 3-quart kettle, sauté the onion and the celery in the butter until limp. Stir in the flour. Remove from the heat. Stir in the milk and chicken broth using a whisk to mix well. Return to the heat and simmer, stirring constantly, until the soup thickens. Add the cheese (please, don't remove the wonderful rind!) and stir until melted. Run all of this through a food processor or blender until very smooth. Correct seasoning with salt and pepper. Serve very hot with chive garnish.

SERVES 6.

Vegetable and Champagne Soup

I do not know whether to call this a soup or a vegetable or an appetizer. It cannot be served on a plate as a vegetable, but it is delicious with just about any other course. In a bowl for the first course? Or the second or third?

- **3 cups shelled green peas (fresh is best, frozen will do)**
- **1 carrot**
- **1 medium onion, peeled**
- **1 ounce salt pork**
- **1 bay leaf**
- **⅛ teaspoon each sage, chervil, and thyme**
- **3 cups Chicken Soup Stock (page 101)**
- **½ cup dry sherry**
- **1 teaspoon fresh lemon juice**
- **Salt and pepper to taste**
- **1 cup whipping cream**
- **1 cup brut champagne, room temperature**

In a saucepan, combine the peas, carrot, onion, salt pork, and herbs. Add water to cover. Cover and simmer until the peas are very soft. Remove and discard the carrot, onion, bay leaf, and salt pork. Purée the soup in a food processor or food mill. Return the soup to the saucepan and stir in the chicken stock, sherry, and lemon juice. Add salt and pepper to taste and bring the mixture to the boiling point. Whip the cream until it holds stiff peaks. Carefully fold the cream into the soup. Remove from the heat and add the champagne. Serve immediately in heated bowls.

SERVES 6.

FISH AND SHELLFISH

Fish must swim thrice—once in water, a second time in the sauce, and a third time in wine in the stomach.

—John Ray, 1627–1705
English Proverbs

Fish and Shellfish • with Wine

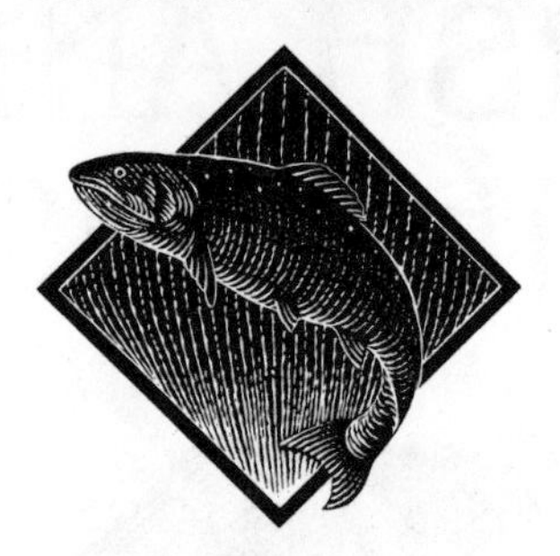

Seafood and wine support each other at the table in a most beautiful way. Try to tell a Greek that he is to enjoy his fish without wine and he will simply not understand what you are talking about. Nor would a Frenchman, or an Italian, or, for that matter, most good souls in Boston.

Certain fish present a problem when eaten with wine. Oily or fatty fish leaves a sharp flavor on your tongue that will often get in the way of the wine. Therefore, when serving oily fish such as trout, herring, mackerel, catfish, tuna, swordfish, or my beloved salmon, be sure to remove the bit of gray fat that runs down the back of the fish or is to be found surrounding the flesh. The taste will be much lighter that way. Regardless, choose a wine that will stand up to and support the oiliness of such fish. I have given wine suggestions for each of the fish dishes. Seafood lighter in flavor, such as whitefish and snapper, will present you with no problem in choosing a lovely white to complement the dish.

•

Salmon with Green Sauce

When my first cookbook came out one reviewer observed, "He's not frugal at all. He eats salmon!" True, but frugal does not mean cheap. It means that you do not waste anything. A good salmon steak has no waste at all. And here in the Pacific Northwest where I live, salmon is not expensive at all. So, here we go again. I shall start the seafood section with my favorite seafood . . . salmon.

	¼	cup olive oil
	2	tablespoons fresh lemon juice
	½	tablespoon dried dill weed
	4	8-ounce salmon steaks
SAUCE:	2	tablespoons peeled and chopped yellow onion
	1	green pepper, chopped
	½	cup chopped parsley
	2	bunches fresh spinach, leaves only, chopped
	1	tablespoon fresh lemon juice
	½	cup Mayonnaise (page 131)
	3	green onions, chopped

THE SALMON:

Whip the oil, lemon juice, and dill weed together. Baste the steaks on both sides and place on a broiling rack. Broil until a light golden brown on each side. This should be done under high heat and very quickly. Less than 4 minutes on each side will do. You don't want to dry out the fish. They could also be pan-fried using this same blend, but broiling is much nicer. Salt and pepper the fish before serving. Remember to remove the dark spot of fat that is just at the back of the fish.

PREPARE THE SAUCE:

Mix all ingredients for the sauce, except the mayonnaise and green onion, and chop very fine in a food processor or by hand. Do not grind it into mush, but do chop it very well. Stir in the mayonnaise and the finely chopped onions by hand. Refrigerate for several hours before serving. Serve a generous portion of the sauce with the fish. Try the sauce on other meats or fish.

Variation: For low-salt/low-fat dining, use Mock Sour Cream (page 289) instead of mayonnaise in the sauce recipe.

Serve with Carrots and Vermouth (page 261), Pasta with Olives (page 148), and a green salad with White Wine Vinaigrette (page 128).

Wine Suggestion: Fumé Blanc or very dry white.

SERVES 4.

Prawns Sautéed in Garlic and Wine

The combination of prawns, wine, and garlic is just basic to my soul. This recipe is from one of San Francisco's best seafood restaurants, and that city has some of the best seafood restaurants in the country. All that wonderful California wine and great seafood besides! You must go try Scott's Seafood Grill & Bar. You will be most happy with everything there. I have changed the frying oil from butter to olive oil in this dish.

- **1 pound large prawns (16–20 per pound), peeled and deveined**
- **2 tablespoons flour**
- **4 tablespoons olive oil**
- **1 garlic clove, peeled and sliced**
- **1/16 teaspoon salt (pinch)**
- **1 tablespoon chopped shallots**
- **1/4 cup dry white wine**
- **2 tablespoons fresh lemon juice**
- **2 tablespoons butter**
- **2 tablespoons chopped parsley for garnish**

Dust the prawns with the flour, shaking off the excess. Heat a 12-inch sauté pan over medium heat and add the oil. Add the prawns to the pan. Brown lightly on one side, turn and add garlic, shallots, and a pinch of salt. Brown prawns on their second side. Deglaze the pan (page 282) with white wine and lemon juice. Reduce the liquid, swirling the pan to form a sauce. Toss the prawns to ensure that they cook through. The color of the meat will change from translucent to opaque when done. Finish the sauce with the butter, swirling it into the sauce quickly. Remove from the heat at once to prevent the sauce from breaking. Sprinkle with chopped parsley.

Serve with Real Garlic Toast (page 341), Green Onion Pasta (page 144), and salad with Pesto Vinaigrette (page 130).

Wine Suggestion: Light Riesling.

SERVES 2–3.

Scallops in Cheese Sauce

Coquilles St. Jacques
(France)

The variations of this dish are endless. The name in French simply refers to scallops, not to a way of preparing them. Most often, however, even in France, the seafood is served in its own shell. Since we cannot buy them in their shell, you must buy a set of shells from your local gourmet peddler. They can be washed and used many times.

- 2 tablespoons olive oil
- 1 carrot, cut julienne (page 257)
- 1 green onion, chopped
- 1 cup Chicken Soup Stock (page 101) or used canned
- ½ cup dry white wine
- 2 tablespoons each flour and butter cooked together for a moment to form a roux (page 288)
- ½ tablespoon chopped fresh basil
- ½ tablespoon chopped parsley
- 1 tablespoon freshly grated Parmesan or Romano cheese
- 3 tablespoons dry sherry
- Salt and black pepper, freshly ground, to taste
- 1 pound scallops
- ½ cup coarsely grated Swiss cheese

Heat a large frying pan and add the oil. Sauté the carrot sticks and green onion for 2 minutes. Add the chicken stock and wine. Simmer for 5 minutes. Add the roux, stirring until thickened. Add the basil, parsley, Parmesan, and sherry. Taste the sauce for salt and pepper. Be careful, you should need little. Remove the sauce from the heat and add the scallops. Divide the mixture among 6 scallop shells and sprinkle on the cheese. Broil under high heat for just a few minutes, until the cheese begins to brown. Serve immediately.

Serve as a first course or with Stuffed Zucchini with Tomato (page 264), Risotto with Mushrooms (page 155), and a green salad with Garlic Dressing (page 129).

Wine Suggestion: Chardonnay or Fumé Blanc.

SERVES 6 AS A FISH COURSE.

Fried Fish New Orleans

I do not deep-fry fish. I absolutely do not. I am a child of the Pacific Northwest and we would never do such a thing. However . . . when I was in New Orleans last I tasted a dish close to this one. I must tell you how it is made.

- 2 pounds red snapper or whitefish, cut into 1½-inch square pieces
- Tabasco sauce to taste
- 2 eggs, beaten
- ¾ cup water
- ¾ cup flour
- ¼ cup cornstarch
- ¼ teaspoon baking powder
- Salt and black pepper, freshly ground, to taste
- Peanut oil for deep-frying

Place the fish and Tabasco sauce in a stainless steel bowl. Let marinate for 20 minutes. Mix the batter by whipping the eggs, adding the water. Blend the flour, cornstarch, baking powder, salt, and pepper together in a dry bowl, using a fork. Gently stir this into the egg/water mixture. Do not try to get out all of the small lumps. It will not matter. Do not overmix.

Heat 4 cups of peanut oil to 375–400°. Dip the marinated fish squares into the batter and then deep-fry until light brown, about 4 minutes.

Serve with Pasta and Green Onion Salad (page 134), and French bread.

Wine Suggestion: Dry Gewürztraminer or dry Chenin Blanc.

SERVES 4.

Oysters with Stolen Sauce

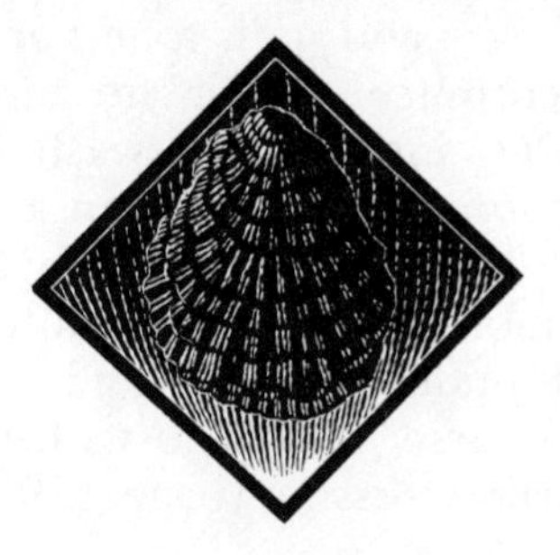

Let's face it. Maybe this wasn't stolen. I asked him for the recipe and he gave me a list of the ingredients. I was expected to work out the amounts. So, here is to John Calihan, who runs one of the best catering services in Chicago, George Jewell Catering. I met John at a party he did for Marshall Fields on State Street in Chicago. Now, that is a store to be seen. Phillip Miller, the chairman of the board, is bringing the wonderful old store back to the glory of the classy days. "Give the lady what she wants" . . . and then some class. He is doing it. And John and his crew are helping with parties and fundraisers for charity that you would just not believe. Well, in any case, I stole this recipe from John. He seemed willing.

- 2 eggs, beaten
- ½ cup milk
- 1 cup flour
- 1 cup cornmeal
- 1 pint small oysters
- Salt and black pepper, freshly ground, to taste
- Peanut oil for frying

SAUCE:
(i.e., The Theft!)

- 2 ripe avocados, mashed
- ¼ cup Mayonnaise (page 131) or store-bought
- ¼ cup sour cream or Mock Sour Cream (page 289)
- 1 garlic clove, crushed
- Tabasco to taste
- Worcestershire sauce to taste
- Salt and pepper to taste

Blend everything together for the sauce. Do not mix too much. A small lump or two of avocado is fine.

Mix the beaten eggs and milk together to form an egg wash. Combine flour and cornmeal on a plate and season with salt and pepper. Dip the oysters into the egg wash and then into the seasoned flour, coating completely. Place in a medium-hot pan with the oil and brown on both sides. Do not overdo this! The oysters should cook for no more than a few minutes on each side. Serve the oysters in a small puddle of the wonderful sauce.

Serve as a first course. It will go with most anything. Follow with a salad with Garlic Dressing (page 129).

Wine Suggestion: Light Chardonnay or light Fumé Blanc.

SERVES 5–6 AS A FIRST COURSE.

Whitefish with Filbert and Lemon Sauce

This dish is close to one served by a fine restaurant in the Pike Place Market. It is called Place Pigalle.

3 pounds true cod or any fresh whitefish such as a sole or flounder
Butter or olive oil
Salt and pepper to taste
½ cup filberts, coarsely ground
Juice of 1 lemon

SAUCE:
2 tablespoons butter
2 tablespoons flour
1 cup clam juice or fish stock
Salt and pepper to taste
¼ cup white wine
Juice of ½ lemon

Divide the fish into 8 portions and place each in a buttered individual baking dish. Add salt and freshly ground pepper to taste. Brush each portion with melted butter and top with a tablespoon or so of coarsely chopped filberts. Sprinkle with a bit of fresh lemon juice. Bake at 350° for 20–25 minutes, or until the fish is tender but not dry.

For the sauce, melt the butter in a small saucepan and add the flour. Cook for a moment and then add the clam juice or fish stock. Stir over medium heat until the sauce thickens. Add the salt and pepper and the white wine. Just before serving add the lemon juice. Pour a bit of the sauce over the fish.

Serve as a first course or with Pasta and Fresh Asparagus (page 143) and Carrot and Zucchini Salad (page 134).

Wine Suggestion: Chardonnay.

SERVES 8 AS AN APPETIZER OR 6 AS A MAIN COURSE.

•

Fish in Champagne Sauce

Matelote Champagne

(France)

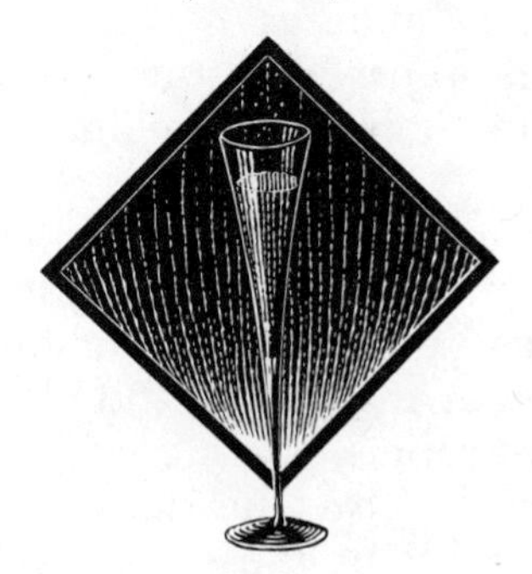

The old rule about white wine with fish has often been put aside when the French cook whitefish in red wine. The color is disgusting but the flavor is delightful. In this case we will use a champagne and a bit of brandy. Remember that brandy is distilled wine. Don't buy expensive wines for this dish . . . just something dry and drinkable.

1 cup sliced mushrooms
3 tablespoons butter or olive oil
3 large yellow onions, peeled and sliced
4 garlic cloves, crushed
3 pounds fresh whitefish (cod, bass, snapper) cut into serving pieces of equal thickness
1 bouquet garni (page 44)

1 bottle brut or dry champagne (750 ml or a fifth)
1 cup brandy
Roux: 5 tablespoons flour cooked in 5 tablespoons butter or olive oil
Parsley, chopped, for garnish

In a heated frying pan, sauté the mushrooms in half the butter or olive oil. Set aside.

Heat a 3-quart covered Dutch oven and sauté the onions and garlic in the remaining butter until they begin to brown. Place the fish pieces on top of the onions and place the bouquet garni on top of that. Add the champagne and bring to a light boil. Warm the brandy in a small saucepan so that you can set it aflame. It is necessary to remove the heavy alcohol. Be careful with this; just heat it until it is fairly warm. Light it with a match and pour it over the fish. Cover the pot and simmer until the fish is tender but still holds together, about 20 minutes.

In the meantime, prepare the roux by cooking the butter and flour together for a few minutes in a small pan. Do not discolor the flour. Set aside.

Remove the fish to a heated platter along with the onions on the bottom of the pot. Remove the bouquet garni and discard. Reduce the pot juices by one third over high heat. Thicken the sauce with the roux, stirring quickly off the heat. Return to the heat and add the mushrooms, stirring until the sauce is thick and the mushrooms warmed. Taste the sauce to see if salt is needed. It probably will not be. Pour the sauce over the top of the fish and add the parsley garnish.

Start the meal with Cream of Lentil Soup (page 103) and follow the fish with a green salad with Dijon Mustard Dressing (page 131).

Wine Suggestion: Macon or light Chardonnay (Italian).

SERVES 6.

◆

Oysters in Champagne Sauce

(France)

My wife and I were fascinated by a restaurant in Tours, France. Called The Pepper Mill, it is run by an Englishwoman and her French husband, the chef. She served a dish to us that was similar to the one here. It was delicious, but she told us how difficult it was for her to get the French to eat a *cooked* oyster. She is having success with this dish.

2 tablespoons butter or olive oil
2 garlic cloves, peeled and sliced
1 cup dry champagne
½ cup cream or Mock Cream (page 289)
1 pound small oysters
1 pound fresh spinach, carefully washed
1 tablespoon *each* butter and flour cooked together for a roux (page 288)
Salt to taste

In an enamel or stainless pan, melt the butter and sauté the sliced garlic for a moment. Add the liquid from the oysters along with the champagne and cream. Simmer to reduce by about one third liquid volume. Add the oysters to the sauce. Place the spinach on top and cover. Cook for just a moment. You do not want to overcook the oysters.

Remove the lid and place the spinach on a heated plate. With a slotted spoon remove the oysters and place them on the spinach bed. Thicken the sauce with the roux and pour the sauce over the oysters.

Serve with Risotto with Mushrooms (page 155), a green salad with Pesto Vinaigrette Dressing (page 130), and French rolls.

Wine Suggestion: French Chablis or Chardonnay.

SERVES 4–5.

HINT: How to Clean Squid

Squid is probably the most maligned fish from the sea. You remember the great stories from Jules Verne's classics about gigantic squid that swim under the sea. What a horrible fright to put upon the squid lovers of the world. While it is true that squid grow to great length, the kind that you and I buy in a fish market, either frozen or fresh, are little rascals, being about 5 or 6 inches long total. They are easy to clean. You simply cut the head off each and remove the filling from the tube, or body. Don't forget the plasticlike backbone of the squid. You will find it within the tube of the fish while digging around. Rinse the tubes, and you are ready to begin. I also save the tentacles, though not the head, for other dishes.

Squid in Mustard and Ginger Sauce

This one has you wondering, doesn't it? I had a similar dish for lunch one afternoon at a fine restaurant in the Pike Place Market in Seattle. Place Pigalle always has some new creative thing to teach me. I suppose that is really how I judge the creativeness of a restaurant . . . whether or not I learned something new. This dish is perfect for a first course.

- **1 pound squid, cleaned and cut into circles (page 123)**
- **½ cup Chicken Soup Stock (page 101) or used canned, not bouillon**
- **½ cup dry white wine**
- **¼ cup whipping cream or half-and-half or Mock Cream (page 289)**
- **½ teaspoon grated fresh ginger**
- **1 tablespoon *each* butter and flour cooked together for a roux (page 288)**
- **Salt and black pepper, freshly ground, to taste**
- **1 tablespoon Dijon mustard**

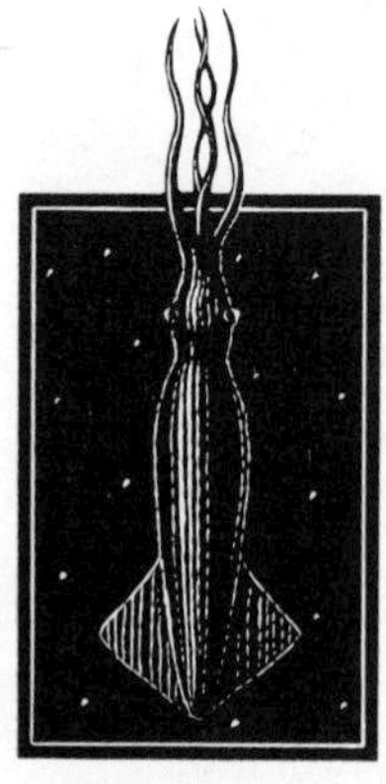
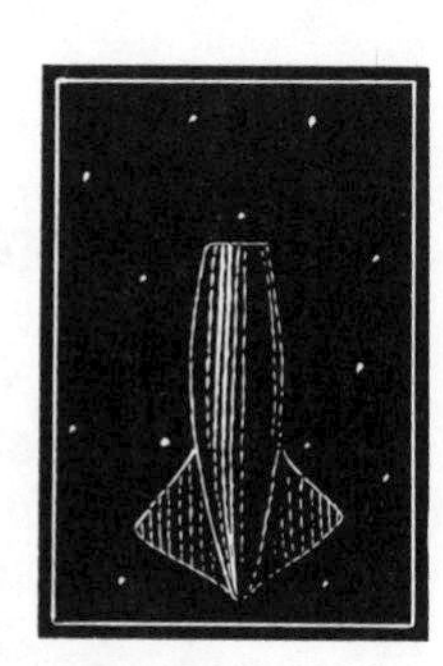

Clean and cut the squid.

Bring the stock, wine, and cream to a heavy simmer and allow to reduce by one third. Add the ginger and the roux. Cook, stirring, until thickened. Taste for salt and pepper. Careful with the pepper. Little, if any, is needed. Stir in the mustard. Add the squid and cook just until the squid are tender, about 5 minutes.

Serve in small boats or bowls with plenty of good French bread for sopping up the very rich sauce.

This is a wonderful dish for a first course. It is very rich.

Wine Suggestion: Chenin Blanc or Vouvray.

SERVES 2–3 AS A FIRST COURSE.

◆

Scallops in Pesto

I had not thought of this until Dennis Terczak, chef at Avanzares in Chicago, brought it to my table. Utter simplicity and light flavors. It is great!

- 1 carrot, cut matchstick or julienne style (page 257)
- 1 garlic clove, crushed
- 2 tablespoons olive oil
- 1 green onion, chopped
- 1 small ripe tomato, diced
- 3/4 pound scallops
- 3 tablespoons dry white wine
- 1 tablespoon lemon juice
- 1 tablespoon Pesto Sauce (see following recipe)
- Salt and pepper to taste

In a large frying pan, heat the olive oil and sauté the carrot matchsticks and the garlic, just for a minute or two. Add the green onion and the tomato. Sauté until the tomato is soft. Keep the heat on high and add the scallops. Sauté just until tender, less than 5 minutes. Add the wine, lemon juice, pesto, salt, and pepper. Toss quickly and serve on a small seashell or a small warmed plate.

Serve this as a first course as it is very rich.

Wine Suggestion: Orvieto (Italian white) or a light Chardonnay.

SERVES 3–4 AS AN APPETIZER.

Pesto Sauce

(Italy)

This is a wonderful uncooked sauce from Genoa. I first tasted it twenty years ago in San Francisco. Now it is very "in." You can buy it canned or frozen or in glass bottles. Avoid the can and buy it frozen or in glass. Better yet, make your own and freeze it in small batches for later use.

- 4 cups tightly packed fresh basil
- ½ cup olive oil
- 2 garlic cloves, crushed
- 6 sprigs parsley
- Salt and pepper to taste
- ¼ cup pine nuts, walnuts, or almonds
- ½ cup freshly grated cheese (Parmesan or Romano)

Place the basil in a food blender (don't bother trying this with dried basil; it won't work). Add the oil, garlic, parsley, salt, pepper, and nuts. Blend until all are chopped very fine. Remove from the blender and add the grated cheese.

Use in the scallop recipe above, or put in soups or on pasta.

MAKES ABOUT 2 CUPS.

SALADS

The better the salad the worse the dinner.

—Italian Proverb

· Salad and Wine ·

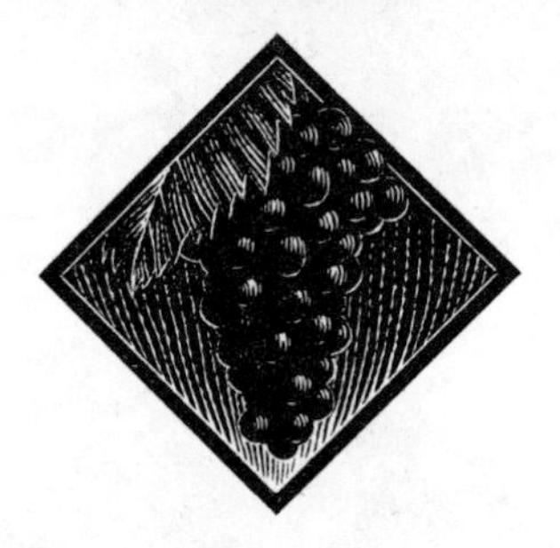

Great problem here. Vinegars are great for salads but they tend to get in the way of the wine. Any vinegar you use must be very mild and played down.

Rule: If you are going to serve a salad with a wonderful vinaigrette dressing, simply do not serve a wine with the salad course. That is all there is to it. Or try a dry German Riesling with your salad course. It will work with many good dressings.

HINT: Enjoy Olive Oil

There is growing evidence that points to olive oil as being quite good for you. It seems to have the ability to help the body clear itself of the harmful part of cholesterol, the part that stays in your arteries as fat. Called a monounsaturated oil, olive oil seems to be more helpful in this cleansing process than even polyunsaturated oils. But oil is oil and we still tend to use too much. Since olive oil has such a bright flavor you may just be better able to cut down by simply using less oil. And olive oil has the advantage of keeping longer than most other oils.

White Wine Vinaigrette

This is very simple to make. It will help with the problem described above if you use a good-quality white wine vinegar, or make your own (page 376). Try this on any of your favorite green salads.

- ¾ cup dry white wine
- ½ cup olive oil
- ¼ cup white wine vinegar
- 1 teaspoon oregano
- ½ teaspoon dry mustard
- Salt and black pepper, freshly ground, to taste

Blend all in a food blender or by shaking in a jar. Store covered in the refrigerator. Keeps very well.

MAKES 1½ CUPS.

Garlic Dressing

You will enjoy this dressing best with a rather heavy wine. If you think that it has too much garlic in it you are welcome to cut down. Please note that soaking the garlic in the oil before blending makes the flavor much brighter.

- 4 garlic cloves, crushed
- ½ cup olive oil
- ¼ cup salad oil (not peanut oil)
- 1 egg yolk at room temperature
- 1½ tablespoons lemon juice
- Dash of cayenne (about 1/16 teaspoon)
- Salt and black pepper, freshly ground, to taste
- ¼ cup dry white wine

Soak the crushed garlic in the salad oil for ½ hour. Place the egg yolk, lemon juice, and seasonings in a food blender. Blend a moment more. Mix the garlic oil and olive oil and then add in a stream. Remove the mixture from the blender and stir in enough wine to thin it to your taste.

This is great with plain green endive or romaine lettuce.

MAKES 1 CUP.

Burgundy and Herb Dressing

This is a very rich dressing but suitable for any kind of meal. Though the list of ingredients may look a little long to you, I promise you this takes no time at all.

- 2 eggs, room temperature
- 1 garlic clove, crushed
- 1 tablespoon lemon juice
- 1 tablespoon red wine vinegar
- Salt and pepper, freshly ground, to taste
- 1/8 teaspoon thyme, whole
- 1/8 teaspoon oregano, whole
- 1/8 teaspoon basil, whole
- 1/16 teaspoon marjoram
- 3/4 cup olive oil
- 1/4 cup dry Burgundy wine
- 1 tablespoon chopped yellow onion
- 1 tablespoon chopped parsley

Place the eggs in a food blender. Add the garlic, lemon juice, vinegar, spices, and herbs. Blend for a few seconds and then, the machine on high, pour in the oil in a steady stream. Stir in wine, onion, and parsley by hand.

MAKES 1½ CUPS.

◆

Pesto Vinaigrette

This dressing is very light due to the rice wine vinegar. This would be a fine dressing for a salad that is to accompany a dish of delicate flavor.

- 1/4 cup Pesto Sauce* (page 126)
- 1 cup olive oil
- 1/2 cup rice wine vinegar
- Salt and black pepper, freshly ground, to taste

Mix all ingredients together with a wire whip or food blender. Use on any green salad. This would also be good on many cooked vegetables that are to be served cold, such as carrots or zucchini.

MAKES 1¾ CUPS.

*Pesto sauce can be purchased in any delicatessen or Italian food shop. Buy it frozen or in glass. Avoid the canned varieties. Or, you can make your own.

Dijon Mustard Dressing

This is served often at our home. I do many variations on it, such as adding oregano now and then. You can have some fun with your herb ideas as well.

1 egg
½ cup olive oil
⅛ cup red wine vinegar
Salt and black pepper, freshly ground, to taste
1 tablespoon Dijon mustard (Grey Poupon is fine)
⅛ teaspoon oregano or any other herb you wish
Pinch of sugar

Coddle the egg by placing it in a bowl of very hot tap water. Let stand for 15 minutes.

Place all ingredients in a food blender and mix.

MAKES ¾ CUP.

•

Mayonnaise

I enjoy good mayonnaise, and it does not seem to fight with wine at the table. Usually, I simply buy a jar of Best Foods or Hellmann's mayonnaise. Sometimes it is fun to make your own. This is the simple food blender method.

It is very easy to prepare fresh mayonnaise by using a 2-cup glass measuring cup and a cordless mixer with the balloon whip attachment. Proceed with the recipe below, but add the oil slowly while whipping all the time. It is a snap, and you don't have to clean the food blender!

2 egg yolks, room temperature
⅛ teaspoon salt
1/16 teaspoon ground white pepper
Pinch of cayenne
½ teaspoon dry mustard (I prefer Colman's)

3 tablespoons lemon juice
2 tablespoons olive oil
1 cup salad oil (not peanut oil)

Put all ingredients into a food blender, except for ¾ cup of the salad oil. Blend for 15 seconds. Turn machine to high and pour in the rest of the oil within about 3 seconds. Keep refrigerated. If the mayonnaise curdles when making, add an egg yolk and continue with the mixing. You should have no trouble with this.

MAKES 1½ CUPS.

◆

Eggs and Mayonnaise

(France)

I had forgotten how good this is for a salad course until I was eating in a workers' restaurant in Paris. So simple that I had not done this in years.

Lettuce leaves for a bed
Red onion rings
Hard-boiled eggs, peeled and cut in half lengthwise
Mayonnaise (page 131)
Salt and pepper to taste

Arrange a bit of romaine or endive on each plate. Add a few onion rings. Place the eggs on the lettuce, cut side down, and place a dollop of fresh mayonnaise on the top of each. Pass salt and pepper to each individual.

Cold Brussels Sprouts Salad

Please don't think this is a weird dish. It is just delicious because you don't overcook the sprouts. Please see the hint on page 261 about cruciferous vegetables.

- **2 pounds fresh or 2 boxes (10 ounce) frozen Brussels sprouts, defrosted**
- **1 bunch green onions, chopped**
- **1 red sweet bell pepper, diced, or 2 ripe tomatoes, diced**
- **½ cup White Wine Vinaigrette (page 128)**
- **¼ cup sliced almonds for garnish**

Boil or steam sprouts until barely tender. This should take no more than 10 minutes. Add a bit of peanut or olive oil to the water when you begin. It helps them remain green instead of that awful gray that you remember from your childhood. Do not put salt in the water. When tender but still crunchy, drain and immediately immerse in cold water. This will stop the cooking. Drain and chill. (If using frozen Brussels sprouts, do not cook them at all. Simply defrost and cut for the salad.)

Cut each sprout in half and place in a large salad bowl. Toss with chopped green onions, chopped red bell pepper or tomatoes, and the vinaigrette. Top with a bit of pepper and some sliced almonds for garnish.

SERVES 6–8.

◆

Cold Brussels Sprouts Salad with Caraway

Prepare the salad above and add some caraway seeds to the dish. You will be surprised at how delicious this is.

Carrot and Zucchini Salad

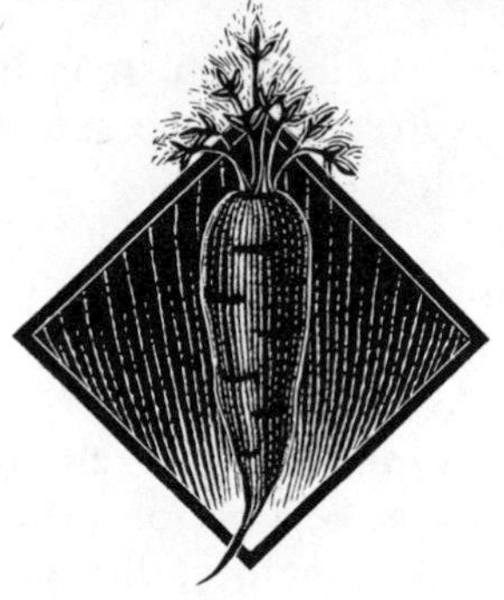

Toss julienne-cut (page 257) carrots and zucchini with Garlic Dressing (page 129). This is great as a first course, a salad course, or a vegetable course during the meal.

◆

Pasta and Green Onion Salad

Read this and you are going to say, "Hey, that sounds good. And no work at all!"

Pasta, cooked al dente, drained and cooled
Green onions, cleaned and chopped, to taste
Mayonnaise (page 131)
Salt and black pepper, freshly ground, to taste

Prepare the salad and chill. Serve as a first course or along with dinner. Do not put too much mayonnaise on this or it will be too rich to eat. Use lots of onions and lots of pepper.

Egg in Tomato

This one is kind of cute, and it is very tasty.

- Lettuce leaves for a bed
- ½ ripe tomato for each person
- Eggs, hard-boiled and peeled, 1 for each person
- White Wine Vinaigrette (page 128)
- Salt and black pepper, freshly ground, to taste

Place lettuce leaves on each plate. Cut the tomatoes in half, from top to bottom. Lay each cut side down and make several cuts in the tomato. Insert a wedge of egg in each cut of the tomato. Place a small puddle of vinaigrette on the lettuce and set the tomato/egg in the dressing. Pass salt and pepper to each individual.

Cauliflower Salad

(Italy)

I had this in a workers' restaurant in Italy. It had never occurred to me to prepare such a thing. I think that you will like it. Children will prefer cauliflower this way since the flavor is much milder when the vegetable is cold.

1 head cauliflower
White Wine Vinaigrette (page 128)
Salt and black pepper, freshly ground, to taste
Parmesan or Romano cheese, freshly grated

Using a stainless steel vegetable steamer (page 25), cook the cauliflower whole until fork tender, about 15 minutes. Allow the vegetable to cool, core it, and break it up into flowerets. Toss with the dressing, salt, and pepper, and top with the cheese.

This works well for a salad course with a nice lettuce garnish. Or you may serve it as a vegetable course at any time of the year.

•

Tuna and Potato Salad

(Italy)

This kind of salad is common in Italian communities such as those in San Francisco or New York. It is very delightful and can be used as a first course, a side dish, a vegetable dish, or a main course in the summertime. Now this is Frugal versatility!

1 package (10 ounce) frozen green beans, defrosted
6 small new potatoes, unpeeled, cooked and diced
1 tin (6 ounce) tuna in water, drained
3 flat anchovies, mashed (optional)
2 tablespoons Pesto Sauce* (page 126)
1 cup Mayonnaise (page 131)
Salt and black pepper, freshly ground, to taste
3 tablespoons chopped parsley

Blanch the defrosted green beans for 2 minutes in boiling water. Drain and plunge into cold water. Drain.

Place the cooked potatoes, beans, and tuna in a salad bowl. Mix the anchovies and pesto with the mayonnaise and pour onto the salad. Add salt and pepper and toss. Garnish with the parsley.

SERVES 4.

*Pesto sauce can be purchased in any delicatessen or Italian food market. Buy it frozen or in glass. Avoid the canned variety. Or, you can make your own.

◆

Baby Shrimp with Butter Lettuce Salad

This dish makes a fine first course. It is easy to do, and if the shrimp are fresh, it is delicious. You can use some other form of chopped lettuce if you wish.

3 ounces cooked shrimp per person
1 small head butter lettuce per person

DRESSING:
(for two persons)

½ cup olive oil
1 tablespoon red wine vinegar
2 tablespoons fresh lemon juice

¼ teaspoon dry mustard (I prefer Colman's)
¼ teaspoon oregano
1 garlic clove, crushed
Salt and black pepper, freshly ground, to taste
Parsley for garnish

Blend all ingredients for the dressing in a food blender or with a wire whip. Chill before serving.

Remove a few of the center leaves of the head of butter lettuce. Chop and mix with the shrimp.

Place the lettuce "bowl" on a plate and pour a bit of the dressing over it. Place the chopped lettuce and shrimp mixture in the center of the "bowl." Add just a bit of the dressing and serve. Garnish with parsley.

Green Bean and Filbert Salad

I whipped this one up one day when I came into a free bag full of filberts. Actually, these nuts are not at all expensive if you can find some kind of a source for them in bulk. Try food co-ops and health food stores.

2 cups whole filberts (hazelnuts)
1 bag (20 ounce) frozen green beans, french cut or julienne style
1 large white salad onion, peeled and sliced very thin
8 green onions, cleaned and chopped

DRESSING:

- 1 egg
- ½ cup olive oil
- 2 teaspoons fresh lemon juice
- 3 tablespoons white or red wine vinegar
- 2 tablespoons Dijon mustard (Grey Poupon is fine)
- ⅛ teaspoon sugar
- 3 garlic cloves, crushed
- Salt and black pepper, freshly ground, to taste

Prepare the filberts: Place the nuts on a baking sheet and roast in a 375° oven for about 15 minutes, or until they are light brown. Cool. Remove the husk by simply placing a few nuts in your hands and then rubbing your hands together. The husk will come off and you can blow away the unwanted coating. Chop the nuts very coarse.

Prepare the dressing: Coddle the raw egg by letting it stand in 2 cups very hot tap water for 15 minutes. Mix all other ingredients for the dressing with the coddled egg. I prefer to use a food blender.

Thaw the beans and drain them well. Place the beans, sliced white onion, and the green onions in a large salad bowl. Toss with the dressing. Top with the filberts.

SERVES 6.

◆

Tortellini and Green Pea Salad

Pasta salads are so "in" at the moment that I thought I should offer one of my favorites. You do not find this kind of cooking in Italy . . . except in places that cater to many American tourists.

VINAIGRETTE DRESSING:

- 4 teaspoons red wine vinegar
- Juice of 1 lemon
- 1½ teaspoons Dijon mustard
- ½ teaspoon salt
- 3 garlic cloves, crushed
- ½ cup olive oil

Whisk all ingredients together to form an emulsion.

Tortellini
Frozen green peas
Parsley, chopped
Grated cheese (Romano or Parmesan)

Boil either fresh or dried tortellini until barely tender. Strain from the water and throw into the kettle a package or two of frozen peas. Cook for only a minute and drain. Mix with the pasta and the dressing. Add parsley and cheese. Chill well before serving. You may wish more salt and black pepper.

PASTA, RICE, AND DUMPLINGS

O Lord, . . . Give us pasta with a hundred fillings, and rice in a thousand variations.

—Robert Farrar Capon
The Supper of the Lamb

• Pasta •

The glories of pasta seem to be endless. Surely, in our time, we see more new pasta dishes each week than just about any other food form. And why not? Pasta is a grand food product, well balanced in terms of its ability to offer excitement in flavor with low fat and complex carbohydrates. At least it *can* be low in fat. The heavy cream sauces negate the lack of fat . . . but there is nothing mundane about a dish of pasta with garlic and olive oil. Wonderful!

The argument over who invented pasta goes on and on. The common notion is that Marco Polo brought pasta into Italy from his trips through China. Since I love the Chinese culture so much I am glad to credit them with the invention of almost everything I enjoy, but not pasta. While they may have had it first, there is good evidence that shows that Italians were eating pasta before the Marco Polo trip, but not around his area, Venice. It could have come into Italy through the Arabs or the Indians. Both had pastas . . . the Indian dish being called *sevika,* meaning "thread," and the Arab's *rishta,* also meaning thread. In any case, the practice, which was unknown in Venice prior to Marco Polo's trip, was probably known in other regions of Italy. Italians chose a similar name to thread, spaghetti, from *spago,* which means "string."

Since pasta refers to any paste made of flour and water, we can also credit other cultures. The dish can be made from rice, wheat, or corn flour, and still qualify. Even a pancake, cut into ribbons for soup, as they do in Austria, is technically a pasta. So let us be done with the argument of who, and simply be thankful that they did. From the days of your first bowl of bad macaroni and cheese at P.S. 13, to the dishes served at fine Italian-American restaurants in our time, you must admit that we have come a long way.

I do not think that you have to go to the work of making your own fresh pasta. Buy it fresh if you can. Make it yourself when you have time, but dried pastas, of good quality, abound. Enjoy them!

Pasta with Fresh Asparagus

If you are a serious asparagus lover then we both will admit that we will do anything for asparagus, at any time. I have bought the stuff in San Francisco during the off-season and paid a fortune for it! But when I brought it home and cooked for Patty, my wife, all was healed and the financial ruin forgotten. This dish is simple and elegant.

½ pound fettuccine
1 large bunch fresh asparagus
1 garlic clove, sliced
1 tablespoon olive oil
1 egg, beaten
3 tablespoons freshly grated Parmesan or Romano cheese
½ cup whipping cream or half-and-half or Mock Cream (page 289)
Black pepper, freshly ground
Salt, if you must

Bring a pot of salted water to a boil for the pasta.

Clean the asparagus and slice across the stalks into pieces ¼ inch long. Try to do this on the diagonal. Place a wok or large frying pan on to heat and place the pasta in the boiling water.

Add the oil to the hot wok, along with the garlic. Toss for a few seconds and then add the cut-up asparagus. Toss until the asparagus is bright green in color and barely tender, about 2 minutes on high heat. Quickly mix in the beaten egg and the grated cheese. Add the cream and salt and pepper. Bring to a simmer for a few minutes while the pasta finishes cooking.

Do not overcook the asparagus!

SERVES 4.

Green Onion Pasta

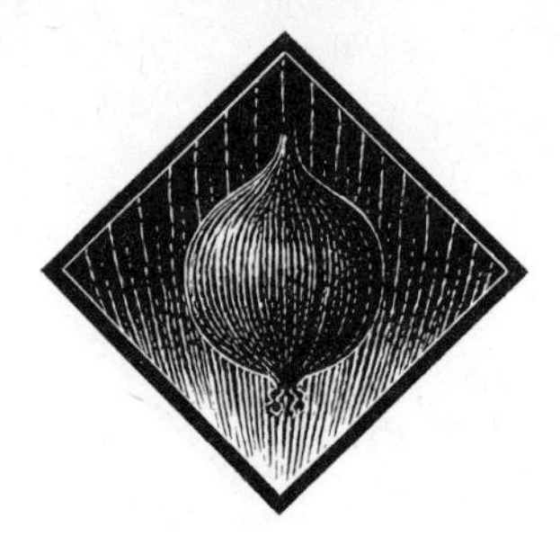

This is only for green onion lovers. The rest of you must not try this. Promise me, or the first thing you know you will be eating this dish often.

- 3 bunches green onions or scallions
- 1 cup Italian Gravy (page 341) or your favorite spaghetti sauce
- 4 tablespoons olive oil
- 1 garlic clove, chopped
- ½ pound pasta, cooked al dente
- 3 tablespoons dry vermouth
- Black pepper, freshly grated, to taste
- ½ cup freshly grated Parmesan or Romano cheese

Clean the green onions by cutting them lengthwise once, and then into 1-inch pieces. Heat the Italian Gravy. Heat a small frying pan and add the olive oil and garlic. Cook for just a moment and then add the green onions. Stir for just a moment and then put the onions and oil on the cooked pasta, pasta cooked al dente, of course. Add the hot Italian Gravy, the vermouth, and the pepper to taste. Toss and top with the cheese.

SERVES 4.

Rigatoni con Pepperoni

(Italy)

I was served this very simple lunch at a workers' restaurant near the airport in Venice. I expected something more elaborate, but I found that this dish was delicious and satisfying.

- 1 garlic clove, crushed
- 1 small yellow onion, peeled and diced
- 2 tablespoons olive oil
- 2 ripe tomatoes, diced
- ½ pound pepperoni, sliced thin
- ¼ cup whipping cream or Mock Cream (page 289)
- Salt and pepper to taste
- ½ pound rigatoni, cooked al dente
- Parmesan or Romano cheese, freshly grated, for topping

Heat a frying pan and sauté the garlic and onion in the olive oil, just until clear. Add the tomatoes and pepperoni. Sauté until the tomatoes cook down a bit, about 3 minutes. Add the cream, salt, and pepper. Toss with the rigatoni and top with the cheese.

SERVES 4.

◆

Spaghettini in Clams and Cream Sauce

I always have a few cans of Gorton's minced clams on hand, even though I do live in the clam center of the country. I know that I will always be able to whip out a dish at that moment when the unexpected guest appears.

- 2 garlic cloves
- 4 tablespoons olive oil
- 2 cans (6½ ounce each) minced clams
- ½ cup whipping cream or half-and-half or Mock Cream (page 289)

3 tablespoons dry vermouth
Salt and pepper to taste
3/4 pound spaghettini, cooked al dente
Parmesan or Romano cheese, freshly grated, for topping

Sauté the garlic in the olive oil. Drain the clams, reserving the juice. Add the juice to the pan and reduce by more than half. Add the cream, clams, and vermouth. Cook only until heated and add salt and pepper to taste. Careful with that salt! Toss with the cooked pasta and top with the cheese.

This will make a complete meal if served with a cold cauliflower salad or a green salad with Garlic Dressing (page 129).

Wine Suggestion: Italian Frascati or Vernaccia.

SERVES 6.

◆

Pasta with Three Meats and Peas

(Italy)

My son Channing and I developed this recipe while doing a live special in Chicago. There he stood on the set, telling me that he had an improvement on my basic pasta carbonara recipe. He began to prepare his portion over a gas burner and his potholder caught on fire. Right there on live television! Being fifteen at the time, he nearly died. When we made this dish together later, however, he told me that he still liked it, regardless of its history. I think you will like it, too. It is a whole meal.

¼ pound bacon
½ cup (1 stick) butter or ½ cup olive oil
1 cup milk
2 tablespoons red wine vinegar
1 pound pasta
1 bag (20 ounce) frozen peas
½ pound sliced Italian salami, cut into sticks
½ pound sliced Italian mortadella, cut into sticks
2 eggs, beaten
⅓ cup Parmesan or Romano cheese, freshly grated
Salt and pepper to taste

Dice the bacon and sauté in the butter until clear. Add the milk and the vinegar. This will turn the milk to cheese. Simmer about 15 minutes, or until the sauce cooks smooth.

Boil the pasta al dente. When the pasta is finished, dump the entire bag of peas into the kettle with the pasta. Bring to a quick simmer again and drain.

Toss the pasta with the salami, mortadella, eggs, and cheese. Toss with the sauce and add salt and pepper to taste. I like a lot of pepper in this dish.

SERVES 8–10 AS A FIRST COURSE AND 6 AS A WHOLE MEAL.

◆

Pasta with Anchovy and Onion

You have got to be in the right mood for this dish, or just a lover of anchovies. I don't serve it to everyone, just to people that I like. It is very different and I think wonderful. The secret is to wash the salt off of the anchovies and then soak them in a bit of milk. Works wonders!

1 can (2 ounce) flat anchovies
½ cup milk
3 tablespoons olive oil
½ cup yellow onion, peeled and diced

2 garlic cloves, crushed
¼ cup Italian Gravy (page 341) or your favorite spaghetti sauce
¼ cup whipping cream or Mock Cream (page 289)
Black pepper, freshly ground, to taste
½ pound pasta, cooked al dente (I like penne with this dish)
Parmesan or Romano cheese, freshly grated for topping

Rinse the anchovies with lukewarm tap water and place in the milk. Let them soak for ½ hour.

Heat a frying pan and add the olive oil. Sauté the onion and garlic until clear. Dice the anchovies and add to the pan, discarding the milk. Cook for 2 or 3 minutes until the anchovies begin to cook apart. Add the Italian Gravy or spaghetti sauce and cream. Add black pepper to taste. Toss with the hot pasta and top with cheese.

SERVES 4 AS A FIRST COURSE.

◆

Pasta with Olives

This dish is just great, if you like olives. It was given to me by a cabbie in Chicago while we were racing in and out of traffic. I have no amounts, but then, you will not need them.

Large green olives, pitted and chopped
Olive oil
Garlic
Cream or half-and-half or Mock Cream (page 289)
Grated cheese (Romano or Parmesan)
Pepper, freshly ground

Pit and chop the olives. Cover them with olive oil and allow to marinate for 2 days, unrefrigerated. Sauté with garlic and oil. Add cream. Toss with hot pasta along with the cheese and pepper.

Pasta Bagna Cauda

Yes, this is full of garlic and salt. No, you should not make it every night. Yes, you should make it tonight!

- ½ cup olive oil
- ¼ pound butter
- 3 to 5 garlic cloves, chopped fine
- 6 flat anchovy fillets, chopped or mashed
- 1 pound pasta, cooked al dente
- 1 egg
- Grated cheese (Parmesan or Romano)
- Pepper, freshly ground

Heat the oil and the butter together in a small pan on very low heat. In another pan cook the garlic in a bit of the oil until the garlic is soft. Add the anchovy fillets and cook until the fish dissolves into a paste, about 5 minutes. Add to the pan of olive oil and melted butter. Stir briskly.

Toss the cooked pasta with the sauce. Add 1 whipped egg and cheese and pepper to taste.

SERVES 4 AS PASTA COURSE.

Hooker's Pasta

Spaghetti alla Puttanesca
(Italy)

That's not a very nice name, it it? However, the Italians love to tell a story behind this dish; something about the women of the night preparing this dish for their customers late in the evening. It could be quickly made from things that would normally be on hand in any Italian kitchen; thus the gals could keep the operation going easily.

This recipe is from a chef in San Francisco that I respect very much. His name is Carlo Middione. You must go to his wonderful restaurant and Italian take-out store called Vivande Porta Via.

- 3 tablespoons olive oil
- 2 garlic cloves, minced
- 2 ounces or more Calamata black olives, pitted and chopped

- 1 teaspoon capers, coarsely chopped
- 1 large fresh tomato, peeled and coarsely chopped
- 4 or 5 anchovy fillets, coarsely chopped
- 1 pound spaghettini
- ⅓ cup finely chopped parsely
- ½ teaspoon salt
- ½ teaspoon pepper, freshly ground
- 1 teaspoon crushed red pepper flakes (optional)

Place the olive oil in a frying pan and add the minced garlic. When it is golden, add the olives, capers, tomato, and anchovy fillets. Stir well and heat through for about 6 minutes.

Cook the pasta al dente and drain it. Place in a warm bowl and add half the sauce. Toss well. Add the remaining sauce on top and sprinkle on the parsley with some salt and pepper to taste. Optional: Sprinkle red pepper flakes over the top before serving. Serve hot.

There is no cheese used with this dish. It can also be eaten later, cold.

SERVES 4–6.

Stuffed Shells

This is a dish that children always seem to love. It is a kind of spaghetti that behaves itself. It will not run off the plate or slap you on the side of the mouth when entering. Maybe I have taken all of the fun out of spaghetti!

1 pound large shells
1 package (10 ounce) frozen spinach, thawed and water squeezed out
½ pound Italian sausage
½ pound cottage cheese, small curd, drained
3 garlic cloves, crushed
Juice of ½ lemon
¼ cup grated cheese (Parmesan or Romano)
Salt and black pepper, freshly ground, to taste
½ teaspoon oregano
1 egg, beaten
2 cups tomato, spaghetti sauce, or Italian Gravy (page 341)
2 cups coarsely grated Swiss or mozzarella cheese

Boil the pasta until firm but tender. Rinse in cold water and drain.

Sauté the sausage and break up into small pieces. Mix with the drained spinach, drained cottage cheese, garlic, lemon juice, grated cheese, salt, pepper, and oregano. Stir in the beaten egg.

Stuff the shells with the above mixture and place in a greased baking dish. Top with a bit of tomato or spaghetti sauce and, finally, the cheese.

Bake at 350° until all is hot and the cheese melted, about 20 minutes.

Serve this for a complete meal, along with Zucchini and Carrots (page 257) and a crisp green salad.

Wine Suggestion: Chianti or Zinfandel.

SERVES 6.

Pan-Fried Ravioli with Bleu Cheese Dressing

This one looks a bit strange to you, I know. But you will love it. It is from an excellent restaurant in Washington, D.C., called Mrs. Simpson's. The name refers, of course, to Mrs. Wallis Simpson, a fine cook from Baltimore who wound up sleeping with the King of England. The whole restaurant is filled with memorabilia from King Edward's short reign, and the food is excellent. The chef deep-fries this dish. I prefer it as follows:

	1	pound fresh or frozen ravioli
	3	tablespoons olive oil
		Parsley for garnish
BLEU CHEESE DRESSING: (This makes plenty— but it keeps)	1	quart Best Foods or Hellmann's mayonnaise
	2	cups buttermilk
	4	ounces bleu cheese
	2	garlic cloves, crushed
	1	dash Worcestershire sauce
	1	tablespoon dried parsley flakes

For the dressing, use a fork to mix a bit of the buttermilk with the cheese until the cheese is soft, but not smooth. Stir in remaining ingredients. Do not use a food blender or food processor. Refrigerate. Stir before each use. Makes 6½ cups.

Boil the ravioli until just tender but firm. See instructions on the package. Drain well. Pan-fry in the olive oil. When light brown on both sides, place on a serving plate and dribble a bit of blue cheese dressing on the top. Garnish with parsley.

SERVES 4.

Ravioli with Vegetable Sauce

(Italy)

I tasted this dish in Italy and was so surprised by its simplicity that I decided I would do it at home. It is a winner every time for a quick and creative meal. No, I don't expect you to make your own ravioli. The frozen brands that are on the market will do just fine for this dish. Of course, homemade would be better if you have the time . . .

Since the sauce is cooked for so little time, all the vegetables retain a fresh and lively flavor.

1 cup diced eggplant
1 teaspoon salt
1 pound frozen ravioli
3 tablespoons olive oil
2 garlic cloves, crushed
½ cup peeled and diced yellow onion
1 carrot, cut julienne style (page 257)
½ cup frozen green beans or peas, defrosted
1 cup diced ripe tomatoes
¼ cup cream or half-and-half or Mock Cream (page 289)
¼ cup Italian Gravy (page 341) or your favorite spaghetti sauce
¼ cup red wine
1 tablespoon chopped fresh parsley
½ teaspoon oregano
Salt and pepper, freshly ground, to taste
Parmesan or Romano cheese, freshly grated, for topping

Dice the eggplant and mix with the teaspoon of salt. Place in a drainer for ½ hour while you prepare everything else for the recipe.

Cook the ravioli according to instructions. Heat a large frying pan and add the oil, garlic, and yellow onion. Cook for a moment and add the eggplant, drained and wiped dry with a paper towel. Sauté or stir-fry on medium-high heat for 4 minutes. Add the carrot, green beans, and diced tomatoes. Cook for another 4 minutes and add the remaining ingredients, except the cheese. Simmer for a few more minutes while you drain the ravioli.

Pour the sauce over the drained ravioli and top with the cheese. This dish will bring forth applause!

SERVES 4–6.

• Rice •

Rice was common in Italy long before it came to this country. Tom Jefferson, a great food authority in his time, found rice in Italy when he was there representing us before the Italian government. He had never seen such a thing. We had wild rice from the lakes in the Colonies, but nothing like what he found in Italy. The story goes that Jefferson decided to bring back some seed, since he was an agricultural genius. The only problem was that he decided to do this during a famine in Italy. As he approached the ship to return to the Colonies he was met with a great sign that said, "Anyone attempting to smuggle grain or seed out of Italy during the famine will be shot without trial." The author of our Declaration of Independence, dressed in his burgundy-colored velvet coat, and flashing his gorgeous red hair, nodded to the captain, and walked aboard the ship, his pockets filled with rice seed. By the late 1790s we had rice in the Carolinas. Now, to rice as it is cooked in Italy.

HINT: Wine to Cut Down on Salt Addiction
As we grow older our taste buds begin to wear out. We begin to overdo on fats, alcohol, sugar, and salt. Salt is the most overused item here, and wine in your cooking will help you cut down. Wine contains a great deal of natural potassium chloride and calcium chloride. These chemicals, related to salt, or sodium chloride, react on your tongue very much like salt. When you are told to cut down on salt, put wine in your food. It contains natural salts and acids that will help in the replacement of salt.

Risotto with Mushrooms

(Italy)

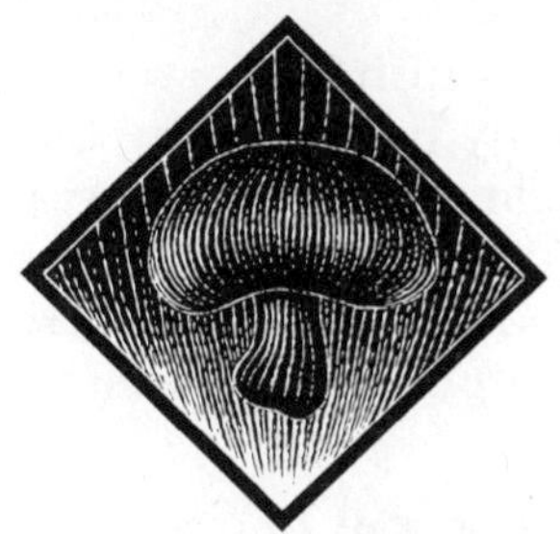

This dish is a great replacement for the boredom of potatoes or plain rice. Since it is quickly made, you can serve it often, and with almost anything.

- 2 ounces dried European mushrooms
- 2 tablespoons butter or olive oil
- ¼ cup diced yellow onion
- 1½ cups short-grain rice
- 3 cups Chicken Soup Stock (page 101), boiling, or use bouillon
- ½ cup Italian Gravy (page 341) or your favorite spaghetti sauce
- ¼ cup dry sherry
- Salt and black pepper, freshly ground, to taste
- ¼ cup freshly grated Parmesan or Romano cheese
- 2 tablespoons chopped fresh parsley

Soak the mushrooms in 2 cups water for ½ hour. Drain, saving the water for a later use in soup. Chop the mushrooms and set aside.

Heat a 2-quart heavy saucepan with a cover and add the butter and onion. Sauté until clear and then add the rice. Sauté until the rice begins to turn very light brown, and pour in 1½ cups of the boiling broth, along with the mushrooms. Cover and let simmer for 10 minutes. Add the remaining boiling broth, the Italian Gravy, sherry, salt, and pepper. Cover and simmer until the broth is absorbed, about 10 more minutes. Stir in the grated cheese and parsley, and serve.

SERVES 6.

Risotto and Vegetables

(Italy)

My wife and I tasted this dish in Torcello, a tiny community outside Venice, reached only by boat. The food was superb, and the day a delight. We bought a bottle of wine and hired a taxi (speedboat) to take us to Venice. Between the beauty of the day, the speedboat, the wine and my wife, and the memory of this dish, I was in heaven. I have duplicated it as best I can.

- 2 tablespoons butter
- ¼ cup diced yellow onion
- 1½ cups short-grain rice
- 3 cups Chicken Soup Stock (page 101), boiling, or use bouillon
- 3 tablespoons olive oil
- 3 green onions, chopped
- ¼ cup coarsely grated zucchini
- 1 cup chopped fresh spinach
- 1 cup chopped kale or Swiss chard
- 2 tablespoons chopped parsley
- 3 ripe tomatoes, diced
- 1 ounce dried European mushrooms (page 37)
- 1 teaspoon dried basil
- ¼ cup cream or Mock Cream (page 289)
- ¼ cup dry white wine
- ¾ cup freshly grated Parmesan or Romano cheese
- Salt and black pepper, freshly ground, to taste

Heat a 2-quart heavy saucepan and melt the butter. Sauté the yellow onion and rice until the rice is a very light tan. Add half the boiling broth and cover. Cook over low heat until the broth is absorbed, about 10 minutes.

In the meantime, in another large frying pan or wok, heat the olive oil and sauté the remaining vegetables, including the mushrooms. Cook just until everything begins to collapse.

Add the remaining boiling broth to the rice, along with the vegetables, basil, cream, and white wine. Simmer for another 10 minutes, or until most of the liquid is absorbed.

Mix in the cheese, salt, and pepper. Place all in a covered casserole and bake in a 350° oven about 30 minutes.

SERVES 6–8 AS A PASTA COURSE.

Rice and Peas

Risi e Bisi
(Italy)

My wife's Aunt Suzy told me about this dish. Her Italian background has given me many recipe ideas, although she just describes the dish and says "Do it!" A recipe is out of the question. You will enjoy this simple dish from Romeo Salta.

- 4 tablespoons olive oil
- 4 tablespoons butter
- ¾ cup peeled and chopped yellow onion
- 1½ cups long-grain rice
- 3 tablespoons dry sherry
- 3 cups shelled fresh peas, or 2 packages (10 ounce) frozen peas, thawed
- 1 cup diced smoked ham (about ¼ pound)
- 3 cups hot Chicken Soup Stock (page 101) or bouillon
- 1½ teaspoons salt
- ¼ teaspoon black pepper, freshly ground
- ¼ cup freshly grated Parmesan or Romano cheese

Choose a heavy 2-quart saucepan with a tight-fitting lid. Heat the saucepan and then add the oil and 2 tablespoons of the butter. Sauté the onion for 5 minutes. Mix in the rice and stir until translucent. Add the sherry; cook over low heat 1 minute. Add the peas, ham, 2 cups of the hot stock, salt, and pepper. Cover, bring to a boil, and cook over low heat for 10 minutes. Add the remaining broth, re-cover, and cook for 10 minutes longer, or until the rice is tender and dry. Taste for seasoning; mix in the cheese and the remaining butter.

SERVES 6–8.

Green Rice

Riso Verde
(Italy)

I wish Americans would eat as much rice as the Italians do. Many household cooks are afraid to learn the simple process of cooking rice and so they resort to instant rice, which tastes like the cardboard box in which it is packed. No, the box tastes better than the rice!

This dish is common all over Italy and in the Italian communities in this country. This is a wonderful rice dish that I found in Romeo Salta's cookbook.

- **2 tablespoons olive oil**
- **4 tablespoons butter**
- **1 cup minced green onions or scallions**
- **1 cup minced parsley**
- **1½ cups finely chopped fresh spinach**
- **2 cups short-grain rice**
- **3½ cups hot Chicken Soup Stock (page 101)**
- **1½ teaspoons salt**
- **¼ teaspoon black pepper, freshly ground**
- **Parmesan or Romano cheese, freshly grated, for topping**

Choose a 2-quart heavy saucepan with a tight-fitting lid. Heat the pan and add the oil and 2 tablespoons of the butter. Add the onions, parsley, and spinach. Cover and cook over low heat for 5 minutes. Mix in the rice and stir until translucent. Add 2 cups of the hot chicken stock, salt, and pepper. Cover and cook over low heat. Add the remaining broth, cover, and cook another 10 minutes, or until the rice is tender and light. Lightly mix in the remaining butter with a fork. Garnish with the cheese topping.

SERVES 4–6.

Rice with Chilies and Cheese

(Mexico)

This is great as a molded dish. The advantages here are many. The dish is delicious, and it sits in the oven until you are ready for it.

- 2½ cups cooked rice
- Salt and pepper to taste
- ¼ teaspoon oregano
- 1 can (4 ounce) diced green chilies (I like Ortega brand)
- 1 pint sour cream or Mock Sour Cream (page 289)
- ½ pound grated jack cheese
- 2 tablespoons chopped parsley
- Paprika for garnish

Mix the salt, pepper, and oregano with the rice. Blend the green chilies with the sour cream and cheese. Gently fold into the rice. Bake, uncovered, in a buttered casserole or mold for 30 minutes at 350°. You may wish to put a bit more cheese on the top during the last 5 minutes of baking. Garnish with parsley and paprika.

SERVES 4–6.

• Dumplings •

Semolina Dumplings

Gnocchi alla Romana
(Italy)

While this dish of baked wheat dumplings is supposed to be a Roman specialty, it is found all over Italy. I tasted a wonderful version in Venice. It was rich with eggs and cheese and baked until crisp on top. I promised my wife that I would learn to make it the moment I returned home. This is a good dish for entertaining since the dumplings can be made ahead and baked at the last minute.

3 cups milk
1 teaspoon salt
⅛ teaspoon ground nutmeg
Pinch of black pepper, freshly ground
¾ cup semolina or farina (regular cooking cream of wheat will do, though it is not the same flavor)
2 eggs
1 cup freshly grated Parmesan or Romano cheese
5 tablespoons butter, melted

In a 2-quart heavy saucepan bring the milk, salt, nutmeg, and pepper to a boil. Gradually stir in the semolina, using a wooden spoon. Keep stirring until it is so thick that the spoon can stand up in the pan. Remove from the heat.

Beat the eggs and stir them into the semolina, along with ½ cup of the cheese. Oil a large baking sheet and spread the mixture out to a thickness of ¼ inch. Place a piece of wax paper over the top of this and just pat it into shape. Refrigerate until well chilled.

Using a 1-inch-diameter round cookie cutter or glass, cut the dough into circles. Place in an oiled baking dish, overlapping the slices like tiles. Top with the melted butter and the rest of the cheese. Bake in a 400° oven for about 15 minutes, or until bubbly hot and browned lightly on the top. You may wish to put the pan under the broiler for a short time in order to brown the top.

Serve immediately with more cheese or with Italian Gravy (page 341) or your favorite spaghetti sauce. I like mine best just as they come from the oven.

SERVES 4–6.

Semolina Dumplings with Ham

(Italy)

Prepare the recipe above but add ½ cup chopped proscuitto or smoked ham. Stir the ham in along with the eggs and cheese and proceed as above.

Baked Polenta

(Italy)

Corn was a gift to Europe from the New World. It is a strictly American product, having been given to the Colonists by the first Americans, the Indians. It is now popular in all of Europe and China. This dish is very easy and delicious with any kind of meal.

- **1 quart water**
- **1½ teaspoons salt**
- **1 cup yellow cornmeal or polenta**
- **1 cup diced Swiss cheese**
- **1 teaspoon whole thyme**
- **1 cup diced fresh red sweet pepper or 3 tablespoons chopped pimientos**
- **⅛ teaspoon black pepper, freshly ground**
- **½ cup butter (1 stick), melted**
- **½ cup freshly grated Parmesan or Romano, for topping**

Bring the water to a boil in a heavy 2-quart saucepan. Add the salt and slowly add the cornmeal, keeping the water boiling. Use a wooden spoon and stir until the mixture begins to thicken. Reduce the heat and simmer the polenta, stirring frequently, for 20 or 30 minutes, or until the wooden spoon will stand up in the polenta. Remove from the heat and stir in the remaining ingredients, except the butter and the grated cheese. Spread the mixture in a 9x13-inch baking dish that you have greased with a bit of the melted butter. Pour the remaining melted butter on the top and sprinkle on the grated cheese. Bake in a 375° oven for 20 minutes, or until browned on top. Cut into squares to serve. You might wish to put Italian Gravy (page 341) or your favorite spaghetti sauce on the top of this.

Variation: Omit the thyme and red pepper above and add instead 1 teaspoon crushed rosemary and 6 garlic gloves, crushed. Bake as above. Delicious!

SERVES 4–6.

◆

German Dumplings

Spaetzle
(Germany)

These are little fat noodles that can be made in a hurry. They are a basic in the German diet and go very well with the many gravies and sauces that we have made in this book.

- **2 eggs, beaten**
- **½ cup milk**
- **2 tablespoons water**
- **1½ cups flour**
- **½ teaspoon salt**
- **½ teaspoon baking power**
- **Pinch of nutmeg, grated**

- **2 quarts boiling salted water**
- **5 tablespoons butter**
- **½ cup toasted bread crumbs**

Beat the eggs and add the milk and water. Stir in the flour, salt, baking powder, and nutmeg, mixing well. Bring the water to a boil and add 2 teaspoons salt. The spaetzle should be light and delicious, so check the batter by dropping ½ teaspoon into the boiling water. Cook for 6 to 8 minutes and check the noodle. If it is not

light, add a couple more tablespoons of water to the batter. Force the dough through a spaetzle maker or use a plastic bag for forming the noodles. Put all the dough into a heavy 1-quart self-sealing plastic food bag and cut one corner off. Make the cut fairly small so that you can extrude noodles about the size of a pencil. Squeeze on the bag and cut the noodles off into 1-inch pieces. Do this quickly into the boiling water. Boil 6 to 8 minutes. Remove and drain. Heat a large frying pan and melt the butter. Lightly brown the spaetzle in the butter. Top with the bread crumbs and serve.

I like this dish with Basic Brown Sauce (page 283) or brown gravy.

SERVES 4.

Fried Rice Balls

Arancini

(Italy)

Very often these rice balls from southern Italy contain a bit of tomato in one form or another. I tasted the following delicious recipe, without tomatoes, while judging a cooking contest in, of all places, Mobile, Alabama. A young fellow, Jon Fusco by name, entered these arancini as his contribution. They are just terrific, and you can make them ahead and freeze them. Do not be put off by the complexity of this recipe. It is really very simple.

- 2 cups short-grain rice
- 1 teaspoon salt
- ½ cup butter (1 stick), melted
- ¼ cup chopped parsley
- ½ cup grated cheese (Parmesan or Romano)
- 2 eggs, well beaten
- ¼ pound lean ground beef
- ½ cup each (diced)
  - Genoa salami or Italian salami
  - Fresh mushrooms
  - Provolone cheese
  - Mozzarella cheese
- 2 additional beaten eggs for dipping
- Bread crumbs for coating, about 2 cups
- Oil for deep-frying

Wash the rice and drain well. Place in a 2-quart saucepan with a tight-fitting lid. Add 4 cups of water and the salt. Bring to a boil without the lid. Then, cover and turn the heat to low. Simmer for 20 minutes and remove from the heat. Do not take the lid off the pot for this entire process. Allow the rice to sit for 15 minutes.

Add the melted butter, parsley, grated cheese, and eggs to the rice. Stir well to blend. Set aside.

Sauté the ground beef, drain, and cool. Mix the beef, salami, mushrooms, provolone, and mozzarella together.

Lightly moisten your hands. Shake off excess water. Form a ball of rice just smaller than a golf ball. Using your thumb, poke a hole into the center and put in some of the salami and cheese stuffing. Seal up the hole by pinching it together. Finish all before cooking.

Heat the oil to 350°. Dip the arancini in egg and then in bread crumbs. Fry in deep fat, a few at a time, until light brown. Keep warm in the oven.

May be made ahead and frozen. Defrost before frying. Use leftover filling for omelets or toss with hot pasta.

MAKES 25 ARANCINI. THANKS, JON!

POULTRY

CHICKEN • DUCK • TURKEY
CONFITS

. . . poultry is for the cook what canvas is for the painter.

—Brillat-Savarin

CHICKEN

I want there to be no peasant in my kingdom so poor that he is unable to have a chicken in his pot on Sundays.

—Henri IV of France
1553–1610

• Chicken in Wine •

I am glad that I do not have to do a selling job to you on chicken. Lamb, tripe, tongue, rabbit, maybe so, but not chicken. It has been with us from the beginning of the European invasion of this country, and it remains. Coming first from China about three thousand years ago, it is still a blessing adaptable to a million tastes. And the bird is very efficient in terms of the food chain. It takes much less grain or food to make a pound of chicken than it does for any red meats. The Chinese prized the bird because it was so efficient. They have never understood our love for beef because it is so costly to raise. Chinese favorites such as chicken, duck, and pig, on the other hand, are affordable and delicious.

So, to the chicken. It marches about on two feet, halfway between the red-meated creatures with four feet and the white-meated creatures of the sea with no feet. And the chicken's meat is right in between. Versatile!

Wine and chicken are a natural blending. You will have no trouble with any of these dishes.

Chicken in Red Wine

Coq au Vin
(France)

There are a thousand variations on this classic dish. In this case I am going to use a beef stock along with the wine. In this way we will come closer to that dark brown sauce served with the chicken when you see it in France. The darkness of the dish in France is due to the use of chicken blood in the pot. I am just not up to that. You will understand this variation, I am sure. It is easier than the classic dish, and therefore frugal.

¼ cup olive oil
2 yellow onions, peeled and sliced
4 garlic cloves, crushed
1 pound white mushrooms, sliced
¼ pound bacon, diced
2 fryer chickens, 3 to 4 pounds each, or use 5 pounds breasts, thighs, and legs
2 cups Basic Brown Soup Stock (page 100)
2 cups dry red wine, such as Burgundy
2 bay leaves
1 teaspoon whole thyme
Salt and pepper, freshly ground, to taste
½ cup minced parsley
4 tablespoons brandy
Roux: 6 tablespoons flour cooked in 6 tablespoons butter

Heat a large frying pan and add the olive oil, onions, and garlic and sauté until they are tender. Add the mushrooms and sauté, on high heat, until the mushrooms are barely tender. Remove from the pan and deglaze the pan with a little of the red wine. Pour the pan drippings over the onions and mushrooms. Set aside.

In the same pan, sauté the bacon until clear. Remove the bacon from the pan, leaving the fat. Set the bacon aside. Cut the chicken into serving pieces, reserving the backs and necks for a later soup stock. In small batches, brown the chicken in the bacon fat. Place the chicken and bacon in a large kettle and add the stock, red wine, bay leaves, thyme, salt, pepper, parsley, and brandy. Bring to a simmer and cook until tender, about 1 hour. Add the onions and mushrooms and continue to simmer while you prepare the roux. Lightly brown the flour in the melted butter and stir this mixture into the cooked chicken and sauce. Stir over the heat until the sauce thickens.

Serve the chicken and sauce over noodles or rice pilaf.

You might serve this with Pan-Fried Broccoli (p. 263) and a green salad.

Wine Suggestion: Burgundy or Pinot Noir.

SERVES 6.

Chicken Marsala

(Italy)

The spiciness and sweetness of Marsala adds wonderful depth to this quick chicken dish. Normally, of course, the dish is made with veal, but I cannot and will not eat veal. The poor animal is treated in such an unkind way that I cannot bring myself to eat the meat. So, on to the chicken and Marsala instead.

8 chicken breasts (each chicken has two breasts)
Flour for dredging
Salt and black pepper, freshly ground, to taste
Olive oil for frying
1 yellow onion, peeled and sliced
2 garlic cloves, crushed
¼ cup dry white wine, Chablis type
½ cup sweet Marsala

Debone the chicken breasts and remove the skin. Save the skin and bone for a later soup stock. Pound the breasts thin between two pieces of plastic (page 175). Dredge the pieces in flour seasoned with a bit of salt and pepper. Set aside.

In a large frying pan, sauté the onion and garlic in a bit of olive oil. Sauté only until the onions are clear, not browned. Remove from the pan and deglaze the pan with the white wine. Pour the white wine over the onion and garlic.

Rinse the pan and heat it again. Add a bit of olive oil for frying and sauté the chicken pieces, a few at a time, quickly on both sides. They should just begin to brown. Remove them to a warm plate and finish the remaining chicken pieces. Add the onion and garlic to the pan and deglaze with the Marsala. Allow the wine to reduce a bit and then pour the sauce over the chicken pieces.

Serve with Rice and Peas (page 157), a green salad with Garlic Dressing (page 129), and French bread.

Wine Suggestion: Zinfandel or Côtes du Rhône.

SERVES 6–8.

Chicken with Mustard and Wine Sauce

This dish was created for a live special at my studio in Chicago, Channel 11, WTTW. The place is filled with wonderful people, but during pledge week there is no way that I can give them all a taste. There are several hundred people in the building at once, and they *all* wanted to taste this dish. I am warning you. Make plenty.

1 whole frying chicken
2 tablespoons peanut oil
2 large garlic cloves, peeled and sliced thin
2 tablespoons chopped shallots (may substitute red onion)
½ cup dry white wine (more may be needed)
1 cup leeks sliced into 2-inch lengths, washed and drained
Salt and pepper to taste
3 tablespoons Dijon mustard (Grey Poupon is fine)
¼ cup whipping cream, unsweetened and unwhipped, or Mock Cream (page 289)

Hack the chicken, i.e., cut it into serving pieces. Use a cleaver and have the pieces no larger than 2 inches square. Heat a large frying pan or wok and add the oil. Sauté the chicken pieces over high heat, stirring as you cook, until they are browned.

Remove the chicken from the wok; drain the oil and discard.

Sauté the garlic and shallots or red onion in the pan for a minute. Add the white wine and the chicken. Cover and simmer until the chicken is tender, about 15 minutes.

Increase heat to high. Add the leeks. Toss and cook for a moment. Add salt and pepper to taste. Cover and cook over medium heat for 3 minutes.

Add the mustard and cream. Toss and serve. You may need to add more wine if the sauce is too thick.

Try this with Ravioli with Vegetable Sauce (page 152), and a green salad with Burgundy and Herb Dressing (page 129).

Wine Suggestion: Chenin Blanc or Vouvray.

SERVES 2–3.

HINT: Don't Add Water!

That is not really such an exaggeration. Recipes that tell you to add more water if needed, or "simply add water," would often be helped by the addition of wine or soup stock. This is true of sauces, soups, stews, gravies, meat and fish dishes. This is not true of waffles.

Chicken and Ham Rolls

This is another dish that is usually done with veal. But as I have said before, I cannot think of eating veal when you think of the pain the poor animal has gone through. So I use chicken instead.

8 chicken thighs, skinless, boneless, and pounded thin (see Chicken Marsala, page 170)
½ cup coarsely grated Swiss cheese
¾ cup cooked, sliced ham cut into strips
Salt and pepper to taste
3 tablespoons butter
2 tablespoons olive oil
½ cup dry white wine
Chopped parsley for garnish

Pound each of the thighs until thin (page 175). Lay each piece out flat and spread a portion of the Swiss cheese and ham on each. Add salt and pepper. Roll up and tie with thread.

Place the butter and olive oil in a hot frying pan and sauté the chicken rolls until brown. This should be no more than 6 minutes. Add the wine, cover, and continue to cook for another 6 to 10 minutes, or until the rolls are tender but not dry. Remove the rolls to a heated platter, reduce the sauce in the pan, and pour over the rolls. Add a chopped parsley garnish.

This would go well with Eggplant Stuffed Turkish Style (page 269) and a cold Cauliflower Salad (page 136). Rolls as well.

Wine Suggestion: Beaujolais, Gamay Beaujolais, or Riesling.

SERVES 4.

Chicken with Tomatoes, Shallots, and Vermouth

This is one of those dishes for one of those days. Late to work, late home, late for dinner . . . Relax and cook something good for those that you love.

- 1 frying chicken, cut into serving pieces
- Olive oil for frying
- ½ cup chopped shallots (can substitute red onion)
- 3 very ripe tomatoes, diced
- ½ cup dry vermouth
- 1 teaspoon oregano
- Salt and black pepper to taste

In a large frying pan, one with a cover, sauté the chicken in the olive oil. Remember, heat the pan first and then add the oil. When the chicken is brown, remove it to a heated platter and add the shallots or onions to the pan. Sauté for 3 minutes and then add the tomatoes and vermouth. Cook this until the tomatoes are soft and tender and then return the chicken to the pan. Add the oregano, salt, and pepper, and cover. Simmer until the chicken is tender, about 20 minutes.

Serve with Green Rice (page 158), Onions in Herbs and Wine (page 259), and rolls.

Wine Suggestion: Chardonnay or Zinfandel.

SERVES 2–3.

Garlic Chicken with Garlic, Garlic

It is always fun to receive recipes from viewers and friends. This one will scare you to death, since it calls for one chicken and forty cloves of garlic. I cannot even thank the person in this book since he or she did not put a name on the recipe . . . and I have long since lost the envelope. So, you know who you are, and you are going to have the whole country smelling of wonderful garlic. Do try this. It is not strong at all and very good for you.

1 whole frying chicken, about 3 pounds
40 unpeeled garlic cloves
Salt and pepper to taste
¾ cup dry white wine

Pat the chicken dry. Rub inside and out with one split clove of garlic. Lightly salt and pepper. Preheat oven to 450°. Place chicken on a roasting rack in a baking pan and arrange cloves of garlic around in the pan. Place in the oven and reduce heat to 350°. Bake 20 minutes and then pour wine over chicken. Baste again in 10 minutes and again 10 minutes later. Roast a total of 1 hour. You may wish to bake your chicken longer.

My friends serve the chicken on a platter with the garlic on the side. In this way, you can squirt the cooked garlic cloves onto bread, rolls, or potatoes. Or you can make the following sauce:

SAUCE:

½ cup Chicken Soup Stock (page 101)
½ cup whipping cream or Mock Cream (page 289)
The cooked garlic cloves

Put the chicken stock in a small saucepan and add the cream. As this is heating, squirt all of the garlic cloves into the sauce, discarding the peel. Simmer for a few minutes. Correct the seasoning with salt and pepper and enjoy the sauce on the chicken. They call it Grand Garlic Gluttony. I cannot understand why!

Try this with Fried Cabbage (page 262), Carrots in Champagne and Dill (page 265), and a green salad with White Wine Vinaigrette (page 128).

Wine Suggestion: German Riesling or Merlot.

SERVES 3–4.

HINT: To Pound a Piece of Meat or Fish Thin and Flat
Purchase a 2x2-foot piece of 8-millimeter vinyl at a lumberyard or hardware store. Ask to be sure that the material can be used on food. Wash and then fold the sheet in half, and place the thin-sliced meat in between. Pound with a wooden meat mallet or a piece of two-by-four wood. The meat will spread very thin and will not tear because of the protection of the plastic. This works well for fish and meat.

Chicken in Port

This does sound strange, doesn't it? Cooking chicken in a heavy red wine seems to be against all the rules. Red wine with beef and lamb, white wine with chicken and fish. This will convince you that most rules were made by people with little imagination. (Boy, I hope Channing and Jason don't read this chapter!)

- Olive oil for frying
- 10 chicken thighs
- 2 garlic cloves, crushed
- Salt and pepper to taste
- ½ cup peeled and chopped yellow onion
- ½ cup finely chopped mushrooms
- 1 cup ham steak cut into julienne (page 257)
- 2 cups dry port or tawny
- ½ cup whipping cream or Mock Cream (page 289)
- Roux: 2 tablespoons flour cooked with 2 tablespoons butter

Heat a large frying pan and then add the olive oil. Season thighs with salt and pepper and fry until brown on both sides. Remove to a heated platter. Sauté the garlic, onion, and mushrooms until the onions are clear. Add the ham to the onions and cook for 3 minutes. Add the chicken thighs and port to the pan and cover. Simmer until the chicken is tender, about 15 minutes.

Remove the chicken to a heated platter and add the cream to the sauce. Reduce the sauce a bit and thicken with the roux. Correct the seasoning for salt and pepper.

Return the chicken to the sauce and serve over pasta or rice.

I like this with German Dumplings (page 162) and Brussels Sprouts Polonaise (page 264.)

Wine Suggestion: Petite Sirah.

SERVES 4.

HINT: Don't Buy Cooking Wine

Cooking with wine and "cooking wine" are two different things. Products labeled as cooking wine are wines of cheap quality and then loaded with salt so that the shipper may avoid the taxes placed on wine. My rule is simple: If you can't drink it, don't cook with it. The only exception to this rule pertains to those households in which a member is condemned to alcoholism. In such a case undrinkable cooking wine is better than testing your loved one with temptations of the vine.

Chicken Stuffed in the Front

I don't know what else to call this dish. While it is delicious, it is a bit different in terms of preparation. Sara Little, a fine cook and a dear friend, told me about this and I just had to try it. It is so easy and the results are just spectacular.

1 whole frying chicken, about 3 pounds
Olive oil
2 garlic cloves, crushed
Juice of 1 lemon
Salt and pepper to taste

KASHA STUFFING:
1 cup kasha (Wolff's brand is great)
1 egg, beaten
Giblets, neck, and wing tips from the chicken
½ yellow onion, peeled and chopped
Fat from the chicken

Remove fat from the tail of the chicken and render the fat by gently cooking in a small frying pan. You may also use the skin from the neck for rendering. Allow the fat to cool. You should have about 3 tablespoons.

Place the giblets and the tips of the wings, (the first joint), along with the neck, into a small saucepan and cover with water. Bring to a boil and add a bit of salt and pepper. Cook for 1 hour, covered. Remove from the broth and cool, reserving the broth. Chop the giblets and sauté them, along with the onion, in the chicken fat, just until the onion is clear.

Now, the stuffing. Heat a heavy 2-quart saucepan with lid and add the kasha. Stir in the beaten egg and stir over the heat until the egg is absorbed by the kasha. Add the giblets, onions, and fat along with 2 cups of the leftover broth from the giblets. You may have to add additional water or chicken broth to make up the 2 cups. Cover and simmer for 30 minutes, much as you would cook rice. Test for the need of salt.

The Grand Construction:

Cut the chicken along the backbone from the bottom to the top. Open it like a book and lay it skin side up on a board. Remove the tail with a knife and then gently raise the skin of the bird, starting with the bottom front section. Simply poke your fingers under the skin and loosen it all over the front of the chicken so that you can stuff the bird's front. Push the kasha under the skin, being careful not to pack it too tight. Arrange the chicken on a baking rack or sheet.

Brush the bird with olive oil, garlic, and lemon juice. Add salt and pepper and then place in a 375° oven for 1 hour, or until done to your taste.

Cut up and serve with a bit of dressing on each plate.

Variation: Use your own favorite stuffing and proceed as above. It will be moist and delicious.

Great with Sammy's Eggplant Salad (page 274) and Egg in Tomato Salad (page 135).

Wine Suggestion: Light dry white.

SERVES 2–3.

Chicken with Olives

(Greece)

You will become very fond of this dish. It is simple to prepare and offers such bright flavors that your dinner party or family evening will go very well indeed.

1 chicken, 3½ pounds, cut up
3 tablespoons olive oil
5 garlic cloves, chopped
3 yellow onions, peeled and chopped
3 cups coarsely chopped very ripe fresh tomatoes
1 jar (6 ounce) green olives, stuffed with pimientos, drained (buy the cheaper ones called salad olives)
Black pepper, freshly ground, to taste
1 tablespoon oregano
1 cup dry red wine
Salt to taste

Brown the chicken in the olive oil. Use a large pan and do not try to do the whole batch at once. Remove the chicken from the pan and drain most of the oil. Sauté the garlic and onions until limp. Add the tomatoes and olives and sauté until tomatoes are soft. Add the pepper, oregano, wine, and the chicken. Cover and simmer until the chicken is tender, about 30 minutes. Taste for salt. You should use very little as the olives are salty.

Serve with Pan-Fried Ravioli with Bleu cheese (page 152) along with a watercress and mushroom salad.

Wine Suggestion: Rich Italian red such as Barolo or a Zinfandel.

SERVES 4.

Chicken Under a Brick

When you want your children to think that they have driven you over the edge, serve them this dish. Let them see the brick in the oven, the whole works. That should stop them!

I have a friend Sue, who is a serious New Yorker. She claimed that she could not make this dish in a frugal manner. "After all, I would have to drive clear to New Jersey to get a brick!" I hope you have less trouble finding bricks in your neighborhood.

1 chicken, about 3 pounds

MARINADE:

5 garlic cloves, crushed
3 tablespoons olive oil
1 teaspoon whole oregano
1 teaspoon whole rosemary
Salt and pepper to taste
Juice of 1 lemon
3 tablespoons dry white wine

Preheat the oven to 375°. Place two bricks, each wrapped in aluminum foil, in the oven to heat for 1 hour before baking the chicken.

Cut the chicken in half. Prepare the marinade by blending together the garlic, olive oil, oregano, rosemary, and salt and pepper to taste. Place the chicken halves in a large bowl and pour the marinade over them. Rub the chicken well with the marinade. Allow to sit for 1 hour, turning and rubbing again once or twice more.

In a large frying pan, brown the chicken skin side down. No need to turn. Place in a baking pan and cover each piece with a hot brick, wrapped in foil. Bake at 375° for ½ hour.

Remove from the pan. Deglaze the pan with the lemon juice and white wine. Reduce the sauce and serve over the chicken. Leave the bricks in the kitchen!

The advantage to this method of cooking is that it drives all the excess water out of the chicken and you get a bird of very firm but tender flesh.

Try this with a Baby Shrimp in Butter Lettuce Salad (page 137) and Rigatoni con Pepperoni (page 145).

Wine Suggestion: Cabernet.

SERVES 2–4.

HINT: Substitute for Wine in Cooking

If you really do not wish to use wine in your cooking, look for new wines on the market that contain no alcohol. Grape juice will also help, along with a small shot of good-quality wine vinegar.

DUCK

One cannot think well, love well, sleep well, if one has not dined well.

—Virginia Woolf
A Room of One's Own

• Duck with Wine •

Duck was one of the primary meat sources in China as early as the second century B.C. One of the reasons for the popularity of the duck is that it is quite able to take care of itself. Respected by the Chinese as a forager, the duck is capable of marching out into the front yard in the morning and returning home that evening, well fed.

While the chicken was brought into this country by Europeans, the duck was already common food for natives as early as the fifteenth century. The Incas of South America and the early Aztecs of Mexico prized the bird, and evidently cooked it well and often.

Duck and wine go well together. While the duck is rich and bright in flavor, the wine is cleansing and supportive. Duck with wine dishes are popular in Europe, Greece, and China. Here we rarely see it except in restaurants. I think that this is due to the commonly held belief that duck is hard to cook. Not so! The following recipes will prove my point.

•

Duck in a Pot

(France)

This is a very lovely dish that amounts to something like a duck stew. It is great on a winter evening since you have a bit of soup as well as the duck.

1 duck, about 4 pounds, defrosted if frozen
Salt and black pepper, freshly ground, to taste

- ½ cup brandy
- ½ cup dry white wine
- 1 garlic clove, sliced thin
- 1 tablespoon chopped parsley
- ¼ pound salt pork, diced and rinsed
- 1 teaspoon thyme, whole
- 3 tablespoons butter or olive oil
- ¼ pound bacon, diced
- 3 yellow onions, peeled and chopped
- 3 carrots, chopped
- Chicken Soup Stock (page 101) or bouillon as needed

Cut the duck into four pieces and salt and pepper each. Place in a stainless steel or glass bowl along with half the brandy and half the white wine. Add the garlic and parsley. Marinate the duck in this for 2 hours.

In a small saucepan, place the salt pork, diced and rinsed, the remaining wine and brandy, and the thyme. Add a bit of black pepper if you wish. Bring to a boil, cover, and simmer on very low heat for 10 minutes.

Drain the marinade from the duck and reserve it. Pat the duck pieces dry with paper towels and sauté them in a frying pan in the butter. Just lightly brown each piece, turning once.

Place the duck pieces in a 2-quart ovenproof lidded casserole. Add the pork and sauce, the marinade from the duck, the bacon, and the onions and carrots. Cover the mixture with chicken stock and place the lid on the pot. Bake in a 325° oven for 1½ hours, or until the duck is very tender. Correct the seasoning before serving.

Add a Green Bean and Filbert Salad (page 138), Risotto with Vegetables (page 156), and a green salad with Burgundy and Herb Dressing (page 129.)

Wine Suggestion: Cabernet or Merlot.

SERVES 4.

Duck with Cabernet Sauce

This dish is heavenly. Duck cooked in this manner is very "in" at the moment but I cannot help it. It is so delicious that I must make it for myself. I would just love to have a backyard full of ducks and rabbits. But I would become so attached to them that I would soon be calling them by name and that would be the end of my career in agriculture. Cook this dish without naming the duck!

- 1 duck, about 3½ pounds, defrosted if frozen
- 1 medium yellow onion, chopped
- 1 garlic clove, sliced thin
- 2 carrots, chopped
- 2 celery stalks, chopped
- ¼ teaspoon thyme, whole
- 1 bay leaf, whole
- ⅛ teaspoon black pepper, freshly ground
- 1 tablespoon tomato paste
- 1 cup water
- 2½ cups red wine, Cabernet if you can afford it
- 1½ cups Chicken Soup Stock (page 101) or use canned broth (Do not use bouillon. Too much salt, and we are going to reduce this sauce.)
- 1 tablespoon Glace de Viande (page 284)

Remove the loose fat that is to be found around the tail section of the duck and render the fat by gently cooking it in a small saucepan, along with a tablespoon of water. The fat will turn liquid. Be sure not to have the heat too high or you will burn the fat. A medium-low should do. Remove the cracklings or brown fat solids and discard. Set the rendered fat aside.

Remove both breasts of the duck. Use a very sharp paring or boning knife and simply begin at the breastbone and gently pull away the meat while stroking the bones with the knife. Trim any extra skin but leave the breast skin attached. Remove the leg and thigh in one piece. Set the breasts and the leg and thigh pieces aside.

With a cleaver or with kitchen shears, cut the duck carcass into 8 or 10 pieces. Place in a roasting pan and roast for 35–40 minutes in a 400° oven, or until the bones and carcass are browned a bit. Remove from the oven and add the liquid fat to the rendered fat. Save the fat for later use with a confit (pages 195 to 200).

Heat a 2- to 3-quart heavy saucepan and add 3 tablespoons of the rendered fat. Sauté the yellow onion, garlic, carrots, and celery until they just begin to brown. Add the thyme, bay leaf, pepper, tomato paste, and red wine. Place the roasted bones in the pan and add the water, wine, and stock. This should just cover the bones. Otherwise, add a little more wine and stock. Bring to a boil, turn down the heat, and gently simmer this for 3 hours, covered. Drain the stock through a sieve or strainer and discard all solids. Return the stock to the saucepan and reduce by one half or more. It should be thick and very rich. Add the glace de viande and correct the seasonings. I am sure that you will not need more salt.

Place the leg pieces, skin side up, on a broiler rack. Roast in a 400° oven for 15 minutes and then add the breasts. Continue roasting for 20 more minutes.

Place a puddle of the sauce on each person's plate. Slice the breasts very thin and arrange in the sauce. Separate the leg from the thigh and serve along with the breasts. You may wish salt with this, but I doubt it.

Serve with German Dumplings (page 162), Vegetables North Beach (page 258), and a green salad with Garlic Dressing (page 129).

Wine Suggestion: Cabernet.

SERVES 2.

Duck with Olives

(Greece)

There is a restaurant just outside of Athens, Greece, that serves a dish like this. This is as close as I could come. I have eaten in this place only once, this Taverna Anna, and I shall never forget it. I will eat there again, I know.

- Salt and black pepper, freshly ground, to taste
- 1 duck, cut into 4 pieces
- 3 tablespoons olive oil
- 1 yellow onion, peeled and diced
- 2 garlic cloves, crushed
- 5 very ripe tomatoes, chopped
- 2 tablespoons chopped parsley
- 1 cup dry red wine
- 1 teaspoon oregano
- 1 cup green olives, stuffed with pimiento

Salt and pepper the duck pieces and place them on a broiling pan and roast in a 400° oven for 20 minutes. The pieces should just begin to brown.

While the duck is baking, prepare the sauce. Heat a frying pan and add the olive oil, the onion, and the garlic. Sauté until transparent. Add the remaining ingredients, except the olives. Simmer, uncovered, for about 20 minutes, or until the tomatoes have collapsed. Place the duck pieces in a Dutch oven with a lid. Rinse off the olives and add to the sauce. Pour the sauce over the duck, cover, and simmer until the duck is tender, about 1 hour.

I like this with Baked Polenta (page 161), Carrots in Champagne and Dill (page 265), and Eggs and Mayonnaise (page 132) for a salad.

Wine Suggestion: Barolo or Zinfandel.

SERVES 4.

Pickled Duck

(France)

No, this dish does not quite come out in the way that you expect. We use the word "pickled" to refer to the presence of vinegar in a dish. In France, the word refers to meat that has been preserved with salt, much as we would do with corned beef. This is simple to prepare and the result is a tender and very flavorful dish.

- 1/4 cup salt
- 1 tablespoon thyme, whole
- 3 bay leaves, whole
- 1 bunch of parsley, stems and all
- 1 duck, 4 to 5 pounds, cut in half, defrosted if frozen
- 1 yellow onion, peeled and stuck with 2 whole cloves
- 6 leeks
- 2 celery stalks, chopped, leaves and all
- 1/2 pound turnips
- 1 pound carrots
- 1 cup Basic Brown Soup Stock (page 100) or canned (do not use bouillon)
- 1 cup whipping cream or Mock Cream (page 289)
- 1/2 cup dry Marsala
- Salt and pepper to taste

Place 3 quarts of water in a deep lidded kettle and add the salt, thyme, bay leaves, and parsley. Bring to a boil and drop in the duck halves. Remove from the heat. Cover and let sit for 8 hours. (This can be done in the morning.)

Cut the yellow onion in half. Insert a clove in each half. Cut the leeks in half, lengthwise, and then into 2-inch pieces, using only the tender ends. Chop the celery and peel and dice the turnips. Chop the carrots. Bring 2 quarts of water to a boil and boil the turnips and carrots for 15 minutes. Drain and set aside.

Remove the duck from the pickling bath. Pat dry with paper towels. Place the duck halves, skin side up, in a baking pan side by side, with 1/2 onion stuck with a clove under each duck. Spread the vegetables around the base of the duck and bake in a 400° oven for about 45 minutes.

Meanwhile, prepare the sauce. In a 1-quart saucepan, mix the beef stock and whipping cream. Bring to a light boil and reduce by half. Add the Marsala and correct the seasoning if salt and pepper are needed. Keep warm.

Remove the duck halves from the baking dish and cut each in half again. Arrange with the vegetables and sauce. Serve immediately.

Serve this with Fried Rice Balls (page 163), Cold Brussels Sprouts Salad with Caraway (page 133), and lots of crisp French bread.

Wine Suggestion: Dry German Riesling or dry California Riesling.

SERVES 4.

HINT: Low-Salt/Low-Fat Eating

Some rules that will help you and your heart.

1. Eliminate as much animal fat as possible. Trim your meats well before cooking.
2. Use more fish and poultry.
3. Cut down on salt in your diet. Use wine, herbs, garlic, lemon juice, and wine vinegar instead.
4. Replace much of the butterfat in your diet with olive oil. That is how it is done in Europe. Use it in cooking, sauces, even Real Garlic Toast (page 341).
5. Choose low-fat foods. Low-fat mayonnaise, Mock Sour Cream (page 289), milk, or half-and-half instead of cream in cooking.

Duck with Mustard and Leeks

I love the taste of good Dijon mustard, cream, and poultry. This is just a natural and very easy to create. You might train your junior-high student to cook this one for you while you are at work. It is that simple.

1 cup leeks
1 duck, defrosted if frozen, cut into 4 pieces
Salt and pepper to taste
2 tablespoons peanut oil

2 garlic cloves, sliced thin
2 tablespoons chopped shallots or chopped red onion
½ cup dry white wine
½ cup whipping cream or Mock Cream (page 289)
2 tablespoons Dijon mustard (Grey Poupon is fine)
½ cup brandy

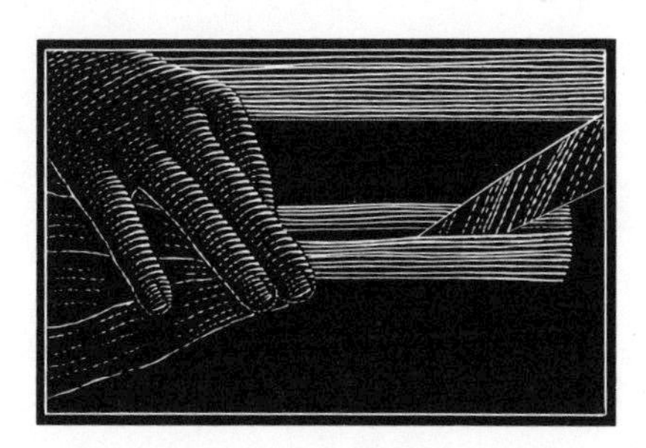

Slice the leeks lengthwise, and then into 2-inch pieces, using only the tender portions.

Hack the duck into small pieces, each about 2 inches square. Cut the legs and thighs into 2 pieces. Use your cleaver or poultry shears for this. Season with salt and pepper to taste.

Heat a large frying pan or wok. Add the oil and sauté or stir-fry the duck pieces over high heat until they are browned. Remove the duck from the pan and discard the oil.

Heat the pan again and sauté the garlic and shallots or red onion for a minute or two. Add the white wine and the duck. Cover and simmer until the duck is tender, about 25 minutes.

Increase the heat to high and add the leeks. Toss and cover. Reduce heat to medium and cook for about 3 minutes. Add the cream and mustard. Toss. Barely warm the brandy in a small saucepan, ignite it, and pour over the duck. Be careful doing this, but it is important to burn off the alcohol. Toss again. No, you don't want to do this in front of your guests. You may just burn up the whole dining room. Do it in the kitchen.

Serve with Semolina Dumplings with Ham (page 160), and Carrot and Zucchini Salad (page 134).

Wine Suggestion: Chenin Blanc or Vouvray.

SERVES 4.

TURKEY

I wish the bald eagle had not been chosen as the representative of our country; he is a bird of bad moral character; like those among men who live by sharping and robbing, he is generally poor, and often very lousy.

The turkey is a much more respectable bird, and withal a true original native of America.

—Benjamin Franklin

• *Turkey with Wine* •

People who grow turkeys tell me that they are one of the dumbest creatures known to mankind. They don't even have enough sense to come in out of the rain. So be it. The turkey does have the ability to offer wonderful meals for us. I do not mean the meals during the holidays when we are always too filled with turkey. Try turkey at other times of the year. Jason wants turkey in July. We barbecue it, simmer it, and cook it with sauces. Now that you can find moist and inexpensive cuts of the bird all year, there is no reason not to serve it more often.

•

Turkey with Salsa Mole Poblano

(Mexico)

Can you believe that you are making turkey with pepper and chocolate sauce? This is actually a very old dish in Mexico. The story goes that some nuns in a priory were suddenly informed that the bishop was coming for dinner. The sisters had little to eat and threw together almost everything that they could get their hands on, thus the birth of this dish. Who knows, and what's the difference? I like that story.

3 turkey thighs, defrosted
Peanut oil for browning

MOLE SAUCE:
3 dried ancho chilies
3 dried pasilla chilies
2 tablespoons peanut oil

- 1 medium yellow onion, peeled and chopped
- 2 garlic cloves, minced
- 1 red sweet bell pepper, chopped
- 1 green sweet bell pepper, chopped
- 1 cup whole canned tomatoes
- ¾ teaspoon ground cinnamon
- ½ teaspoon ground cloves
- ¼ teaspoon ground coriander
- ¼ teaspoon ground anise
- ¼ teaspoon ground cumin
- 1 dry wheat tortilla, torn into pieces
- ¼ cup sesame seeds
- ¼ cup raisins
- 2 cups chicken or turkey broth
- 2 squares (1 ounce each) semi-sweet baking chocolate

Brown the turkey thighs in a bit of oil in a very heavy skillet. Place them in a kettle, barely cover with water, bring to a boil, cover, turn down the heat, and simmer for 45 minutes. Turn off the heat, cover the pot, and leave the turkey in the broth for another 45 minutes.

For the sauce, stem and seed the chilies and tear them into pieces. Be careful with this as the chili oil that you will get on your hands will burn your eyes if you should rub them. Discard the seeds unless you wish for a much hotter dish. Place the pieces in a small bowl, cover with boiling water, and allow to sit for 30 minutes. Discard all the water except ¼ cup.

Heat oil in a skillet and sauté the onion and garlic until limp. In a blender or food processor, combine the chilies and reserved liquid, the two bell peppers, onion and garlic, tomatoes, and spices. Purée until smooth. Then add the tortilla pieces, sesame seeds, and raisins. Purée again until all is quite smooth.

Add the chicken or turkey broth.

Simmer this mixture in a saucepan for 10 minutes. Add the chocolate and stir until the chocolate melts.

Remove the turkey from the kettle, slice, and place on a platter. Mole sauce is served over the turkey with additional sauce served on the side.

Try this with Rice and Chilies with Cheese (page 159) and a green salad with Garlic Dressing (page 129).

Wine Suggestion: Heavy Pinot Noir.

SERVES 8–10.

CONFITS

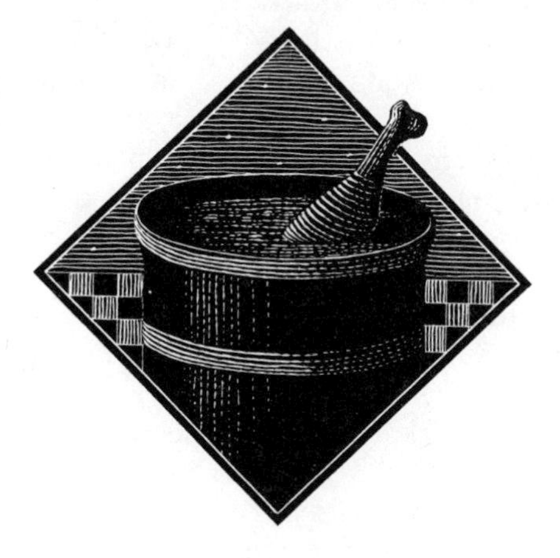

Cook everything until it falls apart!

—Nettie L. Smith 1886–1958
Wobbly and Democratic Member of the
Washington State Legislature

Grandmother of the Author

Confit Recipes

If you have never tried to make a confit you are in for a treat. It goes back to peasant times in France, obviously as an effort at preserving food for the winter.

Sometimes the dish was called a potted meat, because in earlier times the meat was first cooked in its own fat. It was then stored in crocks with a covering of fat, thus preserving the meat for up to three months in the cellar. I am not urging you to cook the meat for this reason, though it is good to know that the dish will keep fine in your refrigerator for several days, providing you have enough fat on it. It will thus help you in your planning for a fine meal with little to do at the last minute.

Recipes vary. Generally the dish is made from goose, though duck is also common. I have tried it with turkey and chicken, and both are delicious. Pork is used in the Gascon region of France. The method of cooking intensifies the flavor of the meat. Moisture is drawn out by the salt but the flavor remains. It is also a good method of tenderizing tougher cuts of meat.

I know that you are wondering about my concern over fat and salt here. These dishes contain less salt than you think, however, as the salt is washed off before cooking. In the old days salt was used as a preservative, but we need not be concerned about that. The fat is already in the goose or chicken. We are simply going to render it and then cook the meat in it. Since the fat is drained before eating the meat, you are probably eating less fat than you normally would with the meat dish.

All of these meats go great with beans and legumes of every kind. Goose or duck confit is common in the classic French bean dish known as cassoulet.

The recipes that I have found vary in the amounts of herbs and spices used. I have several different combinations in the following recipes, depending on how the meat was going to be finally used or served. You can change any of the meats around for any of the recipes. They will all work for each kind of meat.

Confit of Goose

Confit d'Oie
(France)

This is the most common form of confit to be found in France. Geese are hard to find in this country, however, so warn your butcher ahead of time and he will locate a frozen bird for you. It will work just fine.

- 1 whole goose, defrosted if frozen
- 2 bay leaves
- 1 teaspoon dried thyme, whole
- 1 teaspoon dried rosemary, whole
- 3 tablespoons salt

Remove the giblets from the bird and reserve for another use. You might also wish to remove the tips of the wings and reserve them for soup. Remove all fat that you can see from the rear end and the neck area of the goose. Save the fat in the refrigerator. You might also save the skin of the neck, which is very fatty.

Cut the goose up into 6 to 8 equal pieces. Mix the herbs with the salt, crushing the herbs as you mix. Dry the goose pieces with paper towels and rub each with the salt/herb mixture. Place the pieces in a glass or stainless steel bowl and cover with a plate. Place a weight on the top, such as a brick, and place in the refrigerator for 2 days.

To cook: Place a large Dutch oven or metal casserole on the stove and add to it all of the reserved fat. Add 1 cup water. Heat slowly so that the fat is rendered without burning. This will take about ½ hour over moderate heat (medium low). Cover the pan during this process.

Rinse the salt and herbs from the meat and dry each piece. Place the meat in the pot and turn each so that it is coated with fat. Cover and cook over moderate heat for 2½ hours, or until the goose is very tender when pierced with a pot fork. Watch the pot closely during this entire time so that the meat does not overly brown or go dry. You may need to lower the heat or turn the meat once.

The meat can be served at this point, but it is much better if you place the meat in a glass or stainless bowl and pour the fat over the meat. Allow it to sit in the refrigerator in its own fat for anywhere from 1 to 3 days. When ready to serve, remove a piece, sauté it in a pan, browning lightly, and serve.

The meat can also be used in salads, soups, and stews. It is particularly good with bean dishes.

Prepare a pasta with Confit of Goose and Marsala. A green salad and lots of French bread would be perfect.

Wine Suggestion: Chardonnay or Zinfandel.

SERVES 6 OR MORE, DEPENDING ON THE FINAL PREPARATION AND TYPE OF DISH.

◆

Confit of Duck

Confit de Canard
(France)

You should have no trouble finding duck in your supermarket freezer. If you do not see it, then ask the butcher. This makes a smashing dish for a dinner party. Or you can make this and leave it in the refrigerator for a few days and be comforted by the fact that you have a duck ready to warm up at a moment's notice. It is delicious! Duck may be prepared just like the goose above. Or try this variation.

1 duck, about 3 pounds
2 tablespoons salt
½ teaspoons fresh cracked black pepper
¼ teaspoon ground ginger
¼ teaspoon ground nutmeg
¼ teaspoon dried thyme
1 bay leaf, crumbled
Pinch of ground allspice

Proceed as in the goose recipe. Remove the wing tips and cut the duck into 4 pieces. Cook for about 2 hours.

This is just wonderful served with a light salad and perhaps a good pasta.

Use in the Duck, Pork, and Sausage Casserole. Salad and bread will be all that is needed.

Wine Suggestion: Chardonnay or Zinfandel.

SERVES 4.

Confit of Turkey

Proceed as in the goose recipe. Buy a small turkey, perhaps 10 pounds, so that you can serve people easily. This is great for using turkey at other times of the year, and the old bird will not be tough and dry as it generally is during the holidays. You may have to add some lard or olive oil to this dish.

For an interesting variation, try the herbs and spices suggested for the duck on the turkey.

Try this with Pumpkin Soup (page 106), Hooker's Pasta (page 149), and a green salad with Pesto Vinaigrette (page 130). What a meal!

Wine Suggestion: Chardonnay or Zinfandel.

SERVES 6–8.

Confit of Pork

Proceed as in the goose recipe. This is the most common way the dish is prepared in France. Choose a large pork butt of 4 to 5 pounds and ask the butcher for extra pork fat. Trim the roast of the fat and proceed as above. Cut the roast into 4 or 5 pieces.

For a very delicious variation try the following mixture on your pork:

2 tablespoons salt
1 tablespoon grated fresh ginger
¼ teaspoon ground cumin
¼ teaspoon ground coriander
6 garlic cloves, peeled and sliced

Mix the spices and salt together and rub over the pork pieces. Place a few slices of garlic on the top of each piece and proceed with the pressing in the refrigerator. Discard the garlic when you wash off the salt.

Serve with Tortellini and Green Pea Salad (page 139), along with Red Cabbage and Wine (page 262).

Wine Suggestion: Petite Sirah.

SERVES 5–6.

Confit of Chicken

Proceed as in the goose recipe. You may want to find a large chicken, say, 5 pounds. If using a smaller one, cut down on the amount of spices, salt, and herbs.

Serve with your favorite Sunday dinner.

Wine Suggestion: Chardonnay or Zinfandel.

SERVES 3–4.

◆

Pasta with Confit of Goose and Marsala

- ½ pound boneless confit of goose, sliced into matchstick-size pieces or julienne (page 257)
- 2 tablespoons goose fat
- 1 tablespoon flour
- 3 green onions, chopped
- Salt and black pepper, freshly ground, to taste
- ½ cup dry Marsala
- ½ cup half-and-half or Mock Cream (page 289)
- ½ pound pasta of your choice, cooked and drained
- Grated Romano or Parmesan cheese for topping

Melt the goose fat in a frying pan and add the flour, green onions, salt, and pepper. Cook until the flour is lightly browned and then add the wine, stirring with a wire whisk until thick. Add the cream and the goose and toss with the pasta.

Use very little cheese on the top so that the goose flavor is not hidden. This will wow them!

SERVES 4 AS A FIRST COURSE.

BEEF

Better is a dinner of herbs where love is, than a fatted ox in the midst of hatred.

—Proverbs 15:17

• *Beef in Wine* •

I must defend the beef industry. Beef is a perfectly fine food product, and good for you, if you do not eat too much of the fat. Beef fat is hard on our hearts and entire system. And how is most beef eaten in this country? Hamburger, that's how. And hamburger can be up to one third fat, and still be legal. Avoid the fat. I trim all pot roasts and steak very well, and I do not buy prime cuts but rather the cheaper cuts that have the fat in large chunks so that I can remove it. Meat marbled with fat, the sign of prime cuts, may be more tender and more expensive, but it is also tough on your heart. So trim your meat well, buy only the very leanest of hamburger, or better yet, trim the meat and grind your own.

•

Pot Roast with Port and Mushrooms

This one sounds as if the port will be too sweet for the beef. But remember that in many Eastern European countries a bit of sugar is added to the beef stew in order to give it richness and depth. This will happen in this dish as well. It is simple and delicious.

2 tablespoons olive oil
2 pounds pot or chuck roast
1 cup tawny port
1 cup Basic Brown Soup Stock (see page 100)
2 tablespoons flour
2 tablespoons butter

½ pound fresh mushrooms, chopped
3 garlic cloves, crushed
Salt and pepper to taste
Parsley for garnish

In a heavy metal casserole, heat the oil until smoking and brown the meat well on all sides. Add the wine and simmer, uncovered, until the wine is reduced by half. Add the beef stock and simmer, covered, for 1 hour.

Meanwhile, in a small frying pan, prepare the roux (the flour and butter mixture). Lightly brown the flour in the melted butter. When the meat has simmered for 1 hour in the wine and broth, add the roux to the sauce, stirring to thicken. Add the mushrooms, garlic, salt, and pepper. Cover and simmer until very tender, at least another ½ hour. Garnish with parsley.

This is a plain and simple dish that goes well with noodles or rice.

Try this with Cauliflower Salad (page 136) and Eggplant Cheese Rolls (page 273).

Wine Suggestion: Zinfandel.

SERVES 4–6.

HINT: Don't Salt That Meat
I am convinced that one should not salt the meat prior to browning, grilling, or broiling. Salt draws out the moisture in meat. It is a better practice to salt the meat following cooking. You will also find that you use less salt.

Beef in Red Wine and Mushrooms

Does this dish look similar to the one above? Not so! The dried mushrooms are very rich and the red wine must be dry or the wine sugar will make this dish wonderfully rich, so rich that you cannot eat it. This is the kind of thing that I expect to find in the southern regions of France. Or in North Tacoma. You can use cheap stewing beef, which has wonderful flavor but is tough, since you are going to marinate the meat in the wine overnight. Tender! Wine was the first meat tenderizer.

- **4 pounds beef stew, lean, cut in 1-inch pieces**
- **4 tablespoons olive oil**
- **4 garlic cloves, peeled and sliced**
- **2½ cups red wine (dry Burgundy type)**
- **1 cup Basic Brown Soup Stock (page 100)**
- **½ ounce dried mushrooms (page 37)**
- **1 bay leaf**
- **1 teaspoon thyme**
- **Salt and pepper to taste**

Heat a large frying pan, add the oil, and brown the meat. Do so in small batches so that the meat is not crowded and can cook quickly. Remove the meat from the pan and add the garlic. Sauté for a few moments and deglaze the pan with 1 cup of the red wine. Use a wooden spoon to scrape the brown richness from the bottom of the pan. Pour the pan mixture over the meat and add the rest of the wine. Place all in a covered baking casserole and marinate overnight, covered, in the refrigerator.

The next day, add the remaining ingredients to the pot and place in a 325° oven, covered. Allow to simmer until tender, about 2½ hours. You may wish to thicken with a roux (page 288).

I love this over German Dumplings (Spaetzle) (page 162). It is rich and satisfying and the marinating overnight in the wine tenderizes the beef.

Add German Dumplings (page 162), green salad, and Onions in Herbs and Wine (page 259) to this menu.

Wine Suggestion: Pinot Noir.

SERVES 8–10.

Beef with Bleu Cheese

I have tried bleu on everything from pasta to pears. It is always delicious. This dish is rich so you need not plan on a large cut of meat for your friends or guests . . . or family. Everyone at our house loves this except Channing. I have never been able to get him to appreciate bleu cheese. He loses!

Olive oil for frying
1½ pounds round steak
½ cup dry white wine (Chablis type)
2 garlic cloves, crushed
2 tablespoons chopped yellow onion
1 tablespoon Glace de Viande (page 284)
¼ teaspoon dried whole rosemary
2 tablespoons softened butter
2 tablespoons bleu cheese (mixed well with the butter)
Salt and pepper to taste
Chopped parsely for garnish

Heat a large frying pan. Add the oil and the steaks and cook to your preference. (I like mine rare, very rare.) Remove to a warm plate and add the white wine and the garlic and onion. Sauté just a minute and deglaze the pan by scraping the bottom with a wooden spoon. Allow the wine to reduce by half and then add the glace de viande and rosemary. Simmer for a moment and add the butter mixed with the cheese. Mix with a wire whip until smooth.

Place a bit of the sauce on each plate and then a piece of the steak on top of the sauce. Add the salt and pepper at the very last, as salt will dry out the meat during the cooking process. Garnish with parsley.

Serve with Pasta with Olives (page 148) and Zucchini and Carrots (page 257.)

Wine Suggestion: Chenin Blanc or Riesling.

SERVES 5–6.

Beef Stew, Peasant Style

This dish is common in terms of history . . . but delicious in terms of the table. Allow everything to marinate overnight so that the blending of flavors results in a wonderful and smooth flavor. Remember, marinating in wine really does tenderize meat. And please note that this dish does not need salt. The use of wine will help you cut down on your need for the taste of salt in food (page 154).

- **2 pounds beef chuck roast**
- **2 carrots, unpeeled, sliced**
- **3 celery stalks, sliced**
- **1 large yellow onion, peeled and sliced**
- **3 garlic cloves, crushed**
- **1 teaspoon freshly ground pepper**
- **½ teaspoon whole thyme**
- **1 bay leaf**
- **½ teaspoon whole rosemary**
- **3 cups Zinfandel**
- **3 tablespoons olive oil**
- **2 tablespoons tomato paste**

Place all ingredients, except olive oil and tomato paste, in a glass or ceramic casserole. Or you can use an iron casserole if it is covered with procelain enamel. Cover and place in the refrigerator for 24 hours.

The next day, remove the meat from the marinade, saving everything. Heat a heavy frying pan and add the oil. Brown the meat over high heat, using small batches so that the pan is not crowded. Return the meat to the casserole containing the wine and vegetables and add the tomato paste. Bring to a boil and then place in a 350° oven, covered, for 1½ to 2 hours. Meat should be tender.

Remove the meat to a warm platter. Purée the sauce and vegetables in a food processor or run them through a sieve. Bring the sauce to a boil, skim off the fat, and correct the seasoning. Be careful with the salt!

I like this with Semolina Dumplings (page 159), along with a green salad with Garlic Dressing (page 129).

Wine Suggestion: Zinfandel.

SERVES 6–8.

HINT: Wine as a Meat Tenderizer

Wine was the first meat tenderizer that cooks used. Early in history they found that soaking tough but flavorful meat for several hours in wine caused the meat fibers to break down a bit, thus making the meat more appetizing. This also means that you can buy meat that contains little fat and tenderize it with wine. I buy stew meat that has no fat on it at all . . . and then let it sit in wine overnight.

I do not want you to tenderize with chemicals and salt. Salt simply draws the moisture out of the meat . . . and you are stuck with the salt. The alcohol in wine also draws out a bit of the moisture, but it tenderizes without the use of any chemicals at all. Soaking meat for a few hours in wine is a wise practice.

Al Cribari's Barbecued Pot Roast

This dish is pretty basic fare, and it is from a man who makes good, basic wines. Al Cribari, a friend of several years, is a serious cook and the grandson of the founder of the Cribari winery in California. He hates the idea of wine as a snobbish event, so I have included a good old pot roast recipe, soaked in wine of course, for the sake of Al's concern. He is right. Wine is basic, and the two of us are done with the romanticizing of this wonderful food beverage.

- 1 4½- to 5-pound chuck roast
- Freshly ground black pepper to taste
- 1 tablespoon good curry powder
- 4 tablespoons olive oil

SAUCE:

- 1 cup dry red Burgundy wine
- 1 cup catsup
- ½ cup vinegar
- ½ cup water
- 2 tablespoons brown sugar
- 2 tablespoons Worcestershire sauce
- Several drops of Liquid Smoke
- Dash of Tabasco sauce

½ teaspoon dry mustard (I prefer Colman's)
1 medium yellow onion, peeled and chopped

Rub the roast with the freshly ground pepper and the curry powder. Heat a large frying pan and add the oil. Brown the meat on all sides, using high heat.

Prepare the sauce by simmering all the sauce ingredients until the onions are soft. Place the roast in a large piece of aluminum foil and place on a baking sheet. Pour the sauce over the roast and fold the foil over to seal the roast well. Place on a grill or in a 350° oven for about 2 hours, or until tender.

You may wish to add a bit of salt when serving. I find that it is not needed.

Serve with Green Rice (page 158), Carrots in Vermouth (page 261), and a green salad with a Burgundy and Herb Dressing (page 129).

Wine Suggestion: Fruity Cabernet.

SERVES 6–8.

Quick-Fried Beef Venetian Style

(Italy)

My wife, Patty, and I had a dish similar to this one during a stay in Venice. Just behind the Square of San Marco is a restaurant called Naomi. This is a fine place offering typical dishes of this lovely Italian city. This one is quickly prepared and the results taste as if you have been working for days. That's Frugal!

2 pounds thinly sliced beef (I use a beef roast and ask the butcher to cut it on his meat slicer)
Olive oil for frying

SAUCE:
1 medium yellow onion, chopped
2 tablespoons olive oil
2 garlic cloves, crushed
⅛ pound (2 ounces) bacon or prosciutto, diced
2 tablespoons pitted and chopped green olives

1 red sweet bell pepper, coarsely diced
1 very ripe tomato, diced
¾ cup red wine (dry Burgundy type)
1 tablespoon capers
¼ teaspoon oregano
¼ teaspoon basil
Salt and black pepper to taste

Prepare the sauce by sautéing the yellow onion in the oil, along with the garlic and bacon. When the onion is a bit soft, add the remaining ingredients and simmer until all is tender and flavorful. Correct the seasoning with the salt and pepper. You should need little salt, if any.

Heat a frying pan and then add a bit of olive oil. Quickly sauté the meat and then serve on heated plates with a bit of the sauce on the bottom of each plate.

Try this with Pasta with Anchovy and Onions (page 147), as well as a Green Bean and Filbert Salad (page 138). French bread, of course.

Wine Suggestion: Light Cabernet.

SERVES 4–6.

Channing's Greek Hamburgers

You cannot believe my frustration when we were in Greece. Every time that I was ready for a meal the boys had just finished a "meal" on the street. Street vendors around Omunia Square sell wonderful food, and my son Channing was inspired by these people to create the following variation on our hamburger. It is terrific!

1½ pounds hamburger, very lean
2 tablespoons olive oil
3 garlic cloves, minced
3 tablespoons red wine (dry Burgundy type)
2 teaspoons oregano
2 tablespoons Dijon mustard (Grey Poupon is fine)
Salt and black pepper, to taste

Fried onions for topping
Lettuce
Tomatoes, sliced

Mix the hamburger with the following six ingredients. Cook as per your favorite method and top with fried onions on a toasted bun. We always add lettuce and tomato. Go easy on the mayonnaise, mustard, or relish. You will not need much additional flavoring.

Wine Suggestion: Chianti or Greek Retsina.

MAKES 6 HAMBURGERS.

Beef in Wine on Skewers

The whole concept behind such a dish goes back to the desert, the birthplace of wine. It can be easily done in the normal kitchen if you will simply seek out some bamboo skewers. Or if you are really into this kind of quick and flavorful cooking you might invest in some metal skewers. Any import shop, such as Pier Who Knows Where, will have both kinds of skewers for you.

2 pounds good beef
2 yellow onions, peeled and quartered
2 green peppers, seeded
2 tablespoons olive oil
1 tablespoon lemon juice
1/4 cup Zinfandel
1/2 teaspoon oregano
4 bay leaves
3 garlic cloves, crushed
Salt and pepper to taste

Cut the beef into 1 1/4-inch cubes. Cut the vegetables into 1-inch squares. Put all the ingredients in a large stainless steel bowl and marinate for about 2 hours, tossing occasionally.

Alternate the vegetables and meat on skewers. Broil until lightly browned, about 15 minutes, turning once during the process.

Serve this with Pasta Bagna Cauda (page 149), along with Pan-Fried Broccoli (page 263).

Wine Suggestion: Zinfandel.

SERVES 4–6.

PORK

Just the thought of spareribs, broiled over charcoal or in the broiler and served with a pungent sauce, makes me ravenously hungry.

—James Beard
The James Beard Cookbook

• Pork and Wine •

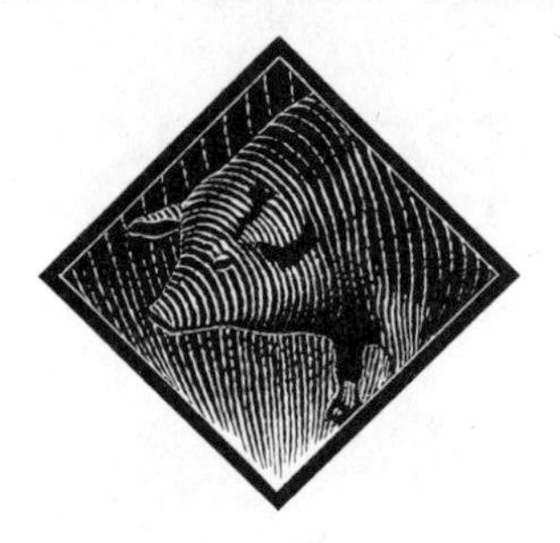

Why has the pig been so maligned in the past? He is not really dirty nor can he sweat, as in, "He sweats like a pig." Pigs can't sweat. He is bright and useful, but mostly as a food product. There is good evidence to show that the biblical admonition against eating it did not stem from the fact that pork meat could carry disease. All meats can carry disease, and we did not even discover the connection between pork and trichinosis until 1860. No, the reason for the Hebrew rejection of the pig as a food product stems from the fact that the Jews were nomads and sheep and goats were best for such a life. Besides, the sheep and goats not only gave meat but also milk and clothing. And, to top it off, the pig ate what man ate . . . grains. The sheep and goat will eat grass. No wonder the tempting and fatty flesh of the pig was forbidden to the Jews. If they had gotten hung up on the pig, they would have had to stay in one place (pigs do not wander about deserts) and compete with the pig for the food and grain and water supply.

Still, the pig is very efficient in terms of converting grain into meat, much more so than beef or lamb. Columbus brought the lovely creatures with him on his second voyage to the New World. The Chinese have recognized the pig as a special food product as early as 5000 B.C. And ancient drawings on cave walls of the Altamira caverns in Spain put the pig as a food product back to fifteen thousand years ago. These creatures were wild, of course, and probably boars. In our time the modern pig is a wonderful and flavorful creature, and it is a great help to our culture. Enjoy the porker with a light red or white. Wonderful!

Pork in Wine and Vinegar Sauce

Normally you would not expect a vinegar to be helpful with the dinner if you are serving a good wine. Vinegars, including wine vinegars, get in the way of most wines. This dish is so delicious, however, and the vinegar flavor so mild, that I suggest you try it. I have even suggested a wine for dinner that will stand up to the flavors.

- **3 pounds pork butt roast, lean and boneless, cut into 2-inch cubes**
- **3 tablespoons butter or olive oil**
- **¼ cup dry white wine**
- **1 cup bread crumbs**
- **Black pepper, freshly ground**
- **2 medium yellow onions, peeled and minced**
- **2 large shallots, peeled and minced**
- **2 garlic cloves, crushed**
- **3 tablespoons minced parsley**
- **1 cup Basic Brown Soup Stock (page 100) or use canned, not bouillon**
- **2 tablespoons red wine vinegar**
- **Salt to taste**

Heat a small covered Dutch oven and add the butter or oil. Brown the meat on all sides. Add wine. Top with bread crumbs and pepper to taste. Mix the onions, shallots, garlic, and parsley together and sprinkle on top of the meat. Put the meat in a 400° oven to brown, about 10 minutes. Baste several times with the pan juices. Turn the oven to 350°, add the stock to the pan, cover, and bake for 50 minutes. Remove the lid, turn temperature to 400°, and bake for 10 more minutes. Remove meat to serving platter. Add the wine vinegar to the pan juices, stir, and pour over the meat. Check for salt.

I like this with Onions in Madeira (page 258), along with Pasta and Green Onion Salad (page 134) and some crunchy bread.

Wine Suggestion: Italian red Dolcetto or Barbera.

SERVES 6–8.

Pork in Mustard Sauce

One of the finest restaurants in Seattle is called Labuznik. The chef and owner, a charming fellow named Peter Cipra, draws on his Eastern European background for wonderful flavors. He did this dish on one of our television shows on NBC, KING in Seattle. I simply added a little white wine to cut the richness of the sauce a bit. Don't let the simplicity of this dish fool you.

- **3 pork tenderloins (2 pounds total)**
- **Black pepper, freshly ground, to taste**
- **4 tablespoons Dijon mustard (Grey Poupon is fine)**
- **2 tablespoons olive oil, for frying**
- **1 teaspoon butter**
- **Salt to taste**
- **2 teaspoons green peppercorns**
- **3 tablespoons whipping cream or Mock Cream (page 289)**
- **3 tablespoons dry white wine**

Slice the pork tenderloins across the grain, ⅓ inch thick. Pepper the meat to taste and spread half the mustard on one side of the slices. Use the back of a spoon for this. Heat a large frying pan and add the oil. Quickly sauté the meat on both sides, until a light brown. Add the butter or olive oil, move the meat in it a bit, and remove from the pan. Place on a platter and add a tiny bit of salt. Add the green peppercorns to the pan, crushing them with a wooden spoon. Add the remaining Dijon mustard and mix with the pepper. Add the cream and wine. Bring to a boil and reduce for 1 minute. Serve the sauce over the pork.

A Chicken and Avocado Mousse (page 293), Fried Rice Balls (page 163), and a green salad with Garlic Dressing (page 129) would make a fine meal.

Wine Suggestion: Vouvray, Chenin Blanc, or Pinot Noir.

SERVES 6–8.

HINT: Don't Butter Your Bread

In France and Italy butter is often replaced with wine. Simply dip your bread into the wine and enjoy. It saves calories and cholesterol.

Piggies Tied Up

This is a dish that would be fun for the kids to make. The name will help their imaginations and the process is not at all difficult. They will need help only with the pounding. (It is all right to make this dish if you are an adult, too.)

- 1½ pounds pork butt roast, boneless, cut into 8 slices (your butcher will do this for you)
- Black pepper, freshly ground, to taste
- 1 cup grated Swiss cheese
- 1 teaspoon oregano
- 4 tablespoons Parmesan or Romano cheese
- ⅓ cup olive oil
- ½ cup dry white wine
- Salt to taste
- 2 tablespoons chopped parsley

Place each slice of pork between two sheets of plastic (page 175) and pound them a bit with a wooden mallet. You don't want them too thin but just spread out a bit. Put a bit of the pepper, Swiss cheese, oregano, and Parmesan or Romano on each slice and roll up like a jelly roll. Tie with string in four places.

Heat a covered frying pan and add the olive oil. Brown the rolls in the oil, on medium-high heat, for about 10 minutes, turning occasionally. Add the wine, cover, and simmer for 20 minutes. Remove the rolls to a platter. Add a bit of salt. Reduce the pan juices if they are not rich enough. Pour juices over rolls, top with parsley, and serve.

Pasta with Three Meats and Peas (page 146), Zucchini and Carrots (page 257), and a green salad would complete this meal.

Wine Suggestion: Heavy red, Petite Sirah, or Zinfandel.

SERVES 4–6.

Grilled Pork New Orleans

The city of New Orleans must use more Tabasco, thyme, and Worcestershire sauce than any other city anywhere. As a matter of fact, I know that they use incredible amounts. I used these three items to prepare a quick marinade for a backyard charcoal dish.

- 4 pork blade steaks, trimmed of the excess fat
- 1 tablespoon Tabasco
- 1 tablespoon Worcestershire sauce
- 1 teaspoon thyme, whole
- ½ cup dry red wine
- 3 garlic cloves, crushed
- Black pepper, freshly ground, to taste
- Salt

Mix all ingredients, except the salt, and marinate the meat for 2 hours. Cook on the outdoor charcoal grill until done to your taste. Check for salt before serving.

Serve with Green Onion Pasta (page 144) and Zucchini Stuffed with Tomato (page 264).

Wine Suggestion: Côtes du Rhône or Zinfandel.

SERVES 4.

Pork in Gorgonzola

This dish is rich, quick, not expensive . . . everything that the Frugal Gourmet loves. I served this at a dinner party one evening and received rave reviews.

- 3 tablespoons olive oil
- 3 garlic cloves, crushed
- 2 pounds boneless pork butt or loin, cut into thin slices, about 1/16 inch thick
- 1 teaspoon rosemary, whole leaves, crushed
- ½ cup dry white wine
- ½ cup crumbled Gorgonzola, bleu, or Roquefort cheese

¼ cup whipping cream or half-and-half or Mock Cream (page 289)
Salt and pepper to taste

Heat a large frying pan and add the oil and garlic. Brown the meat slices quickly on both sides, probably about 3 minutes on each side, depending on the heat of the pan. Do this in two batches on medium-high heat so that you do not overcook the pork. Remove the pieces to a warm platter. Add the rosemary to the pan and deglaze (page 282) the pan with the wine, scraping up the brown goodness with a wooden spoon. Add the cheese, cream, salt, and pepper. Bring to a quick simmer and allow the cheese to melt into the wine. Serve the sauce over the meat.

Baked Polenta (page 161) would complete a fine meal.

Wine Suggestion: Sweet white, Chenin Blanc, or Riesling.

SERVES 6–8.

Pickled Pork Ribs with Lentils

(France)

There is a restaurant in Paris that serves pig's feet and ribs . . . and it is a very fancy restaurant indeed. It is called "au Pied de Cochon," "The pig's foot." My wife and I had a wonderful meal there one afternoon. I have tried to duplicate the French peasant dish that she ordered. This is it. I have not yet figured out how to make the stuffed pig's foot that I enjoyed. Next book? In the meantime, please note that this dish takes a bit of time to prepare. Are you ready for ten days?

PICKLING BRINE:

1 gallon water
1 pound pickling salt (no iodine)
1 teaspoon saltpeter (page 40)
5 pounds pork spareribs, cut into about 10 large pieces
8 black peppercorns, whole
2 bay leaves, whole
1 large yellow onion, peeled and chopped
2 cups dry white wine

LENTILS:

2 tablespoons olive oil
2 yellow onions, peeled and sliced
1 garlic clove, crushed
2 cups lentils
Salt to taste
1 bay leaf
1 cup Chicken Soup Stock (page 101) or canned (if you use bouillon, be careful of adding salt)
½ cup chopped parsley for garnish

In a stainless steel pan or large glass bowl, place the gallon of water along with the pickling salt and saltpeter. Stir until dissolved. Place the ribs in the brine and keep covered in the refrigerator for 10 days. You may have to weight down the ribs with a heavy plate. They must stay under this solution for 10 days.

When pickling is completed, drain the brine and discard. Rinse the ribs thoroughly in fresh water. Drain and place in a stainless pot and add the peppercorns, bay leaves, yellow onion, and the white wine. Add just enough water to barely cover the ribs. Cover the pot and bring to a simmer. Cook for 1½ hours. In the meantime, prepare the lentils.

Heat a frying pan and add the oil. Sauté the onions and garlic until a bit golden. Place the lentils and onions in a heavy saucepan with lid. Add the salt, bay leaf, and stock. Add enough water to cover the lentils. Cover and simmer for about ½ hour, or until the lentils are tender but not mushy.

Remove the ribs to a platter. Serve the ribs on a bed of the lentils.

Try this with Carrots and Zucchini (page 257), Cold Brussels Sprouts Salad (page 133), and French bread.

Wine Suggestion: Beaujolais or California Gamay.

SERVES 4.

Crown Roast of Pork

This dish is one of the most attractive meat dishes that I know. If you bother to trim it with little paper panties you will have a smashing time at the table. And this particular cut of pork is one of the most succulent meat dishes that you will ever eat.

1 crown roast of pork
Black pepper, freshly ground, to taste
1 tablespoon whole sage
1 tablespoon whole thyme
1½ cups dry white wine for basting
Salt to taste

For this dish you must find a real, live butcher. Have him cut and tie a crown roast of pork for you. He will understand what to do. You will have a roast of 16 ribs, enough for 8 persons.

Rub the roast well with freshly ground pepper, along with the sage and thyme. Wrap the ends of the ribs in aluminum foil so that they will not burn during the roasting. Place a ball of loosely crumpled aluminum foil in the center of the roast and place on a roasting rack in a pan.

Bake at 325° for about 25 minutes a pound. I use a meat thermometer and roast until it reaches 165°. Allow the roast to sit a few minutes before you cut it. When ready to serve, remove the foil and place a large bouquet of parsley in the center of the roast. Salt to taste. You may wish to put little paper panties on the rib ends (see below).

I like this with Eggplant Cheese Rolls (page 273), along with a green salad and French rolls.

Wine Suggestion: Merlot or Cabernet.

SERVES 8.

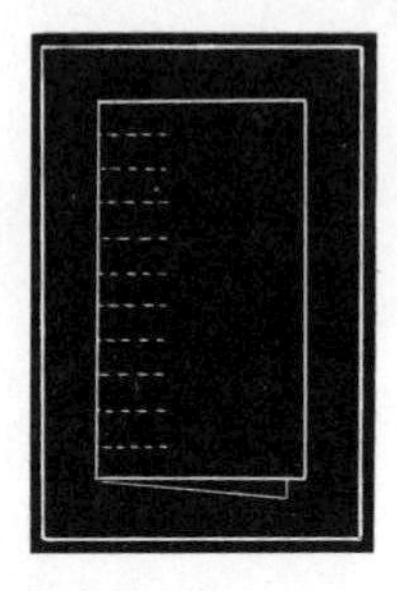 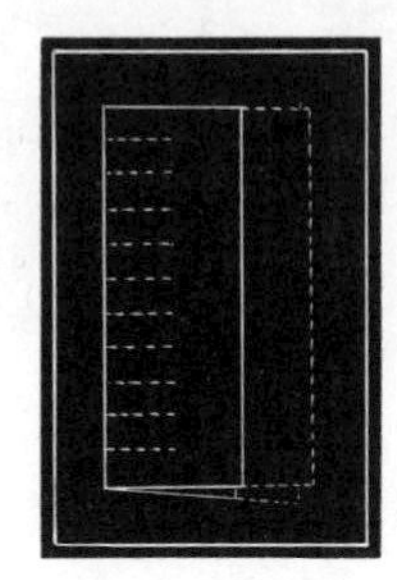 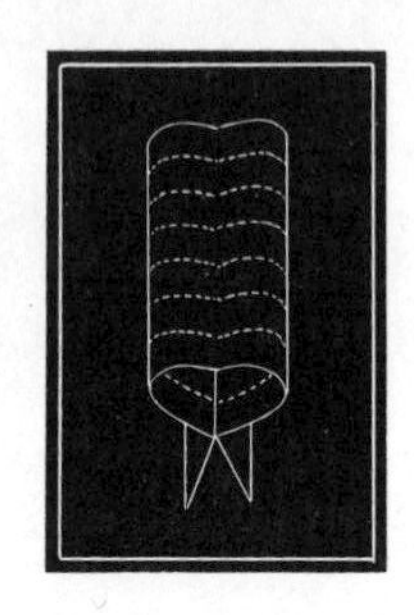 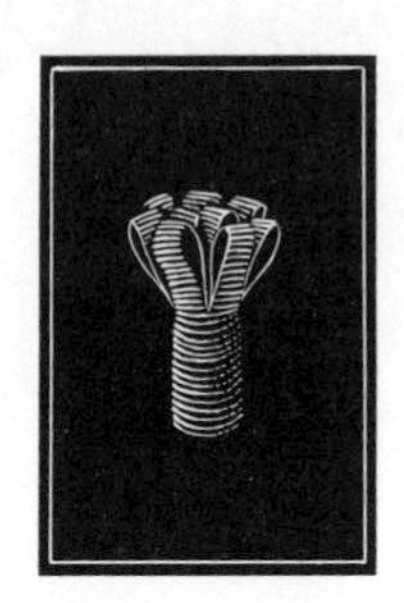

HINT: How to Make Panties for Meat and Poultry

1. Make little cuts long the seam of a paper napkin (each about ⅛ inch apart and about 1¼ inches deep.
2. Cut away all the napkin except a 1-inch border under the cuts.
3. Reverse the fold of the cuts and roll the panties around your thumb. Seal with Scotch tape. You will need to experiment a bit to learn to make them the proper diameter for whatever kind of meat or poultry you wish to decorate.

LAMB

It's not fair! The poor lamb doesn't get much press, does he?

—Patty Smith
Wife of the Author

• *Lamb with Wine* •

Lamb, sheep, and goats were some of the earliest creatures to be domesticated for food. Their use goes back so far into nomadic history in the Middle East that it is hard to trace. And many of us still think that lamb tastes as old as it is!

While in graduate school in theology we were forced to eat in the commons dining room. Some good things came from that experience . . . I met my wife there. But the bad thing, the worst thing, the most disgusting thing was the weekly lamb meal that the cook sacrificed to a dry and tasteless god. That cook (please, I cannot call him a chef) offered us meat that was so desiccated that we could only guess what it was. But it smelled like lamb! All of us have had that experience in our past, either with our mothers or with our schools, or God forbid, with both.

There is no reason not to truly enjoy lamb in our time. The contemporary lamb farmer offers us a meat that is light and moist, of delicious flavor and very controllable fat content. Do not overcook the following dishes, and you will convert all supposedly "lamb haters" in your household.

•

Lamb Shashlik with Wine and Juniper

I hope you do not have any trouble finding dried juniper berries. They import a wonderful flavor to foods and most gourmet shops will have them for you. If not, then a specialty spice shop will have them for sure. If you like gin, you will recognize the flavor of the berries. Juniper is a major flavoring in good English gin. Find the berries. This dish is worth it. The rest is easy.

	2	pounds boneless leg of lamb, trimmed of most of the fat, cut into 1½-inch cubes
MARINADE:	½	cup olive oil
		Juice of 1 fresh lemon
	1	medium yellow onion, peeled and chopped
	½	cup chopped parsley
	½	teaspoon black pepper, freshly ground
	1	tablespoon juniper berries, crushed
	2	garlic cloves, crushed
	½	cup dry red wine
SEASONING:	6 to 8	slices bacon
		Salt

Have your butcher debone the lamb and trim the fat. You cut it into cubes and mix the marinade. Crush the juniper berries in a mortar and pestle or in a small electric coffee grinder. Soak the meat in this marinade for at least 12 hours, refrigerated. Then place the meat on skewers, alternating it with pieces of bacon. Salt and place under a hot broiler or on a charcoal grill. Cook for about 15 minutes total time, turning often, or until the meat is done to your taste. Take care not to overcook the lamb. It should be a bit pink inside.

Serve with Green Rice (page 158) and Vegetables North Beach (page 258).

Wine Suggestion: Rich Pinot Noir or Italian Barolo.

SERVES 5–6.

◆

Lamb with Wine and Cumin Sauce

I hesitate to tell you about this place. It is so small that I have trouble getting in there now. If you were to go I might not ever get near the place again. But I shall tell you that it is one of my favorite restaurants in San Francisco. It is the Nob Hill Café on

Taylor Street, not far away from the fancy hotels. It is not to be confused with the Nob Hill Restaurant, which is in one of those hotels. The Nob Hill Café has about seven tables . . . and the staff is incredible. The chef is French by nature, and his wife, a wonderful woman of Korean descent, adds an interesting touch to the cuisine. I had never thought of serving cumin with lamb, but I had it there one night and was very pleased with the results. This is as close as I can come to the sauce and the dish. And stay away from the restaurant. You would love it!

6 thick lamb chops
2 tablespoons olive oil
1 garlic clove, crushed
½ cup dry red wine
½ cup Basic Brown Soup Stock (page 100) or use canned (do not use bouillon cubes)
¼ cup cream or half-and-half or Mock Cream (page 289)
⅛ teaspoon ground cumin, or more to taste
Salt and black pepper, freshly ground, to taste
Parsley, chopped, for garnish

Heat a large frying pan and add the olive oil. Sear the chops well on both sides, using rather high heat. Do not overcook them as we want them to be a bit pink on the inside. Depending on the thickness of the chops, you should cook them about 4–5 minutes on each side. Remove them to a warm plate and keep them just barely warm.

Drain the fat from the pan. Add the garlic to the pan and stir it around for just a moment. Deglaze the pan with the red wine. Be sure to scrape up all of the brown goodness that has formed in the pan. Use a wooden spoon for this. Add the beef stock and the cream. Continue to boil lightly until the sauce is reduced by half. Add the cumin, black pepper, and taste for salt. Serve the sauce over the chops with a chopped parsley garnish on top.

Try this with German Dumplings (page 162) and Sammy's Eggplant Salad (page 274).

Wine Suggestion: Dry German Gewürztraminer.

SERVES 4–6 (FEWER IF YOU WANT EACH TO HAVE 2 CHOPS).

Leg of Lamb in Balsamic Vinegar

Balsamic vinegar is a wonderfully aged product from Modena, in Italy. It is unlike most wine vinegars in that the flavor is so mild. Normally, I would not urge you to use vinegars when you are going to serve a good wine, since the vinegars fight and get in the way of the flavor of the wine. In this case, however, the flavor of the vinegar is mild to begin with, and the roasting calms it down to a very mellow flavor. You will enjoy this easily prepared dish. The only thing that might get in your way is the fact that it must be marinated for five hours.

- **1 5- to 6-pound leg of lamb**
- **¼ cup olive oil**
- **¼ cup balsamic vinegar**
- **Salt and black pepper, freshly ground, to taste**
- **½ tablespoon dried rosemary, whole, or twice that much if fresh**
- **2 garlic cloves, crushed**

Using a sharp-pointed knife or a pot fork, pierce the leg in several places and soak it for 5 hours in the olive oil mixed with the vinegar.

Place it on a roasting rack and rub with the salt, pepper, rosemary, and garlic. Place a meat thermometer in the thickest part of the leg. Be sure you do not touch the bone. Bake at 325° until the thermometer reaches 140°. This should take about 1¼ to 1¾ hours. Baste with the marinade several times during the roasting. Remove from the oven and let sit ½ hour before carving. The lamb will continue to cook a bit. Slice at the table or buffet.

Risotto with Vegetables (page 156) and a green salad with Garlic Dressing (page 129) would complete a fine meal.

Wine Suggestion: Italian Barolo or California Cabernet.

SERVES 4–6.

Lamb Chops with Olive Paste

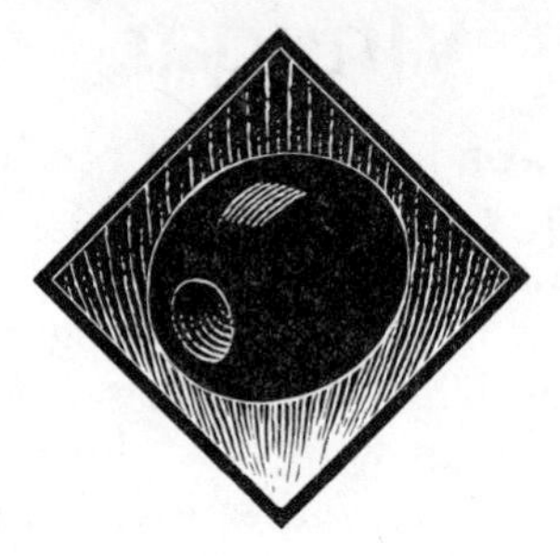

This is a triumph. We combine the best of the flavors of the Middle East, lamb and olives, and eat with wine. What more can you ask for? I do like this dish.

	8	thick lamb chops
		Olive oil for frying
OLIVE PASTE:	1	cup Olive Paste (page 94)
	1/4	teaspoon dried thyme, whole
	1	bay leaf, crushed
	2	teaspoons Dijon mustard (Grey Poupon is fine)
	1	garlic clove, crushed

Stir all the ingredients for the olive paste together.

Pan-fry the chops in a bit of olive oil until they are brown on both sides. Use very high heat and do not overcook them. They should not be anywhere near done. A couple of minutes on each side should do.

Spread a bit of the olive paste on one side of each chop and place it on a broiling rack. Place in a 500° oven (yes, 500°) for about 5 minutes, or until the center of the chop is tender but still pink. Remove to a serving platter. Enjoy.

Try this with Pasta with Fresh Asparagus (page 143) and green salad with French bread.

Wine Suggestion: Cabernet.

SERVES 4.

Lamb Curry

One of the wonderful things about a good curry is that you can make it the day ahead and you can serve it from the buffet. The sauce is rich enough and thick enough so that it will not spill on the carpet. You should never embarrass your guests by giving them a dish that is going to trickle onto the floor.

3 pounds boneless lamb, cut in 1-inch cubes
Olive oil for sautéing
3 yellow onions, peeled and sliced
4 garlic cloves, crushed
2 cups Chicken Soup Stock (page 101) or canned
Curry Powder to taste (see below) (I use about 3 tablespoons)
1 tablespoon grated fresh ginger
Salt and pepper to taste
2 tablespoons cornstarch mixed with 2 tablespoons water

In a hot frying pan, quickly brown the lamb in a bit of olive oil. Do this in three small batches so that the lamb is quickly seared. Remove the meat and place in a 2-quart saucepan, with lid. Sauté the onions, along with the garlic, in a bit of oil until limp. Add to the lamb.

Cover the lamb with the stock and add the curry powder, ginger, salt, and pepper. Simmer, covered, until all is tender, about 1½ hours. Thicken with the cornstarch and water mixture.

Serve with rice, salad, fresh fruit, and bread.

Wine Suggestion: Dry Gewürztraminer.

SERVES 6–8.

◆

Curry Powder

This is largely a matter of personal taste. Try this one and vary what you wish.

½ tablespoon cardamom
1 tablespoon chopped cinnamon stick
½ tablespoon whole cloves
¼ tablespoon whole cumin
¼ tablespoon grated nutmeg
1 tablespoon turmeric
½ tablespoon whole coriander
Black peppercorns to taste
Dried red pepper flakes to taste
1 bay leaf

Grind all of this together in an electric coffee grinder and keep in a tightly closed jar.

RABBIT

But don't go into Mr. McGregor's garden!

—Beatrix Potter
The Tale of Peter Rabbit

• Rabbits and Wine •

Why do Americans eat so little rabbit? In Europe rabbit has been prized as a food product since Roman times. In this country it is seldom used. Has it something to do with our refusal to eat a little furry creature, one of the *Watership Down* cult? Yet we will kill an entire cow and make hamburgers . . . and think nothing of it.

Rabbits are very efficient in terms of the food cycle, more so than beef, lamb, or pork. They also have the distinct advantage of being very low in fat, lower than chicken. So enjoy rabbit. It is good for you and tastes delicious, even better than chicken. You can now find fresh rabbit in most American supermarkets.

•

Rabbit in Red Wine

Rabbit Hunter's Style

(Italy)

In the old days in Italy one went out and shot his own rabbits. The wild creatures tended to be rather tough . . . and they still are. However, if you soak them in wine overnight they become tender and flavorful. Thus, rabbit hunter's style.

- **1 large rabbit, about 3 pounds, cut up**
- **2 cups dry red wine**
- **4 tablespoons olive oil**
- **2 garlic cloves, crushed**
- **2 yellow onions, peeled and sliced**
- **1 cup Chicken Soup Stock (page 101) or use canned**

2 ripe tomatoes, diced
½ teaspoon rosemary, whole
2 bay leaves
½ teaspoon thyme
Salt and black pepper, freshly ground, to taste
1 piece fresh lemon peel, 1 inch by 2 inches

Place the rabbit in a stainless steel or glass bowl and cover with the red wine. Cover the dish and let the rabbit marinate overnight, refrigerated. Drain from the marinade, reserving the wine. Pat dry with paper towels. Heat a large frying pan and add the oil and garlic. Sauté the rabbit parts until brown on both sides. Remove to a stove-top lidded casserole. Sauté the onions in the pan and add to the casserole. Deglaze (page 282) the pan with a bit of the wine marinade and add to the casserole. Add the stock and simmer for ½ hour. Add the wine marinade, tomatoes, the seasonings, and the lemon peel. Cover and cook until the rabbit is tender, about 25 more minutes.

Serve with Rice and Peas (page 157), along with fresh fruit, and a green salad with Pesto Vinaigrette (page 130).

Wine Suggestion: Light red Burgundy.

SERVES 4.

◆

Rabbit in Mustard Sauce

(France)

I am always pleased with the way that rabbit will maintain its moisture providing you do not cook it to death. The meat is very moist in this recipe.

4 tablespoons olive oil
1 large rabbit, about 3 pounds, cut up
2 garlic cloves, crushed
2 yellow onions, peeled and sliced
½ teaspoon rosemary
¼ teaspoon *each* tarragon and sage
½ teaspoon oregano
1½ cups dry white wine

3 leeks, sliced lengthwise once, then in 2-inch slices (wash these very carefully as they may be full of mud)
1½ tablespoons Dijon mustard (Grey Poupon is fine)
½ cup half-and-half or Mock Cream (page 289)
Salt and black pepper, freshly ground, to taste
¼ cup chopped parsley, for garnish

Heat a 6- to 8-quart Dutch oven and add the oil. Sauté the rabbit pieces until brown on all sides, about 10 minutes. Remove to a plate. Add the garlic and onions to the oil and sauté until clear. Add the four herbs to the pot, along with the wine and the rabbit. Cover and simmer until the meat is tender, about 35 minutes. Add the leeks to the pot, cover, and cook 5 more minutes. Remove the meat from the pot to a large heated platter. Add the mustard and half-and-half to the pot, bring to a boil, turn to a simmer, and cook for 5 minutes. Add salt and pepper to taste. Serve a third of the sauce over the chicken, with the remaining sauce being offered for the sake of noodles or rice.

I like this with Risotto with Mushrooms (page 155), Carrots and Zucchini (page 257), and a salad with Pesto Vinaigrette (page 130).

Wine Suggestion: Light red Burgundy.

SERVES 4.

◆

Rabbit in Vermouth

(Italy)

At least I hope someone in Italy serves a dish like this. I cooked this for our family one evening and was very pleased with the results. It felt Italian, and it was very easy to prepare.

4 tablespoons olive oil
1 large rabbit, about 3 pounds, cut up
2 garlic cloves, peeled and sliced
2 yellow onions, peeled and sliced
3 tablespoons flour

Salt and black pepper, freshly ground, to taste
½ tablespoon rosemary
1 cup dry vermouth

Heat a large Dutch oven and add the oil. Sauté the rabbit pieces in two batches until brown on both sides, about 10 minutes total time. Add the garlic and onions to the pot and cook uncovered for another 10 minutes. Stir in the flour, salt, pepper, and rosemary. Blend with a wooden spoon. Finally, add the vermouth. Cover and simmer for 45 minutes, or until the rabbit is very tender.

Eggplant Stuffed Turkish Style (page 269) along with Cold Brussels Sprouts Salad (page 133) would complete this menu.

Wine Suggestion: Fruity Chardonnay.

SERVES 4.

Plain Fried Rabbit

(New Orleans)

There must be a way to do this job simply, and this is simply delicious. There is nothing to it and it will convince you that you should enjoy rabbit more often.

1 large rabbit, about 3 pounds, cut up
1 tablespoon Tabasco sauce
1 cup flour
1 teaspoon thyme
Salt and black pepper, freshly ground, to taste
Peanut oil for pan-frying, about 1 cup

Place the rabbit pieces in a bowl and add the Tabasco. Mix well and let marinate for ½ hour. Mix the flour, thyme, salt, and pepper together in a paper sack. Dredge the rabbit in the flour and pan-fry in the hot oil. Brown both sides evenly on moderate heat, uncovered. This should take about 20 minutes to cook.

Serve with Fried Cabbage (page 262), Rigatoni con Pepperoni (page 145), and a green salad and rolls.

Wine Suggestion: Chianti.

SERVES 4.

Rabbit in Green Peppercorns and Wine Sauce

(France)

Rabbit, wine, and pepper seem to know each other well. One taste and you can tell that these three have been around together for a long time. No, I can't explain it, but it is obviously the case.

- 3 tablespoons olive oil
- 1 large rabbit, about 3 pounds, cut up
- 2 cups dry white wine
- 1 tablespoon green peppercorns
- ½ cup cream or half-and-half or Mock Cream (page 287)
- Salt and black pepper, freshly ground, to taste

Heat a Dutch oven and add the oil. Sauté the rabbit pieces in the oil until brown on all sides, about 10 minutes. Add the wine, cover the pot, bring to a simmer, and cook for 45 minutes. Remove the rabbit from the pot and place on a heated platter. Add the green peppercorns, smashing them in the bottom of the pot with a wooden spoon. Add the cream and bring to a heavy simmer. Cook for 3 minutes and add salt and pepper to taste. Pour the sauce over the rabbit.

Serve with Semolina Dumplings (page 159), along with Zucchini and Carrots (page 257) and a green salad with French bread.

Wine Suggestion: Côtes du Rhône or Petite Sirah.

SERVES 4.

MEAT MARINADES

Garlic is as good as ten mothers.

—Telugu Proverb

Meat Marinades with Wine

The whole concept of marinating meat is very old. During the past several hundred years meat was marinated in order to solve two problems. The first was spoilage. That is to say, the meat was rotten to start with. The flavor had to be covered over or improved. The second was tenderizing. Wine is, was, has been, and will be the solution. It supports the flavors of meat, contains no salt or chemicals, and really does break down the meat fibers. I have not been able to quite figure out who did this first, but it seems to be the Chinese. Wouldn't you know!

Onion Beef

(Chinese)

This dish is really a conglomeration of several cultures, and I love it. You can do it quickly and it will fit in with many different kinds of menus. In this case I am using a Scotch for the marinade. Yes, I know that it is not wine! However, it is close to the nature of the kind of wines that the Chinese use for this process . . . so I urge you to try it. It is very delicious. If you do not care for the flavor of Scotch you may substitute dry sherry.

1 pound flank steak or boneless chuck steak, cut across the grain into thin slices

MARINADE:	3	tablespoons soy sauce
	3	tablespoons Scotch or dry sherry (I prefer the Scotch)
	1	teaspoon grated fresh ginger
	1	teaspoon sugar
	1	tablespoon sesame oil
	1	teaspoon hot bean sauce (page 35) or red chili and garlic paste (page 39)
		Barbecue sauce, bottled (I prefer Woody's)
THE COOKING:	3	tablespoons peanut oil
	2	garlic cloves, crushed
	1	carrot, cut julienne (page 257)
	2	bunches green onions, cut lengthwise once, then into 1-inch pieces
	½	teaspoon black pepper, freshly ground, or to taste

Mix all of the ingredients for the marinade together. Add the meat and allow it to marinate for 1 hour.

Heat a wok or large frying pan. Add the oil and the garlic. Toss for a few seconds and add the carrots. Stir-fry until they are tender. Remove from the wok and add the beef, drained of the marinade. Toss for a few moments over very high heat. When the meat is tender, add the green onions. Toss for a moment and add the carrots and pepper.

Choose a few other dishes from the Chinese section, such as Glass Noodles with Pork and Shrimp (page 328).

Wine Suggestion: Dry Alsatian white or dry California white.

SERVES 3–4.

•

Flank Steak in Mustard Marinade

This is a delight! You marinate the tough flank steak and *then* cook it. What you wind up with is a delightful and tender piece of meat.

2 flank steaks, around 1 pound each

MARINADE:

½ cup salad oil or olive oil
¼ cup dry white wine
4 tablespoons white wine vinegar
½ cup green onions or scallions
2 garlic cloves, peeled and crushed
2 tablespoons Dijon mustard (Grey Poupon is fine)
Salt and black pepper to taste

Prepare the marinade and soak the steaks in it for 1 hour. Place the steaks on a broiler rack and broil under the highest heat possible for 6 minutes on each side, or until the meat begins to brown. You want the inside to be moist and a bit red. Slice the meat across the grain and serve hot. Salt and pepper to taste.

Serve with Rice and Peas (page 157) and Cauliflower Salad (page 136).

Wine Suggestion: Cabernet or heavy red.

SERVES 6.

Basic Chinese Marinade

(China)

The Chinese seem to know more about this whole process than anyone else. It is easy to use and it does not matter whether the marinated creature is fish or fowl . . . or red meat, for that matter.

½ cup light soy sauce
¼ cup dry sherry
½ teaspoon grated fresh ginger

This is a basic marinade for all meats in Chinese cuisine. You may also add hot pepper oil or Tabasco, sesame oil, chopped green onions, and perhaps a touch of brown sugar.

Marinate the meat anywhere from 15 minutes to 1 hour and then proceed with the cooking.

Chicken in Wine and Vinegar

In our time the chickens that we buy in the supermarket are always very moist and tender, providing that you do not cook them too long. This marinade will give you an added bit of moisture and certainly an added bit of flavor.

	1	**fryer chicken, 3 pounds, cut up**
MARINADE:	1	**batch Basic Chinese Marinade (page 238)**
	½	**cup white wine vinegar**
		Peanut oil for frying

Mix the marinade and soak the chicken for 1 hour or up to 8 hours. Drain the marinade and reserve. Pan-fry the chicken in the peanut oil until brown on both sides. Add the marinade to the pan, cover, and simmer until tender, about 20 minutes.

Serve with Rice with Chilies and Cheese (page 159), a green salad, and rolls.

Wine Suggestion: Dry Gewürztraminer.

SERVES 4.

HINT: Dishes to Cook Ahead

If you will cook one day a week, and cook like crazy, you will be ready for the rest of the week. Prepare sauces, casseroles, soups, etc. You will be free to enjoy the meal preparation time since the "prep work" has largely been done.

Some of these dishes keep better than others. Use common sense when working out a weekly menu and you will do well.

Olive Paste
Spinach Crepes
Soups of all kinds
(Chicken stock will last 3 days. Beef stock 6 days.)
Salad dressings of all sorts
Pasta sauces of all sorts
Gnocchi and Polenta
Chicken in Red Wine
Duck in a Pot
Mole Poblano Sauce

Confits of all sorts
Pot Roast with Port and Mushrooms
Beef in Red Wine and Mushrooms
Beef Stew, Peasant Style
Pickled Pork Ribs with Lentils
Lamb Curry
Meat marinades
Sausages
Onion dishes (cooked)
Fried Cabbage
Sammy's Eggplant Salad
Eggplant with Sausages
Sauces of every kind (cooked)
Molded dishes
Casseroles
Many dishes from the International Community

SAUSAGES

Everything has an end, except a sausage, which has two.

—Danish Proverb

• Sausage and Wine •

Sausages go back a thousand years. Many different cultures have made them, but, by definition, they all have one thing in common. They consist of chopped pieces of varied and assorted meats, along with spices and binders, such as flour, eggs, or grains, mixed and stuffed into animal entrails. They range from dried sausages from Italy, to chicken sausages in France, to haggis in Scotland, a questionable mixture of sheep lung, liver, and brain, cooked with oatmeal and stuffed into the sheep stomach. Now, if you can go on after that we shall prepare some wonderful sausage.

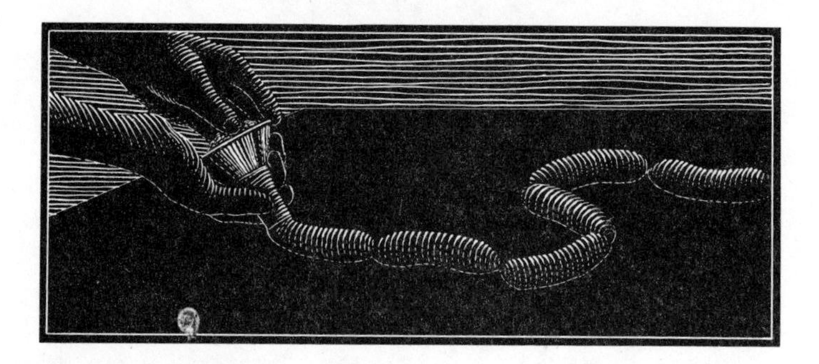

HINT: On Making Sausage

1. *The Casings:* Your butcher can tell you of a source for casings. You will need the size for Italian sausage or garlic sausage. They will probably be packed in salt. They must be washed thoroughly and the inside rinsed of the salt before use.
2. Test out the mixture for seasoning by cooking a tiny amount first. Then correct the seasoning and proceed to stuff the casings.
3. Stuff the filling into casings using a sausage-stuffing funnel (page 25) or a sausage-stuffing tube on your meat grinder. Do not pack the meat in too tight as the sausages will expand a bit when cooking.
4. Prick the casings in several places before cooking. This will prevent them from exploding. I use a little corn on the cob holder for this job.
5. Cook the sausages slowly. High heat will cause them to pop.

6. A pound of filling will fill about 1 yard of casing.
7. Cure the sausages in the refrigerator 1 day before cooking and serving. Do not attempt to keep these sausages longer than 3–4 days, as none of them contains chemicals.
8. Each person will eat about ½ pound of sausage at dinner.

◆

New Orleans Rice Sausage

This delicious sausage shows how frugal one can really be. Nothing was wasted in the old South and the less affluent ended up with the inexpensive cuts of meat. Rice was added as a filler along with enough spice to make one take notice. You will enjoy this one.

- 2½ pounds boneless pork butt or shoulder
- ¾ pound pork liver
- ¼ pound pork kidney
- Salt to taste
- 2 cups long-grain white rice
- 2 tablespoons butter
- 1 large onion, peeled and coarsely chopped
- 1 bunch parsley, chopped
- 2 bunches scallions, chopped
- 3 garlic cloves, peeled and chopped
- ¼ teaspoon ground allspice
- ½ teaspoon whole thyme
- 2 bay leaves, crushed
- Black pepper, freshly ground, to taste (I use about 1 teaspoon)
- Cayenne pepper to taste (Careful! Add up to 2 teaspoons if you really want to smoke)
- 3 yards sausage casings

Place the meats in a saucepan and cover with water. Add a bit of salt, cover, and lightly boil for about 2 hours, or until the meat falls apart. You may have to add a bit more water. Cool in the liquid. Reserve both the liquid and the meats.

Place the rice in a 2-quart saucepan that has a tight-fitting lid. Add the butter and 4 cups of water, along with a teaspoon of salt. Bring to a boil, uncovered, then cover, turn the burner to very low, and simmer for 15 minutes.

Using a coarse blade, grind the meats, along with the onion, scallions, and parsley. Mix all of this with the rice and seasonings. You may taste as you go along since all have been already cooked. Add pepper to taste. Add a bit of the reserved broth so that the mixture is moist but not soggy.

Stuff into casings according to the instructions above. Do not forget to prick the casings.

To cook, simply heat for about 15 minutes in barely simmering water. In New Orleans the sausages are eaten with one's hands. The filling is sucked out of the casing and the casing thrown away.

All you need to complete this meal is bread, wine, and a salad.

Wine Suggestion: Dry Gewürztraminer.

SERVES 6.

◆

White Pudding Sausage

Boudin Blanc

(France)

This is one of my favorites. It is a light sausage, delicate in flavor and with a soft texture, thus the name, white pudding.

- 2 pounds pork shoulder or butt
- 1 pint half-and-half or Mock Cream (page 289)
- 1 yellow onion, peeled and chopped
- 2 garlic cloves, crushed
- 1 teaspoon ground cayenne pepper
- ½ teaspoon ground sage
- 4 teaspoons salt

½ teaspoon freshly ground black pepper
1 bay leaf, crushed or ground
¼ teaspoon ground allspice
½ teaspoon whole thyme
2 cups white bread pieces, tightly packed, crust removed
2 eggs, beaten
1 pound leftover cooked chicken, skinless and boneless, *ground*
3 yards sausage casings

Grind the pork using the coarse blade. Place in a cooking pot along with the half-and-half, onion, garlic, and seasonings. Cook over high heat until the mixture boils and then reduce the heat. Continue to cook for about 10 minutes, with the lid off. Add the bread, torn into little pieces, and simmer for 5 more minutes. Remove from the stove and let cool.

When cool, drain in a colander. Add the beaten eggs and the ground, cooked chicken to the mixture and stuff into casings as per instructions above. Make each sausage about 4 inches long.

To cook, prick the skins and then simmer very gently for about 15 minutes.

Add Egg in Tomato Salad (page 135), Carrots and Zucchini (page 257), and a green salad with Garlic Dressing (page 129).

Wine Suggestion: Light red, Beaujolais, or Gamay.

SERVES 4–5.

◆

Italian Cheese and Red Wine Sausage

(Italy)

You will enjoy this variation on the plain Italian pork sausage. The addition of cheese and wine raises this sausage to dinner-table conversation.

4 pounds boneless pork, shoulder or butt
1 tablespoon coarse-ground fennel seed (grind your own with a small electric coffee grinder)

2 bay leaves, crushed
3 tablespoons chopped parsley
5 garlic cloves, crushed
½ teaspoon dried red pepper flakes
3 teaspoons salt
1 teaspoon freshly ground black pepper
1 cup grated Parmesan or Romano cheese
¾ cup dry red wine
4 yards sausage casings
Olive oil for cooking

Grind the meat using the coarse blade. Mix all ingredients together and allow the mixture to sit for 1 hour before stuffing into casings. Sausage stuffing is explained above. To cook, place in a frying pan with a tiny bit of olive oil and just enough water to cover the bottom of the pan. Cover and cook until the water evaporates. Then, continue to brown, turning once.

Use throughout the book where Italian sausages are called for.

MAKES 4 POUNDS.

◆

Lamb Sausage

This sausage is very popular with the California nouvelle crowd and I have enjoyed it several times in San Francisco. Please do not be put off by the use of lamb. The flavor here is light and delicious.

2½ pounds boneless lamb, shoulder or leg
1½ pounds boneless pork, butt or shoulder
1 yellow onion, peeled and chopped fine
2 teaspoons ground coriander
1 tablespoon ground cumin
4 garlic cloves, crushed
1½ teaspoons freshly ground black pepper
Salt (up to 1 tablespoon)
2 tablespoons paprika
1 teaspoon cayenne
1 teaspoon sugar
½ cup dry vermouth
4 yards sausage casings

Grind the meats using the coarse blade. Mix all ingredients together and stuff into sausage casings as per the instructions above.

To cook, place in an oiled frying pan along with enough water to cover the bottom of the pan. Simmer in the water for a few minutes so that the water evaporates. Continue cooking for about 15 minutes so that the sausages brown. Turn once. Or you can cook these over the charcoal barbecue. Take care that the fire is not too hot. Be sure to prick the sausages first.

Serve with a Tuna and Potato Salad (page 136) and a green salad with rolls.

Wine Suggestion: Cabernet or light Italian Amarone.

MAKES 4 POUNDS.

HINT: Low-Fat Sausage

To prepare low-fat sausage, trim the meat well and discard the fat. Add olive oil or salad oil to the meat mixture to compensate for the lack of fat.

Greek Lamb and Pork Sausage

(Greece)

In the restaurants of Athens it is expected that you are going to order an appetizer before dinner. These sausages are often served. You may make them with pork alone, if you prefer. In any case, when you cook these you will smell the streets of Athens. What a wonderful place to eat!

- **1½ pounds boneless lamb, shoulder or leg**
- **1½ pounds boneless pork, shoulder or butt**
- **1 cup finely chopped yellow onions**
- **½ cup olive oil**
- **Juice of 1 lemon**
- **½ cup dry white wine**
- **4 garlic cloves, crushed**
- **1½ tablespoons oregano**
- **Salt and pepper to taste**
- **3 yards sausage casings**

Grind the lamb and pork using the coarse blade. Mix all ingredients well and stuff into casings. These are cooked in the same manner as the Italian or lamb sausages on pages 245 and 246. They are delicious on the grill as well.

In Greece, it is common to see these stuffed into little pig casings. You might prefer this since they will cook more rapidly.

Try this with Green Onion Pasta (page 144) and a green salad with Garlic Dressing (page 129).

Wine Suggestion: Cabernet or Merlot.

MAKES 3 POUNDS.

Spicy Italian Pork Sausage

Cotechino

(Italy)

While this is an Italian fresh pork sausage, it is not to be confused with regular Italian sausage. This rich variation uses a series of herbs and spices that you will not find in what we normally think of as Italian. I love this cooked in soups. A fine soup using this very sausage is Rich Minestrone, found on page 102.

- **3 pounds boneless pork, butt or shoulder**
- **3 teaspoons salt**
- **2 teaspoons freshly ground black pepper**
- **1 teaspoon ground nutmeg**
- **1 teaspoon ground cinnamon**
- **½ teaspoon cayenne**
- **½ teaspoon finely ground cloves**
- **¼ cup freshly grated Parmesan or Romano cheese**
- **2 teaspoons sugar**
- **¼ cup olive oil**
- **1 cup dry white wine**
- **3 yards sausage casings**

Grind the meat using the coarse grinder. Note that I have put olive oil in this dish so you can cut down on some of the animal fat by trimming away a bit of the fat on the pork. Mix all ingredients together and stuff into casings as per instructions above. Tie off into 4- to 5-inch lengths.

Cotechino is cooked like the Italian sausage on page 245. It is also great in soups. Be sure to prick the sausage well before cooking.

Use in minestrone soup and in heavy pasta dishes.

MAKES 3 POUNDS.

Mexican Sausage

Chorizo
(Mexico)

A favorite Mexican meal at our house is chorizo con huevos, or sausage with eggs. This sausage is also a basic necessity to a good paella. Easy and spicy.

1 pound coarse-ground lean pork
1 teaspoon salt
2 tablespoons chili powder
¼ teaspoon cloves
½ teaspoon cinnamon
1 tablespoon paprika
1 garlic clove, crushed
1 teaspoon oregano
2 tablespoons cider vinegar
2 tablespoons water
1 yard sausage casings

Combine all ingredients. Stuff into casings, or fry plain (best in casings).

Cook with scrambled eggs for breakfast or use in Paella (page 368).

MAKES 1 POUND.

◆

Seafood Sausage

(New Orleans)

The Upperline restaurant in New Orleans is run by a mother/son team, and it *is* a team. The mother runs the place and son is the chef. He is skilled and has a fresh approach to things. He serves a boudin that is made of seafood and it is delicious. I have attempted to create something similar to his own excellent dish.

2 pounds whitefish fillets, boneless (cod, halibut, flounder, all work well)
1 pound raw large shrimp, peeled (optional, but delicious)

- 1 pound scallops (optional, but delicious)
- 1 pound cooked chicken, skinless and boneless
- 3 eggs
- 1 cup cream or Mock Cream (page 289)
- ½ cup dry vermouth
- ⅛ teaspoon cayenne pepper
- ¼ teaspoon thyme
- Salt and black pepper, freshly ground, to taste
- 2 cups bread crumbs
- 5 yards sausage casings
- Chicken Soup Stock (page 101), mixed with white wine for poaching

Grind the boneless fish in a food processor, along with the shrimp, scallops, and chicken. Do this in small batches, adding the eggs, cream, and wine as you go. Blend in the seasonings. Remove from the machine and stir in the bread crumbs. If this mixture is too dry for forming sausages easily, add a little milk.

Stuff the sausage casings.

If you wish to form the sausages by hand, chill the mixture at least 2 hours to firm the filling. To shape the sausages, put a bit of the mixture on a piece of wax paper and roll up like a sausage. Make each about 6 inches long. Then, roll each up in a piece of cheesecloth or muslin and tie the ends like a sausage. These should be firm and rather tight.

Poach the sausages, either in casings or hand rolled, in Chicken Soup Stock (page 101) to which you have added a bit of white wine. They should take about 20 minutes to cook at a simmer. Cover when cooking and turn each when it floats to the surface.

Serve with Real Garlic Toast (page 341) and Tuna and Potato Salad (page 136).

Wine Suggestion: Fumé Blanc.

MAKES 5 POUNDS.

VEGETABLES

ASSORTED VEGETABLES • THE EGGPLANT

Cuisine is when things taste like themselves.

—Curnonsky

ASSORTED VEGETABLES

Tell me what you eat, and I will tell you what you are.

—Brillat-Savarin

• Vegetables and Wine •

It is perfectly logical that we should use wine in the cooking of vegetables. The Chinese have been doing it for hundreds of years. On the other hand, Westerners have been boiling their vegetables in water for hundreds of years. In England they used to believe that peas had to be boiled for at least a hundred years. We are done with that.

The flavor and nutritional value of lovely green foods that are boiled is almost gone. I am for eliminating most of the water and adding a shot of white wine. No, not for every vegetable dish. Of course not! But you will be amazed at how many vegetables will be helped by such gracious treatment.

HINT: Pan-Fry Your Vegetables

People are always asking why vegetables cooked in the Chinese manner taste so good and fresh. It is because they do not cook them. They threaten them! You do the same. Use a wok or a large frying pan with lid. Use a little olive oil or garlic. Sauté or stir-fry thin-sliced or matchstick-cut vegetables for a few minutes and then throw in a few shots of wine. Cover and finish. You will not need butter and you will need little salt.

Zucchini and Carrots

This one will get you started. It is simple and you will begin to think up new mixtures yourself. The trick is learning to cut vegetables julienne style. See my illustrations below for help. Or buy a mandoline (page 25), so called because the cutters are arranged close to each other like strings on a musical mandolin.

- **2½ cups carrots, cut julienne**
- **2½ cups zucchini, cut julienne**
- **2 tablespoons olive oil**
- **1 garlic clove, crushed (optional)**
- **1 tablespoon fresh lemon juice**
- **3 tablespoons dry white wine**

Cut the carrots and zucchini julienne style (see below). Use a large frying pan or a wok. Add the oil to a *hot* pan and then the carrots. Sauté or stir-fry for 2 minutes and then add the zucchini. Toss about for 3 minutes. Add the lemon juice and wine. Toss about and remove from the heat. Serve within a few minutes.

You might like to try garlic with this dish. Add a crushed garlic clove to the pan when you put in the oil. Continue as above.

SERVES 4.

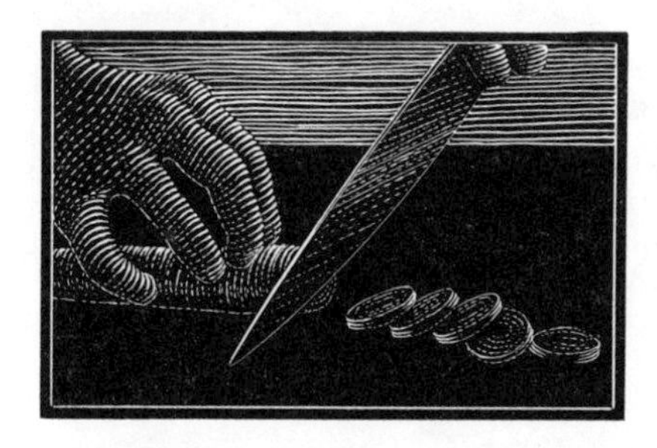

HINT: To Julienne Vegetables
This is simple and it will help your vegetables cook quickly without getting mushy. Cut the vegetables into thin slices. Lay a few slices on top of each other and cut them into matchstick-size pieces. With a little practice you will become very good at this. Or buy a mandoline (page 25). It's quicker.

Vegetables North Beach

The North Beach area of San Francisco is as Italian as you can get in this country. I love the place and the food. Since Chinatown and "Little City," (the Italian community), are back to back, there is a bit of sharing in the cooking techniques. This dish was suggested by Mary Etta Moose of the Washington Square Bar and Grill, a fine place to eat.

- 3 tablespoons olive oil
- 2 garlic cloves, crushed
- 2 small zucchini, sliced thin
- 1 package (10 ounce) frozen Italian green beans, defrosted (drain these carefully and pat dry with paper towels)
- 1 tablespoon tomato paste
- ¼ cup Basic Brown Soup Stock (page 100)
- ⅛ cup tawny port
- 1 teaspoon oregano
- 1 medium red onion, peeled and sliced
- ½ cup cherry tomatoes cut in half, and drained for ½ hour
- Salt and black pepper, freshly ground, to taste

Heat a wok and add the olive oil and garlic. Add the zucchini and the beans, carefully drained and dried with paper towels. Toss in the oil for 5 minutes. Mix together the tomato paste, stock, and port. Add, along with the oregano, onion, and tomatoes. Add salt and pepper to taste and cover the pan. Cook for 3 more minutes and serve.

SERVES 5–6.

Onions in Madeira

This is really an amazing dish in that it is so mild and so flavorful at the same time. It goes very well with any red meat course. You do not have to spend a fortune on imported Madeira. There are several very respectable brands out of California that will do well for both cooking and drinking.

- 4 red onions, peeled and sliced
- 1/4 cup Basic Brown Soup Stock (page 100) or canned, not bouillon
- 1/4 cup Madeira
- Salt and black pepper, freshly ground, to taste

Place the onions in a frying pan that is lined with Silverstone. Add the stock and wine. Simmer gently, uncovered, until the liquid is almost gone. Taste for salt and pepper. You should need little.

Serve as a side vegetable dish with any red meat course.

SERVES 4–6.

◆

Onions in Herbs and Wine

Another easy one that is fine for a side dish.

- 2 tablespoons olive oil
- 2 garlic cloves, crushed
- 4 yellow onions, peeled and sliced
- 1/4 teaspoon oregano
- 1/4 teaspoon basil
- 1/4 teaspoon thyme
- 1/2 cup dry white wine
- Salt and black pepper, freshly ground, to taste

Heat a large frying pan and add the oil and garlic, along with the onions. Sauté until they just begin to brown. Add the herbs and the wine and simmer until the onions are very tender, about 10 minutes. Check for salt and pepper. You should need little.

This can almost be served as an onion relish. It is light enough to be supportive with red or white meat dishes, and it is great with fish.

SERVES 4.

Baked Onions au Gratin

I simply love onions, in any form. I developed this dish because of my love for French onion soup, and you will recognize the flavors. You may not wish to put as much cheese on your onions as I do on mine. This is very rich, indeed!

8 medium yellow onions, peeled and sliced
2 tablespoons butter
¼ cup dry cocktail sherry
⅛ teaspoon nutmeg
Salt and pepper to taste
¼ cup heavy cream
½ cup grated Swiss cheese
¼ cup grated Parmesan or Romano cheese for topping

In two batches, sauté the onions in the butter in a large frying pan. Cook only until limp. Do not brown or discolor.

Deglaze the pan, or remove the onions from the pan and pour in the sherry, scraping the pan with a wooden spoon to dissolve the brown, toasted onion.

Mix the onions, the sherry, nutmeg, salt, pepper, and heavy cream together and place in a baking dish. Top with the Swiss cheese and then the Parmesan or Romano. Bake at 375° until the top is a bit brown and all is bubbling hot, 15 to 20 minutes.

SERVES 8.

HINT: Microwaved Vegetables
You will very much improve the flavor of your frozen vegetables if you do not use water when cooking them. Substitute dry white wine for the water and microwave according to package directions.

Carrots in Vermouth

Your children will like this change. No, I do not worry that children eat foods cooked with wine. The alcohol is gone, absolutely gone!

- **2 pounds carrots, sliced thin or cut julienne (page 257)**
- **2 tablespoons butter or olive oil**
- **¼ cup sweet vermouth**
- **Salt and black pepper, freshly ground, to taste**
- **2 tablespoons chopped parsley for garnish**

Heat a frying pan and add the carrots and butter or oil. Sauté until they just begin to brown. Add the vermouth and simmer for 5 minutes, uncovered. Stir them often. Check for salt and pepper. Little should be needed. Garnish with the parsley.

SERVES 6–8.

HINT: Cruciferous Vegetables and Cancer
What strange and wonderful news! The American Cancer Society and the National Cancer Institute have announced that you can reduce your risk of cancer of the gastrointestinal tract and the respiratory system if you add more "cruciferous" vegetables to your diet.

Cruciferous vegetables are the ones that you refused to eat as a child—cabbages, broccoli, cauliflower, and Brussels sprouts. Generally, they tasted bad because they were overcooked. These vegetables are called "cruciferous" because they all have flowers with four leaves in the form of a cross. Remember the task of the crucifer at church? He carries the cross. Now isn't that good news? No, I didn't think this one up on my own!

Fried Cabbage

Sounds as if we have really hit rock bottom, doesn't it? Cabbage is a wonderful food if you do not cook it long, and it is very good for you. I love this recipe.

- 4 strips bacon, diced
- 2 garlic cloves, crushed (optional)
- 1 large yellow onion, peeled and sliced
- 2 pounds cabbage, cored and sliced
- ½ teaspoon caraway seeds
- ½ cup Chicken Soup Stock (page 101) or bouillon
- ½ cup dry white wine
- Salt and black pepper, freshly ground, to taste

Heat a large Dutch oven and add the bacon. Sauté until cooked, but not crisp. Add the garlic and onion. Sauté until the onion is clear. Add the cabbage, caraway, stock, and wine. Cover and cook until the cabbage collapses, about 5 minutes. Remove the lid and cook until the liquid is reduced a bit, about 10 minutes, stirring now and then. The cabbage should be barely tender. Do not overcook it.

Variation: If you wish to avoid the bacon, use 3 tablespoons olive oil instead.

SERVES 5–6.

◆

Red Cabbage and Wine

This is very delicious and somewhat sweet. My boys call it candied cabbage. And they love it!

Prepare the recipe for Fried Cabbage, as above. Use red cabbage instead of white and omit the garlic. Use red wine instead of white and replace the caraway seeds with 3 tablespoons brown sugar.

Pan-Fried Broccoli

This one may change your children's opinion of broccoli. I hope so.

- 2 garlic cloves, sliced (optional)
- 2 tablespoons olive oil
- 2 bunches fresh broccoli, cleaned and sliced, the heavy part of the stem discarded
- ¼ cup dry white wine
- ¼ cup Chicken Soup Stock (page 101) or canned broth
- Salt and black pepper, freshly ground, to taste
- 3 tablespoons sliced almonds
- 2 tablespoons fresh lemon juice
- 2 tablespoons melted butter or olive oil

Heat a large lidded frying pan or wok and sauté the garlic in the oil. Add the broccoli and toss in the oil. This will help retain the bright green color. Add the liquids and toss. Cover and simmer until the vegetable is barely tender, about 10 minutes. Check for salt and pepper. Garnish with the almonds and top with the lemon juice mixed with the oil or butter. Do not use the lemon juice by itself or you will bleach the vegetable. Mix it with the butter or oil first.

SERVES 5–6.

Brussels Sprouts Polonaise

(France)

Cook your Brussels sprouts with a little white wine in the microwave (page 260).

Sprinkle cooked Brussels sprouts with grated hard-boiled egg and chopped parsley. Pour melted butter mixed with fresh lemon juice over the top at serving time. Or you can use garlic and olive oil, heated, instead of the butter.

Zucchini Stuffed with Tomato

(Italy)

This is a rather cute thing to serve, and it is very tasty. We make a basket of the zucchini and fill it with fresh tomato. Simple!

- 4 zucchini, short and fat
- 2 tablespoons olive oil
- 1 garlic clove, crushed
- 2 tablespoons chopped yellow onion
- 2 cups diced fresh tomatoes, very ripe
- 4 tablespoons dry red wine
- ½ teaspoon dried dill weed (weed, not seed)
- ⅛ teaspoon sugar
- Salt and black pepper, freshly ground, to taste

- ¼ cup freshly grated Parmesan or Romano cheese
- ¼ cup dry white wine

Cut both ends from the zucchini and then cut them in half, crosswise through the middle. Scoop out most of the center pulp from one end, reserving the pulp for a later soup. Leave a round tube of squash that is sealed at the other end. Set them aside.

Heat a frying pan and add the oil, garlic, and onion. Sauté until the onion is clear. Add the tomatoes, red wine, dill, sugar, salt, and pepper. Cook for about 5 minutes, or until the tomatoes are limp but not mushy.

Stand the squash baskets on one end in a baking dish just large enough to hold them. A glass pie plate will work well. Fill each with the tomato mixture and top with the cheese. Pour the white wine around the bottom of the baskets and bake them, uncovered, at 400° until tender but firm, about 35 minutes.

SERVES 8.

♦

Carrots in Champagne and Dill

- 2 tablespoons butter
- 1 pound carrots, peeled and thinly sliced
- ¼ cup Basic Brown Soup Stock (page 100)
- ½ cup champagne
- 1 tablespoon fresh lemon juice
- 1 teaspoon dried dill weed

Melt the butter in a heavy saucepan. Sauté the carrots for a few minutes over medium heat until they begin to brown. Add the beef stock and champagne and cover. Cook until barely tender but still a bit firm. Remove cover and place on high heat until the liquid is almost cooked away. Add lemon juice and dill weed and serve.

SERVES 4.

THE EGGPLANT

The aubergine must surely be one of the most popular vegetables in the world, for it is eaten throughout the Far East, the Near East, Europe, and the Latin countries and the Americas.

—André L. Simon and Robin Howe
Dictionary of Gastronomy

• Eggplant •

Why do a whole chapter and television show on eggplant when doing a series on cooking with wine? Because eggplant is the most beautiful vegetable I know. The shape, the color . . . it looks like an enormous grape!

Originally the vegetable came from India, where it was common even prior to the tenth century. The Arabs were enjoying it then, too, but it did not reach Italy until the Middle Ages. The French have been cultivating the great purple delicacy since the 1600s. They have been taken by the flavor, the shape, and the color. I am taken by the French name, aubergine.

Because it is so pulpy, the eggplant will absorb other liquids, especially oils like olive oil. The vegetable's seemingly endless ability to keep absorbing olive oil gave rise to the wonderful Arab remark about a wealthy man: "He is so rich he doesn't care how much olive oil his wife puts in the eggplant."

I know that there are people in your house who are going to ask you to back off this section since they dislike eggplant. They only *think* they don't like this wonderful vegetable. Cook any one of the following dishes and I am sure that you will be applauded.

HINT: How to Prepare Good Eggplant
Always salt it first if it is to be stewed, baked, or fried. Let it steep for about ½ hour in a colander. Then wipe off the salt and moisture. Don't worry about all of the salt used in drying out the eggplant. It drips off with the moisture.

Eggplant Turkish Style

Imam Bayildi
(Turkey)

This is a surprisingly delicious dish. It is so favored in the Middle East, particularly in Turkey, that the name given the dish is literally "The priest fainted." And, since the dish comes from that ancient and creative portion of the world there are several interpretations as to what was going on. Some say that the Imam, the priest, fainted from sheer gastronomical delight when presented with this dish. Others maintain he loved the dish so that he fainted when he was refused the dish. Another line is that he fell flat on the floor when he realized how much olive oil was used in the dish and how much it cost. The Greeks have eaten this dish for hundreds of years, using the Turkish name. Why? Because the Greeks maintained that the Imam tasted the dish in Greece, and fainted there!

Regardless of which story you choose to tell at the table, your family and friends will love this one.

- **4 medium-size ripe tomatoes**
- **3 medium eggplants, about 1 pound each**
- **2 tablespoons salt for draining**
- **2 tablespoons olive oil**
- **4 garlic cloves, crushed**
- **3 medium yellow onions, peeled and sliced**
- **¼ cup chopped parsley**
- **¼ cup dried currants (optional, but delicious)**
- **Salt and black pepper, freshly ground, to taste**

- ½ cup olive oil
- ½ teaspoon whole thyme
- 2 bay leaves, crumbled
- 1 teaspoon sugar
- Juice of 1 lemon

Dice the tomatoes and drain them in a colander for 1 hour. Discard the juice.

Choose long and narrow eggplants, if possible. Cut off the stems and cut the plant in half, the long way. Using a vegetable peeler, remove 3 long pieces of the peel, each about 1 inch wide, the long way. Move the peeler back and forth. This will help moisture flow out of the eggplant. Using a large metal spoon, scoop out a bit of the eggplant, leaving a boat that has very thick sides and bottom. Coarsely chop the scrapings and reserve.

Sprinkle the salt equally on each eggplant boat and set on a rack to drain, skin side up, for 45 minutes. In the meantime, prepare the filling.

Heat a large frying pan and add the 2 tablespoons of olive oil and garlic. Sauté for a moment and add the onions and chopped pulp from the eggplant. Sauté until the onions are transparent, but not discolored. Remove from heat. Place the onions, garlic, eggplant scrapings, tomatoes, parsley, and currants in a bowl and mix gently. Add salt and pepper to taste.

Wipe the eggplant boats dry with paper towels. Fill each with an equal amount of the above filling and place them in an ovenproof casserole just big enough to take them comfortably. Mix the ½ cup olive oil with ½ cup water, and the thyme, bay leaves, sugar, and lemon juice. Pour 2 tablespoons of this mixture on the top of each eggplant boat and pour the remaining liquid in the bottom of the pan. Bring to a simmer, cover, and simmer until the eggplants are quite soft, about 1 hour and 15 minutes. Remove from the heat and allow to cool with the lid on. Serve cold or at room temperature.

This is great for a nonmeat meal or as an appetizer.

SERVES 6 AS A MEAL, MORE AS A VEGETABLE DISH.

Stuffed Baked Eggplant New Orleans

New Orleans cuisine, a blend of Creole, Cajun, French, and black American, simply fascinates me. They do things with food, they combine certain flavors, that would not even occur to the rest of us. This is such a dish. I first had it at Pascal Manale's, but many other restaurants do a fine job on this. It is costly because of the crab and shrimp, but you do get 8 servings out of this recipe. I can just hear you saying, "No, this is too expensive and too complicated." Please, bear with me. This dish commits neither of those crimes.

- 4 medium-size eggplants
- 3 tablespoons olive oil
- 1 cup chopped yellow onion
- 1 cup chopped green onion
- ¼ cup chopped parsley
- ½ cup chopped green sweet bell pepper
- 4 garlic cloves, crushed
- 1 teaspoon whole thyme
- 2 bay leaves, crushed
- ¼ pound cured ham, diced (buy a slice of good ham from your butcher, not the bland, boiled stuff)
- 2 teaspoons salt
- ¼ teaspoon freshly ground black pepper
- ½ teaspoon Tabasco, or more to taste
- 1 tablespoon Worcestershire
- 2 eggs, beaten
- 1 cup bread crumbs
- 1 pound shrimp, peeled and cut into ½-inch pieces
- 2 tablespoons butter or olive oil
- ½ pound crabmeat
- Grated Parmesan or Romano cheese for garnish

Cut off the stems of the eggplants and cut them in half, lengthwise. Boil in salted water until tender, about 10 minutes. Remove and drain. Scoop out most of the center of each and chop the scrapings coarse. Set aside.

In the oil, sauté the yellow and green onions, parsley, green pepper, garlic, thyme, bay leaves, ham, salt, pepper, Tabasco, Worcestershire, and eggplant scrapings. Simmer gently for ½ hour. Take off the burner and stir in the eggs and then the bread crumbs. In a separate pan, sauté the shrimp in 2 tablespoons butter for 2 minutes, or until it changes color. Add to the eggplant mixture along with the crabmeat.

Divide the mixture among the eggplant boats and sprinkle with cheese. Place on a greased baking sheet and bake at 350° for 30–40 minutes, or until the top is browned.

Serve with Pan-Fried Broccoli (page 263), along with a green salad with Burgundy and Herb Dressing (page 129).

Wine Suggestion: Fumé Blanc.

SERVES 6 AS A MAIN COURSE.

◆

Eggplant Chinese Style

(China)

I tasted this dish for the first time about ten years ago, in San Francisco. The little restaurant that offered this had beaten everyone else to the punch. They were the first, though now it is not unusual to see it on menus in northern Chinese establishments. You will find the dish unusual, however, since it is a most interesting blend of hot and sweet spices and sauces. People who think that they dislike eggplant will love this dish . . . and we will have won them over.

1 large eggplant
2 tablespoons salt
1 teaspoon grated fresh ginger
1 tablespoon red chili paste with garlic*
1 tablespoon Chinese rice wine* or dry sherry
1 tablespoon light soy sauce
1 tablespoon hot bean sauce*
1 tablespoon sweet bean sauce*
3 tablespoons peanut oil
3 garlic cloves, minced

4 green onions, chopped
1 tablespoon toasted sesame oil*
Green tops of 3 green onions, chopped, for garnish

Cut off the stem of the eggplant and cut into ¾-inch slices. Cut the slices again so that you have cubes ¾ inch square. Place in a bowl and mix with the salt. Place in a colander and drain for 45 minutes. Rinse off the cubes and drain for another 45 minutes. Or rinse and pat dry with paper towels.

Meanwhile, mix the sauce: In a small bowl mix the ginger, red chili paste with garlic, wine or sherry, soy sauce, hot bean sauce, and the sweet bean sauce. Stir and set aside.

Heat a wok or very large frying pan. Add the peanut oil and the garlic. Sauté for a moment and then add the eggplant and green onion. Stir-fry over high heat until the eggplant is tender, 7–10 minutes. Add the mixed sauce. Continue cooking for another 3 minutes. Place on a serving platter and drizzle the sesame oil over the top. Add green onion tops for garnish.

SERVES 4–6 AS PART OF A CHINESE MEAL.

*See ingredients list under CHINESE (page 33).

◆

Eggplant Cheese Rolls

I still love eggplant Parmesan, but I think this version is a little more exciting. It will do very well for a first course, or if you serve two or three to each person, you will have a fine main course.

FILLING:
1 cup cottage cheese, small curd, well drained
1 cup coarsely grated Swiss cheese
¼ cup grated Parmesan or Romano
1 egg, beaten
Salt and pepper to taste
¼ cup chopped parsley
½ teaspoon oregano

EGGPLANT:
2 large eggplants
3 tablespoons salt for draining
4 tablespoons olive oil

TOPPING: 2 cups spaghetti meat sauce (homemade or bottled) or Italian Gravy (page 341)
1 cup coarsely grated Swiss or mozzarella cheese

Prepare the filling by mixing all the filling ingredients together. Set aside.

Prepare the eggplant by cutting off the stem portion and cutting the entire eggplant, lengthwise, into slices about ¼ inch thick. Pick out the slices that do not run the full length of the eggplant and set aside. Salt the long slices and place in a rack or drainer. Allow to drain for 30 minutes. Rinse and pat each dry with paper towels, thus removing the salt and water. Fry a few at a time in the olive oil, turning once. Fry only until each is a bit brown on one side and then turn. When all are completed, set aside.

Place a tablespoon or so of the filling on the largest end of each slice and roll up, like a jelly roll. Secure with a toothpick and place in an oiled baking dish. Continue until all are filled and then top with the spaghetti meat sauce and finally with the grated cheese. Bake at 375°, uncovered, about 25 minutes, or until all is hot and bubbly.

SERVES 4 AS A MAIN COURSE, 6–8 AS A FIRST COURSE.

◆

Sammy's Eggplant Salad

I cannot believe that I am telling you about this dish. It is so heavy, it is so rich, it is so full of garlic . . . well, it smells like one of my favorite restaurants in New York. The place is a very high-class dive, in a strange neighborhood, but a neighborhood that has known good times in the past. It was the center of the Orthodox Jewish community on the Lower East Side . . . but that was years ago. Sammy's is still there. They call it a "Roumanian Steak House." The menu is old Lower East Side Jewish from generations ago. I love the place, and the eggplant salad is just wonderful. I will give you the entire recipe, as it is printed on a mimeographed sheet that the waiter will give you, if you have eaten enough schmaltz and onions!

Eggplants are exceptionally adaptable and flavorful. That adaptability is evident here in this excellent eggplant dish that can be served either as a delicious appetizer, a stateful luncheon main course, or as a wonderful accompaniment to a main course. Preparation is somewhat time-consuming, as it is for many good things. Mimi Sheraton, the former *New York Times* restaurant critic, described this dish as "one of the best versions of that salad we have ever had." When shopping for eggplants, remember to select one that is bright purple, smooth-skinned, and heavy for its size.

2 large eggplants
1 large cucumber, peeled, sliced in half lengthwise, seeded, and diced
2 large tomatoes, diced
1 large green pepper, seeded and diced
1 large Spanish (white) onion, peeled and diced
Juice of 1 lemon
3 tablespoons olive oil
Freshly chopped garlic to taste (they must use 15 cloves . . . I would suggest 4)
Salt and freshly ground black pepper to taste
Tongs for turning the eggplants (to avoid piercing them)
Large serving bowl

1. Roast the eggplants over a medium to high flame, turning frequently, until the outside is charred on all sides. The eggplant may be roasted directly on a gas burner or on a metal rack that has been placed over the burner.
2. When all the sides are evenly charred, remove the eggplants and allow them to cool.
3. Peel the eggplants, from the top to bottom, and then dice finely. Place the eggplants in a large bowl that has been rubbed with the garlic.
4. Add the cucumber, tomatoes, green pepper, onions, lemon juice, and oil. Mix well.
5. Season with salt and pepper.
6. Serve at room temperature.

SERVES 6–8.

That is it! The dish is very sharp and wonderful. I would offer the following suggestions: Do use the rack for roasting. Yes, you can use an electric burner. Turn it on high and place the rack over the burner. Or put eggplants in an oven broiler, very close to the elements. That will work as well.

When you rub the bowl with the garlic, be sure to include the remaining garlic in the dish.

This is *not* the dish that you serve when your mother-in-law comes over for the first time. You serve this to her after she has been eating with you regularly for thirty years, minimum. This dish is even better the second day.

◆

Pasta with Eggplant

(Italy)

This may be the easiest way to offer your family and friends the wonderful flavor of eggplant Parmesan without the work. If you put enough cheese on this dish it is almost as good as the baked version that takes much longer to prepare.

1 eggplant, diced
2 tablespoons salt
¼ cup olive oil
2 cups Italian Gravy (page 341) or spaghetti sauce
1 cup dry red wine
½ pound pasta, cooked al dente
Parmesan or Romano cheese, freshly grated, for garnish

Remove the stem of the eggplant. Cut into circles ½ inch thick and then cut each into ½-inch dice. Mix with the salt and place in a colander for 30 minutes. Rinse off and pat dry with paper towels.

Heat a large frying pan or wok. Add the oil and the eggplant. Sauté until brown. Add the eggplant to the spaghetti sauce and cook until tender, about 15 minutes. Pour sauce over the pasta and top with cheese.

SERVES 4.

Eggplant with Sausages

This dish is great for a buffet or for a party "a few days from now." It actually tastes much better after it has sat in the refrigerator for a couple of days. You should have lots of dishes like this one in your repertoire. Cook one day a week, then fill the larder and the freezer.

- 2 medium eggplants (don't bother to peel)
- 2 tablespoons salt
- 3/4 cup olive oil
- 1 pound Italian sausage (pages 245 and 249, or buy from market)
- 3 yellow onions, peeled and sliced
- 5 garlic cloves, crushed
- 1 pound pepperoni
- 4 fresh ripe tomatoes
- 1 cup freshly grated Parmesan or Romano cheese
- Salt and pepper to taste
- 1 teaspoon oregano
- 1 teaspoon basil
- 1 pound Swiss cheese, coarsely grated
- 1½ cups dry red wine

Cut the eggplants into ½-inch slices. Salt each and place in a drainer for ½ hour. Wipe dry with paper towels. Oil a cookie sheet and arrange the eggplant slices on it. Brush the tops with a bit of the oil and broil the slices until browned on one side. Turn and broil the other side.

Pan-fry the sausages until lightly browned. Slice and set aside. In the same pan, sauté the onions and garlic in 2 tablespoons of the oil. Cook the onions just until they are clear.

Slice the pepperoni thin. Slice the ripe tomatoes.

Oil a large glass or metal porcelain baking dish. It must be deep enough to hold all of this.

Construct the dish. Layer half the eggplant slices on the bottom of the baking dish. Cover with half the onions, half the sausages, half the pepperoni, and half the tomatoes. Sprinkle half the Parmesan cheese on top and add salt and pepper to taste. Top with half the basil and oregano. Repeat, adding another layer of each. Top the whole thing with the Swiss cheese. Pour the red wine over the top. Bake in a 350° oven, uncovered, until all is hot and bubbly, about 1 hour.

Serve with a green salad and rolls. That will make this into an ample meal.

Wine Suggestion: Chianti.

SERVES 6.

◆

Eggplant Meatballs

(Italy)

My job is great fun in that I travel all about the country, eating. Once, while racing through Cleveland traffic, our driver began to shout recipes to me. His name is Antonio Iammarono and his parents came to this country from north central Italy. He is a charming gentleman and a fine cook. This dish is his . . . or his wife's. It is just wonderfully easy and it will be a hit with the whole household.

THE MEATBALLS:	1	large eggplant, peeled and diced
	2	pounds lean ground beef
	½	cup freshly grated Parmesan or Romano cheese
	3	garlic cloves, crushed
	½	cup bread crumbs
	2	eggs
	½	teaspoon basil
		Salt and black pepper, freshly ground, to taste
FRYING:	2	tablespoons olive oil
BAKING:	1	cup spaghetti sauce or Italian Gravy (page 341)
	½	cup freshly grated Parmesan or Romano cheese
	¾	pound Muenster cheese, thickly sliced

Place the diced, peeled eggplant in a saucepan with enough water to cover. Bring to a boil, reduce the heat, and simmer for 10 minutes, or until the eggplant is tender.

Meanwhile, mix together the remaining ingredients for the meatballs. Drain the eggplant and allow it to cool for a moment. Mash the eggplant and mix it in with the meatball mixture. Form into 18 meatballs. Heat a large frying pan, add the oil, and brown the meatballs in two batches.

Place the sauce in the bottom of a large baking dish. Set the meatballs in the sauce. Top with the grated cheese and finally with the thickly sliced (⅛ inch thick) Muenster cheese. Bake in a 375° oven for 20 minutes, or until all is hot and bubbly.

Try this with Pasta Bagna Cauda (page 149), along with Vegetables North Beach (page 258).

Wine Suggestion: Chianti or any Italian red.

SERVES 6.

SAUCES

I would eat my own father with such a sauce.

—Grimod De La Reynière
L'Almanach des Gourmands, 1803

• Sauces with Wine •

The quickest and most frugal way that you can prepare a fine sauce is simply to deglaze the cooking pan with a bit of wine. Wine is so cooperative when it comes to making sauces that the wine almost does the job by itself. All you have to do is to get the wine near the pan.

You also need to remember that wine will give great flavors without adding a lot of undue calories and salt. (See page 154 for a discussion of this matter.) I add wine to sauces and gravies as a matter of habit . . . a good habit, I am sure.

You need never worry about the success of a dinner if you are prepared with the makings of a fine sauce. Keep wine on hand and a Demi-Glaze (page 284) or Glace de Viande (page 284) and you cannot go wrong.

There was a time in European history when sauces performed the difficult task of covering over the flavor of meat and game gone foul. This was true as little as a hundred years ago. In our time, due to the blessings of modern refrigeration, sauces may function not as a coverup but as support for the flavor of a fine dish. I do not believe that a dish is defined by the sauce. The sauce becomes too important and overwhelming, too rich and exaggerated. The plate should be lifted by a lightly flavored sauce, not burdened by one. For this reason I favor the lighter sauces rather than the old classics that are so heavy. I really prefer a simple wine sauce made right in the cooking pan, one that you can make at the last minute and pour over the meat or fish. Nevertheless you will enjoy the following collection of sauces. Some are heavy and you will not use them as often as the lighter sauces.

HINT: Deglazing the Pan

The quickest way to make a quick sauce is simply to deglaze the pan with wine. When you have finished browning or cooking any kind of meat or fish, add red or white wine to the pan while it is still hot. With a wooden spoon scrape up the brown goodness stuck to the pan. Do not do this if the pan drippings are black or burned. You may also use dry sherry, Marsala, or vermouth for deglazing.

Basic Brown Sauce

Sauce Espagnole
(France)

This sauce is basic to the French kitchen. It can be served just as it is or it can be further developed with additional seasonings or wine.

- 1 stick butter (¼ pound) *or* ½ cup peanut oil or olive oil
- 1 cup peeled and chopped yellow onions
- 1 cup chopped carrots, unpeeled
- ⅓ cup chopped parsley
- 1 bay leaf
- 1 teaspoon thyme, whole, dried
- ½ cup flour
- 2 cups dry red wine
- 2 quarts Basic Brown Soup Stock (page 100)
- 2 tablespoons tomato paste
- ¼ teaspoon black pepper, freshly ground
- ¼ cup dry sherry
- Salt to taste

Choose a 3- to 4-quart stockpot with a heavy bottom. Heat it and add ½ of the butter or oil. Add the onions, carrots, and parsley. Stir the vegetables on medium-high heat until they begin to brown. Add the bay leaf and the thyme. Put on a low simmer.

In a small frying pan, melt the remaining butter or oil. Add the flour and stir until it is light brown. Stir this roux into the vegetables. Add the remaining ingredients to the pot, except the sherry and salt. Bring to a boil, turn to a heavy simmer, and cook the sauce, uncovered, about 2 hours, or until it has reduced by half. Add the sherry and simmer for 5 minutes. Add salt to taste. Strain before serving or using.

MAKES 1 QUART.

Demi-Glace

Reduced Brown Stock
(France)

This is not really a sauce, but rather a condensed beef broth that will be helpful in preparing other sauces. The flavors are very concentrated and simply need adjusting with wine or some other flavoring such as mustard or mushrooms. It is called demi-glace because it is concentrated to the point that it is syrupy and half-glazed. Add a bit of this to any pan drippings that you have deglazed (page 282) and you are on your way to a terrific sauce.

- 1 **quart Basic Brown Soup Stock (page 100)**
- 1 **cup Basic Brown Sauce (page 283)**
- 2 **tablespoons dry sherry**

Bring the stock and brown sauce to a light boil. Turn the heat to medium and reduce sauce to 2½ cups. This will take about 1½ hours. Remove from the heat and stir in the sherry. Store in a tight container in the refrigerator for up to 7 days, or freeze for later use.

MAKES 2½ CUPS.

Glace de Viande

Meat Glaze
(France)

This takes some time to prepare but it is absolutely basic to a good French kitchen, or a Frugal one for that matter.

- 3 **quarts Basic Brown Soup Stock (page 100)**
- **Cornstarch**

Gently boil down the brown stock until there are about 2 cups remaining. This will require changing pans once. The results will be dark and thick, like molasses. Cool, and place in the refrigerator. Then cut into little blocks, dust each with cornstarch, cover, and refrigerate. Use for flavoring and coloring soups, gravies, and sauces.

MAKES 2 CUPS.

HINT: Alcohol Cooks Out
Do not be concerned about alcohol remaining in food. Alcohol boils out at about 175° while water boils at 212°. If the food was hot when the wine was added, the alcohol evaporated. The flavor and cleansing effect of the wine is left.

Marsala and Mushroom Sauce

This is good with almost anything. It is great with all red meats and most poultry, such as chicken or duck. You are going to scream when you realize that you have several steps to go through before you begin on this sauce, two other recipes that must be made first, the beef stock and the brown sauce. But the results will be grand and your refrigerator will be worth a fortune in compliments. This one can be made a few minutes before the party . . . provided you have made the other preparations a few days before.

- 1 cup chopped mushrooms
- 2 tablespoons butter
- 1 cup Basic Brown Sauce (page 283)
- ¼ cup dry Marsala
- Salt and black pepper, freshly ground, to taste

Sauté the mushrooms in the butter. Stir in the sauce and bring it to a boil. Add the marsala and immediately take off the heat. Check for salt and pepper.

MAKES 1½ CUPS.

HINT: Fat-Free Thickening
If you wish to avoid the fat or oil normally used in thickening sauces, you may use cornstarch mixed with dry white wine. Add about 1 tablespoon cornstarch to 2 tablespoons wine. Stir well and quickly blend into the hot sauce, *off the heat,* and then return the pan to the heat, stirring until it thickens. This can be done with most dishes that call for a roux (page 288).

White Butter Sauce

Beurre Blanc
(France)

This sauce is very rich, very simple, and very expensive in terms of the butter. So we are being frugal only in terms of simplicity. Normally, this sauce is served over fish of almost any kind. It makes the fish! No, I would not try this with margarine. Better you should make this just once in a while than to try it with bad-tasting margarines.

- 2 tablespoons finely chopped peeled shallots
- ½ cup dry white wine
- 2 teaspoons white wine vinegar
- 1½ sticks butter, chilled and cut into small pieces
- White pepper, freshly ground, to taste

Place the shallots, wine, and vinegar in a small saucepan. Bring to a boil, turn the heat to medium, and reduce the contents of the pan to 2 tablespoons. Turn the heat to low and, using a wire whisk, beat in the butter 2 tablespoons at a time. Cook and whip continuously until the sauce is the consistency of thick cream. This is easy to do with a cordless electric mixer.

MAKES 1 CUP AND SERVES AT LEAST 6.

Basic White Sauce

Béchamel

(Greece, France)

This is another basic sauce for the frugal kitchen. It is easy to make and offers many possibilities in terms of creamed meat dishes, fish, vegetables . . . on all kinds of things. I know that there is a canned white sauce out there. It is terrible stuff but people buy it because they don't know how to make a lumpless sauce. This one will be lumpless and you will never buy that canned white paste again.

2 cups milk
3 tablespoons chopped yellow onion
1 bay leaf
Cayenne pepper to taste
4 tablespoons butter
3 tablespoons flour
Salt to taste

Bring the milk to a simmer. Add the yellow onion, bay leaf, and cayenne pepper. Simmer for a few minutes, and strain the milk stock. Return to the stove. In another pan, melt the butter and stir in the flour. Remove the milk from its burner and stir in the flour/butter mixture (roux). Continue to simmer, stirring until thick, about 10 minutes. Add salt to taste.

Variation: Try adding a dash or two of dry sherry to this sauce. It is great on vegetables. I stir cooked onions into this sauce and eat the whole dish by myself!

MAKES 2½ CUPS.

HINT: Immediate Help for Your Brown Gravy
When you are preparing a brown gravy of any kind—chicken, beef, turkey—try adding a few tablespoons of dry sherry. You will be amazed at the polish this will give your sauce.

HINT: A Roux Without Butter

A roux is a mixture of butter and flour cooked together for a moment. It is then used as a thickening agent in sauces and stews. If you wish to avoid the butterfat, make your roux with olive oil. Use half oil and half flour. It will make absolutely lumpless gravies and sauces . . . without any butterfat.

White Cheese Sauce

Mornay
(France)

Another basic flavor from France that you achieve by doing the previous recipe first. I like this sauce with baked pasta, with vegetables, and anything that is left over, such as cooked chicken.

- 1 cup Basic White Sauce (see above)
- ¼ cup freshly grated Parmesan or Romano cheese
- Dash of Worcestershire sauce, to taste
- 1 tablespoon dry sherry
- Salt and black pepper, freshly ground, to taste

Stir the cheese into the hot sauce. Add the remaining ingredients.

Variation: Replace the white cheese with ½ cup sharp Cheddar, or even more if you like. This is great with baked pasta.

Variation: Add a bit of fresh lemon juice to the White Cheese Sauce and enjoy a fresh cheese and lemon flavor on your vegetables.

MAKES 1 CUP.

HINT: Heat Diffuser for Sauces

Use a heat diffuser (page 24) on your burners to even out and reduce the heat. You will save sauces from being burned and prevent lumps from forming.

HINT: To Make Mock Sour Cream
Place ½ pound low-salt/low-fat cottage cheese in a food blender. Add 1½ tablespoons low-fat milk and blend until the consistency of sour cream.

HINT: To Make Mock Cream Sauces
Place 1 pound low-salt/low-fat cottage cheese, along with 1 cup low-fat milk, in a food blender. Blend until very smooth, like cream. You may wish to make it a bit thinner. Use in any sauce recipe that calls for cream. Do not cook it as long in a sauce as you would regular cream. This mock cream will scare you when you first add it to a hot sauce in that it will separate and look grainy. Don't worry. Simply stir over the heat for a moment and it will smooth out beautifully.

Tomato and Garlic Sauce

(France)

This one is simple and useful. It has a very fresh taste because you use very ripe tomatoes and some of them are not even cooked. It has a light flavor perfect for a vegetable terrine or very light pasta dishes. It will support the flavor of fish without covering it. I tasted this first in France and I was surprised that I had not thought of it before. It is that simple.

2 tablespoons olive oil
4 garlic cloves, peeled and crushed

8 **very ripe tomatoes, diced (7 cups) (ripen these in your windowsill if the market cannot provide you with ripe tomatoes)**
½ **cup dry white wine**
½ **teaspoon oregano**
½ **teaspoon basil**
Salt and black pepper, freshly ground, to taste

Heat a 2-quart saucepan and add the oil. Sauté the garlic for just a moment. It must not be burned or discolored. Add three quarters of the diced tomatoes, the wine, and seasonings. Simmer for 20 minutes. Add the remaining diced tomatoes and remove from the stove. Allow to cool and then chill before serving.

This will keep fresh only a few days in your refrigerator. Since it is very light, use it on fresh cooked vegetables, omelets, cold meat dishes, and light pasta salads.

MAKES ABOUT 6 CUPS.

MOLDED DISHES

Enjoy, enjoy!

—Everybody's Jewish Grandmother

• Molded Dishes •

The advantages of serving a molded course should be obvious to everyone. All the work is done ahead of time and the dish is placed on the buffet or table. Guests may help themselves . . . now or later . . . and the host or hostess has to do nothing. I have a collection of molds that are made in glass, copper, French porcelain, English porcelain, tin, aluminum, and on and on. I love to play with them and I do not fill them with fruit-flavored gelatin salads! You will enjoy these recipes because the dishes are a meal, not toy fruit-flavored food.

Salmon Mousse

(France)

My dear friend Nellie Campbell is from France. Whence came the Scottish name? She married my best friend, and he is a Scot. She is a brilliant woman with a Ph.D. in clouds and waves. Somehow she finds time to cook for me . . . and often. This dish just brought the house down. I pleaded for the recipe that night, but she said she would have to translate it from the French for me. I waited days . . . but you will not have to. This is great stuff!

- **¾ cup clam juice or fish stock**
- **2 envelopes unflavored gelatin (I use Knox)**
- **2 cans (7 ounces each) red sockeye salmon**
- **6 flat anchovy fillets**
- **2 tablespoons capers**
- **2 green onions, chopped**
- **Juice of ½ lemon**
- **1 tablespoon chopped fresh dill weed**
- **8 drops Tabasco**
- **1¾ cups sour cream**
- **Parsley or dill for garnish**

In a small saucepan, warm the clam juice together with the gelatin. Stir until dissolved and warm. Do not boil.

Put the remaining ingredients *except* the sour cream in a food processor. Add the gelatin mixture. (Be sure to remove any bones that you found in the salmon.) Process until all is smooth. Add the sour cream and blend for a moment until well mixed.

Spray Pam into a 1½- or 2-quart mold and fill with the mixture. Refrigerate for several hours or overnight. After removing from mold, garnish with parsley or fresh dill weed.

Serve this as a luncheon or a first course.

Wine Suggestion: Fumé Blanc or Chardonnay.

SERVES 8 AS A FIRST COURSE.

Chicken and Avocado Mousse

When I first thought of doing this I was not even sure that it would work. Now I am so proud of this dish that I serve it often. A glass of dry white wine and this dish and you have got to be a happy person.

- **2 cups diced poached chicken, skinless and boneless (please, don't overcook this)**
- **½ cup sour cream**
- **½ yellow onion, peeled and chopped**
- **Juice of ½ lemon**
- **Salt and pepper**
- **2 ripe avocados**
- **2 cups chicken broth**
- **2 envelopes Knox unflavored gelatin**

Place the chicken, sour cream, onion, lemon juice, salt, and pepper in a food processor. Process until smooth. Add the avocados, peeled and pitted, and process just until smooth.

In a small saucepan, warm the broth along with the gelatin until dissolved and warm. Add to the processed mixture and blend well.

Spray a 1½-quart mold with Pam. Fill with the mixture and chill several hours or overnight.

This is a great buffet dish!

Wine Suggestion: Fumé Blanc or Chardonnay.

SERVES 8 AS A FIRST COURSE.

Pressed Tongue and Pork Loaf

(England)

This takes days to make but it is typical of very old recipes from Europe and Scandinavia. Don't reject this too quickly, as the result is just delicious.

- 1 gallon water
- 1 pound pickling salt (no iodine)
- 1 teaspoon saltpeter
- 1 fresh tongue, about 2 pounds
- 1½ pounds pork spareribs
- 2 tablespoons white wine vinegar
- 12 whole black peppercorns
- 8 whole allspice berries
- 2 whole cloves
- 1 teaspoon basil
- 2 tablespoons chopped fresh parsley
- 2 bay leaves
- 1 large yellow onion, peeled and chopped
- 1 envelope Knox unflavored gelatin

In a stainless steel pan or large glass bowl, place the gallon of water, along with the salt and saltpeter. Stir until dissolved. Place the tongue and the spareribs in the brine and keep covered, in the refrigerator, for 10 days. You may have to weight the tongue and ribs with a heavy plate. They must stay under the brine for 10 days.

When pickling is completed, drain the brine and discard. Thoroughly rinse the meats and place in a large kettle with a lid. Barely cover with water. Add the wine vinegar, the herbs and spices, and the yellow onion. Simmer this, covered, for 2 hours. You may need to skim the top of the kettle often so that the broth remains fairly clear. Allow the meat to cool in the broth. Save 1 cup of the broth, without fat, and discard the rest.

Debone the spareribs and cut into 1-inch-square pieces. Remove the skin from the tongue and cut the tongue into 1-inch-square pieces. Place the meat in a large bowl. Strain the 1 cup of broth and place in a small saucepan. Dissolve the gelatin in the broth over low heat. Mix the gelatin with the meat cubes and place in a soufflé dish or medium bread pan. Pour all of the gelatin from the bowl into the dish or mold. Place a weight on the top of the meat and refrigerate until firm, probably overnight.

Slice and serve cold with horseradish sauce or mustard sauce. Delicious.

Serve as a luncheon dish or as a first course.

Wine Suggestion: Dry white.

SERVES 6–8 AS A FIRST COURSE.

◆

Chicken and Lemon Mold

This is most attractive when molded and placed on a buffet. Your guests will be impressed with the flavor and the color.

- 2 envelopes Knox unflavored gelatin
- 1 cup chicken broth
- ½ cup dry white wine
- Juice of ½ lemon
- 3 cups coarsely chopped poached chicken, skinless and boneless (you might try Chinese Boiled Chicken in my first cookbook)

GARNISH:

- Lemon slices
- Carrot sticks
- Stuffed olives
- Hard-boiled eggs

In a medium saucepan, dissolve the gelatin in the broth, wine, and lemon juice over low heat. Stir until dissolved.

Mix the cooked chicken with the gelatin mixture. Spray a 1-quart mold with Pam. You may wish to decorate the inside of the mold with some of the garnishes. Place the chicken and gelatin mixture in the mold and chill for several hours. Garnish and serve cold.

Serve as a luncheon dish or as a summer dinner.

Wine Suggestion: German Riesling.

SERVES 4–6 AS A FIRST COURSE.

Ice Cream Bombe

Your children will think that you are a genius. Actually, this is a very simple dish. Just remember to chill the mold first and then pack it with your favorite ice creams.

Choose a favorite mold and spray with Pam. Chill the mold.

Soften the first flavor of ice cream and smear it into the mold. Freeze. Then, soften the second flavor of ice cream and fill the mold. Freeze.

Remove from the mold by dipping the mold in hot water for just a moment, or press with hot towels.

SANDWICHES

Man can live without spices, but not without wheat.

—Midrash: Psalms 2:16
Leo Rosten's *Treasury of Jewish Quotations*

• *The Sandwich* •

If you ask any schoolchild who invented the sandwich he will say, "The Earl of Sandwich." How narrow our image of history is. It is true that John Montague, Earl of Sandwich (1718–1792), was given credit for eating meat on bread. The reason for this practice, which the English found strange at the time, was that the earl's chef would do anything to get him to eat when he was gambling. He simply would not leave the gaming tables so the chef brought cold food to him. There he would stand, cards in one hand and bread with cold mutton in the other. This is a sandwich?

The real origin of the sandwich is hard to trace. French peasants were eating bread and meat in the fields generations before the Earl of Sandwich was born. And remember that both the Arabs and Jews ate bread on the desert, bread that we now call pocket bread, and since they used no silverware, everything was eaten with the bread between two fingers. Therefore, everything was a sandwich.

The Roman soldiers in ancient times ate sandwiches in the fields of battle. And the Chinese, for hundreds of years, have been eating a flat pancake into which they fold all sorts of food. Finally, at the beginning of the first century A.D., Rabbi Hillel instructed the Passover observers to prepare a sandwich of the matzo, bitter herbs, and the charoses. So it can be quickly shown that while the Earl of Sandwich put his name on the practice for the English, he certainly had the worst sandwich of all. Cold mutton on English bread!

Pocket Bread Sandwiches

Fill Middle Eastern pocket bread with your favorite meats and cheeses. Stuff the salad right in there, too.

Chinese Pancake Sandwiches

Place your favorite meats and cheese on a Chinese pancake and roll up like a jelly roll.

Tortilla Sandwiches

Place your favorite meats and cheeses on a tortilla and roll up like a jelly roll. Salads, such as egg or tuna salad, are particularly good on this bread.

Norwegian Lefse Sandwiches

Moisten the dry lefse sheets under running water for just a second. Drain and place under damp towels until softened. Fill with your favorite meats and cheeses, sliced thin, and roll up like a jelly roll. Slice in 2-inch lengths and secure with toothpicks. Great for the buffet.

The Danish Open-Face

An Art Form

When you wander about the sandwich shops of Denmark you cannot help but stand and stare at the diverse and beautiful creations that these wonderful people put on an open-face sandwich. Some are so involved that I can't even understand them! And most are a whole meal.

Use square slices of good heavy rye or pumpernickel. Butter and top with favorite meats, cooked seafoods, cheeses, caviars, eggs, etc.

Garnish in an artistic way, with onion slices, piped mayonnaise, capers, tomatoes, radishes, lettuce, parsley, baby pickles, cucumbers, olives, etc.

Serve on a fancy tray for your buffet.

French Croque Monsieur

A fancy name for the toasted cheese sandwich. It is the iron that gives the sandwich the shape, and the name. You can do the same thing with a grill or frying pan. Turn the sandwich once.

Butter two slices of bread on both sides. Place ham, Swiss cheese, and a bit of Dijon mustard on one. Cover with the other and toast on both sides in a croque monsieur iron. Try other fillings as well. Very elegant!

◆

Oyster Loaf from New Orleans

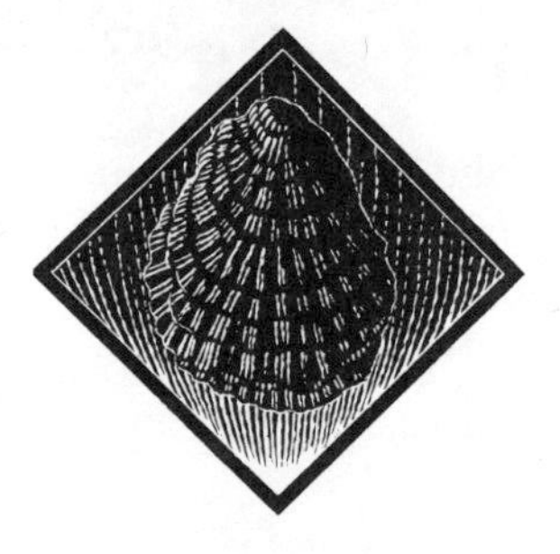

When Calvin Trillin, in his book, *Alice, Let's Eat!,* talks of wandering all over Louisiana looking for the perfect oyster loaf, I could not understand what he was talking about. We had never seen such a thing in the Pacific Northwest. Now I am a convert. I make them for the boys, but the best one is to be found at the Acme Oyster Bar in New Orleans.

Slice a 7-inch piece of poor boy French bread in half, the long way. Scoop out some of the soft white and fill with fried oysters, tartar sauce, sliced lettuce, and tomatoes. Serve while the oysters are still warm.

To fry the oysters, simply dip them in an egg wash, then into seasoned flour (salt and pepper) mixed with a small amount of white cornmeal. Fry in a pan with a good bit of oil until light brown. Do not overcook or they will get tough.

Muffaletta from New Orleans

There is still a battle going on in New Orleans over who invented this dish. It does not matter. All that matters is that you make the olive salad the day ahead . . . with plenty of garlic.

This is a great buffet dish because you can put out all of the makings and let everyone prepare their own meal. It really should be put together at the last minute.

OLIVE SALAD (TO BE MADE THE DAY BEFORE)

- **3 large garlic cloves, crushed**
- **1 cup chopped pimiento-stuffed green olives**
- **1 cup pitted and chopped "black-ripe" olives or Calamatas**
- **½ cup roasted sweet red peppers cut into chunks**
- **1 cup olive oil**
- **3 tablespoons chopped fresh parsley**
- **2 tablespoons white wine vinegar**

Mix all of the above and let stand overnight. Need not be refrigerated for the first night. (You can find the roasted red sweet peppers in jars at any Italian or fancy food shop.)

- **1 large, round, freshly baked Italian loaf**
- **⅓ pound salami, sliced thin (Genoa or Italian wine-cured)**
- **½ pound provolone, sliced thin**
- **½ pound mild cheese (such as Havarti), sliced**
- **⅓ pound mortadella or prosciutto or coppa or ham, sliced**

Make the salad the day before. Cut the bread in half horizontally, as you would for a sandwich. Scoop out some of the center of the loaf and drizzle olive oil from the salad on both halves of the bread. Use plenty! On the bottom half, place the salami, olive salad, provolone, mild cheese, and mortadella. Top with the other half of the loaf. Slice into wedges.

SERVES 6.

Philadelphia Steak Sandwich

This recipe for a Philadelphia classic is from the Society Hill Restaurant and Bar in the City of Brotherly Love. It is fine!

- 1 8-inch round Italian loaf, very fresh
- 10 ounces beef steak or roast, sliced very thin across the grain
- Olive oil for frying
- Pizza sauce
- 4 slices provolone cheese
- Fried sliced yellow onions
- Pickled jalapeño peppers (optional)

Slice the loaf in half through the center and then in half so that you have two half-moon sandwiches.

Grill the beef on a hot griddle in a little olive oil. Do not overcook.

Place the meat on a bottom half of the sandwich. Top with the pizza sauce and cheese. Broil until melted. Top with onions and peppers, if you wish. Place lid on sandwich and enjoy.

Six-Foot-Long Buffet Sandwich

We did this on the sandwich show just for fun. Bosco, the cameraman who sits above my head, is always hungry. We thought this sandwich would stop him in his tracks. It did not. He wanted a doggy bag for what he could not eat at the television station.

Have your baker make you a six-foot-long poor boy loaf. Cut in half the long way and fill with your favorite lunch meats, cheeses, lettuce, onions, tomatoes, relishes, etc. Drizzle on a good vinaigrette dressing. Place on the buffet and let your guests slice off their own portion.

SHOULD SERVE 10–12.

CASSEROLES

Some hae meat, and canna eat,
And some wad eat that want it,
But we hae meat and we can eat,
And sae the Lord be thankit.

—Robert Burns
The Selkirk Grace

· *Casseroles for the Buffet* ·

The wonderful thing about casseroles is that they can be placed on a buffet and our guests can serve themselves. The terrible thing about them is that most of us think of a casserole in terms of those awful dishes that were served at church suppers when we were children. How many pans of macaroni and cheese, along with eight pans of scalloped potatoes, can they get on one table?

In our time a casserole should refer to its more distinguished past. The casserole is simply a cooking vessel in which meat, fish, game, and vegetables are cooked slowly and usually for a long time. It is an ancient method of cooking and a good casserole in our time is made just as it was in the old world of earthenware or terra-cotta. To fully fit the definition, the casserole must have a tight-fitting lid and two handles. I have several of the heavy porcelain-covered iron, as well as my favorite clay pots.

Lamb with Fennel Sausage and Eggplant Casserole

Each time that I go into Place Pigalle restaurant in the wonderful Pike Place Farmers Market, in Seattle, I gain a new recipe. No, the recipes are not printed, but the food is so creative and delicious that I hurry home and begin trying to duplicate the dish. I have done well with this one. Yes, you must eat at Place Pigalle.

- **2 pounds leg of lamb, well trimmed and cut into 1½-inch cubes**
- **Olive oil for frying**
- **¾ pound Italian fennel sausage from the market or Italian Cheese and Red Wine Sausage (page 245)**
- **2 yellow onions, peeled and sliced**
- **3 garlic cloves, peeled and crushed**
- **1 whole eggplant**
- **3 very ripe tomatoes, cubed**
- **½ cup chopped parsley**

2 whole bay leaves
Salt and pepper
2 cups dry red wine

In a large metal casserole, brown the lamb cubes, in two batches, in a bit of the olive oil. Remove from the pot, leaving the oil, and sauté the Italian sausage until lightly browned. Remove from the pan and slice. Set aside. Sauté the onion and the garlic together with a bit more oil until the onions are limp. Cube the eggplant and sauté, with the onions and garlic, over high heat for 5 minutes. The eggplant should begin to soften but not be mushy. Return the lamb and sausages to the pan along with the tomatoes. Add the parsley, bay leaves, salt, pepper, and dry red wine. Bring to a simmer. Cover and simmer until all is tender, about 1 hour.

Watch this carefully so that the dish does not dry out. If it becomes too dry, simply add water during the cooking.

Serve over rice or noodles or serve with a Carrot and Zucchini Salad (page 134) and French bread. Very rich and very delicious!

Wine Suggestion: Hearty Italian red.

SERVES 6.

◆

Duck, Pork, and Sausage Casserole

This is a mild and less fatty version of the classic cassoulet.

1 pound Great Northern white beans
1 duck
2 pounds pork spareribs, cut into bite-size pieces
2 yellow onions, peeled and each stuck with 2 cloves
4 carrots, cut into 1-inch pieces
3 garlic cloves, crushed
Butter
Peanut oil
3 cups peeled and diced yellow onions

3 **more garlic cloves, crushed**
1 **cup tomato purée**
1 **Polish sausage, about 1 pound**

Put beans to soak in ample water overnight. Defrost the duck. Remove the wings and set aside. Remove the giblets from within. Cut the duck into dinner-size pieces. Legs, thighs, breasts each cut in two. Reserve the back and tail for the stock.

Place the wings, giblets, neck, back, and tail in a soup pot. Cover with water and bring to a boil. Simmer for 2 hours. Drain the stock and remove the fat. Reserve the stock.

Brown the duck pieces, along with the pork spareribs, in the oven. Bake at 375° until barely cooked through, about ½ hour.

Drain the beans and place in a 6-quart casserole with a lid. Cover the beans with the duck stock and add the yellow onions stuck with cloves, the carrots, and 3 cloves of garlic, crushed. Cover and cook gently for about 1 hour, or until the beans are about half cooked.

In the meantime, in another frying pan, melt a little butter. Add a little peanut oil and sauté the chopped onions and 3 more cloves of crushed garlic for about 4 minutes on high heat. Add the tomato purée and a little salt and pepper. Set aside.

To the pot of beans and vegetables, add the duck and spareribs. Cut the Polish sausage into 1½-inch pieces and add to the pot. Simmer for 30 minutes more. Finally, add the tomato and onion sauce to the pot. Stir very gently to blend. Cover the casserole with a piece of wax paper. Cover and bake for 1½ hours in a 350° oven, adding water or stock if needed.

Serve with Cauliflower Salad (page 136) and Zucchini Stuffed with Tomato (page 264)

Wine Suggestion: Côtes du Rhône or Zinfandel.

SERVES 12.

Philippine Chicken and Pork Casserole

I have just begun to appreciate and understand the food from the Philippines. This is a very good dish. It will go well at a party or your family dinner table.

- 1 frying chicken, about 2½ pounds, cut up
- 2 pounds boneless pork loin or shoulder, cut into 1-inch cubes
- Peanut oil for frying
- 1 cup red wine vinegar
- ½ cup soy sauce
- 2 bay leaves
- 3 garlic cloves, peeled and chopped
- ½ teaspoon freshly ground black pepper
- Salt to taste
- 1 cup Chicken Soup Stock (page 101) or use canned
- 1 cup coconut milk*

In a large metal frying pan, sauté the chicken in a bit of oil until light brown. Remove and repeat with the pork. You may have to do this in small batches so that you actually brown the meat quickly. Keep the burner on high.

Place all other ingredients, *except the coconut milk,* in the casserole with the meats. Cover and allow to marinate off the burner for about 2 hours. Return to the heat and bring to a boil. Lower the heat and simmer for about 1 hour, or until all is very tender. Add the coconut milk and cook for another 10 minutes, without the lid.

Serve with rice, a fresh fruit platter, and a green salad with Garlic Dressing (page 129).

Wine Suggestion: Rich California Chardonnay.

SERVES 6–8.

*Coconut milk can be found frozen or in cans in specialty food shops and delicatessens. If you cannot find it simply add ½ pound of unsweetened coconut to the pot during the last 10 minutes.

TABLETOP COOKING

I look upon it, that he who does not mind his belly will hardley mind anything else.

—Samuel Johnson

• Tabletop Cooking •

The wonderful thing about this kind of cooking is that it gathers everyone around the table and everyone is in for fun. Most people assume that the Swiss fondue pot is the background of tabletop cooking. Not so! For hundreds of years the Japanese have been sitting about the cooking center, which was placed in the middle of the table. It began as a matter of sheer necessity, this crowding together around the heat source, since they did not have central heating. Thus, cooking from the single heat source in the house was simple and sensible. See a recipe for classic Sukiyaki on page 354.

During the Shang dynasty in China, about three thousand years ago, the use of bronze and iron was quite sophisticated. Similar technology did not come to Europe until two thousand years later. The Chinese had helmets made of wonderful metals, and it was not uncommon for the soldiers to eat in the fields. They removed the metal hats, placed them in the fire, and cooked food in their headpieces. This must have been the beginning of the wok, which still looks like a hat. In any case, everyone gathered around the heat source and cooked for each other. That seems to me to be a very civilized thing to do.

Hoko Pot or Hot Pot

(China)

For this dish you may use a helmet from the Shang dynasty or a Hoko pot or hot pot. This child of the helmet can be found in Chinese markets. Otherwise, use a soup pot on a hot plate or alcohol burner. It is great fun.

2 quarts Chicken Soup Stock (page 101)
2 slices fresh ginger

CHOOSE AND USE ANY OF THE FOLLOWING:

Beef steak, cut in thin strips
Green onions, sliced the long way
Bean curd, cut in ½-inch cubes
Chinese greens of any kind, sliced
Shrimp, large, peeled
Sugar pea pods
Chicken fillet
Abalone, canned, sliced
Chinese dried mushrooms, soaked in water for 1 hour
Cooked ham, sliced into sticks
Chinese egg noodles, cooked, rinsed, and cooled

SAUCE:

3 tablespoons peanut butter
½ cup hot water
3 tablespoons soy sauce
Dash of Tabasco to taste

ANOTHER SAUCE:

2 tablespoons soy sauce
1 tablespoon rice wine vinegar
1 teaspoon sesame oil
Dash of Tabasco to taste
1 tablespoon dry white vermouth

Prepare attractive plates of any of the above food products. Have everything cut or sliced into small, bite-size pieces. Mix the sauces.

Start the charcoal in the backyard. Meanwhile, place the Hoko pot on a tray on the dining room table. Use a protective mat under the tray. Fill the tray with a few cups of water so that the table will not be harmed.

Place the stock and the ginger in the Hoko pot. Cover with the lid and fill the center of the cooker with hot charcoal briquets. When the soup is hot, invite your guests to cook their own supper, each using his own little net or spoon.

The dip sauces go with almost anything. Give all guests a tiny bowl of each sauce and let them dunk anything they wish.

Traditionally, the last course is the noodle course. Then when all is consumed, the soup is finally drunk.

Control the heat of the cooker by placing a Chinese teacup filled with water over the top of the vent. The fire will calm down immediately. This must be done in a well-ventilated room. Otherwise, the charcoal smoke will ruin the evening and your health. Leave the windows open.

Serve as part of a Chinese meal.

Korean Barbecue Steak Strips

While beef became popular in Korea only within the past century, the Korean chef seems to be a master at flavoring the meat in a rich manner and then serving small portions. Our method is exactly the reverse so that we eat too much red meat.

Choose a good 2-pound bottom round and have the butcher slice it across the grain into pieces that are about 1⁄16 inch thick. Marinate for ½ hour in the following mixture:

MARINADE:

- 3 tablespoons soy sauce (I prefer Kikkoman)
- 4 garlic cloves, crushed
- 1 teaspoon fresh grated ginger
- 3 tablespoons dry sherry or gin
- ½ teaspoon sugar
- Dash of Tabasco to taste
- 1 tablespoon hoisin sauce (optional—see your Oriental market for this one)
- 2 green onions, chopped
- 1 teaspoon Liquid Smoke
- 1 tablespoon sesame oil (also available as above)
- Black pepper, freshly ground

Marinate the steak slices, which have been cut across the grain, for about ½ hour. Cook on a hot stone at the table or in an electric frying pan. Be sure the pan is hot. Turn only once.

Serve as a part of a Japanese or Chinese dinner.

Wine Suggestion: Cabernet.

SERVES 6–8.

Onion Rings with Herb and Egg

During the show on tabletop cooking I used a cooking stone. This is a marvelous new gimmick that you can find in most gourmet shops. Please remember, however, that we now have electric cooking stones called Electric Frying Pans. You might want to try something a bit more modern.

2 large yellow onions, peeled and sliced
3 eggs
1 green onion, chopped
1/8 teaspoon basil
1/8 teaspoon thyme
Salt and pepper to taste

Separate the onion slices into rings and arrange on a plate.

Mix the eggs with the remaining ingredients. Place an onion ring on the hot stone or electric frying pan and fill the center with a bit of the egg mixture. Turn once.

Serve along with other meats or vegetables fried on the stone or in the electric frying pan.

SERVES 6–8.

INTERNATIONAL COMMUNITY

THE CHINESE KITCHEN

THE FRENCH KITCHEN

THE ITALIAN KITCHEN

THE JAPANESE KITCHEN

THE SPANISH KITCHEN

The joys of the table belong equally to all countries and all times.

—Brillat-Savarin

THE CHINESE KITCHEN

Better a man should wait for a dish than a dish wait for a man.

—Chinese Proverb

• The Chinese Kitchen and Wine •

I cannot recall when I first realized that the Chinese know more about food than anyone else. I was a child, I'm sure. My opinion has not changed.

There is no other culture in the world that puts as much time, effort, and anticipation into a meal as does the Chinese. They were probably the first cooks, too. Anthropologists are quite certain that the first person ever to cook meat was Peking man. That was hundreds of thousands of years ago.

For the Chinese, eating with another person is a thing of great intimacy and import. This seems to have been the case for thousands of years. The Chinese had the first restaurants, the first cooks, and they were the first to understand the necessity of a balanced diet. To this day the proper greeting to offer a friend is *"Chi fan le, mei you?"* It means, "Have you eaten yet?"

I became more fully aware of the meaning of the polite greeting while in Beijing, China. I had a most wonderful time with students at Beijing University while running about with an Englishman, of Polish descent, who spoke fluent Chinese. Yes! We met on the airplane into Beijing and spent our evenings eating together. He could get us into the few and desperately crowded restaurants.

Lunch was another matter. During the day I toured the beautiful city with a cabdriver, Mr. Lee. You cannot just hire a cab anywhere in town. You must go to one of the few hotels. Therefore, when touring, you hire the cab for the day. It is not expensive and my cabbie turned out to be such a wonderful character that I hired him for all three days in the capital city. That is the general rule. The other rule is that you feed the driver. We went to interesting restaurants and had a fine time, each of us trying to talk to the other when neither of us was sure what was going on. He was practicing his English lessons as we drove about, and I was expected to help. I then asked to go to a very famous restaurant that served Mongolian Hot Pot. It is called Donglaishun, and its popularity caused Mr. Lee to shake his head in refusal when I mentioned the place. "Busy!" he said. I pleaded without language and away we went, only to find the place jammed, even early in the day. I did not want to give up and so I talked and begged until I found the manager. An ancient gentleman appeared. I told him, through a translator, that I must try his food. Since all places were taken on the first three floors we were ushered to the formal dining rooms on the top floor, there to be seated in a room that was already prepared for a party of twelve. We were seated in a corner, at a special table for two that had to be carried in by the manager and his helper. Mr. Lee was mortified. You do not do that kind of thing in China. We should not be in a dining room set up for a private party. I agreed. I was hungry. We stayed.

The din from the hallway indicated that the expected party was about to appear. In they came, laughing and arguing over who was to sit where, a sign of politeness among these gracious people. They began with toasts and more toasts and I sank into my chair. This was a very important family party, and I had invaded. I could understand nothing except that the event was joyful and of great consequence. I sank further. Suddenly, a young fellow at the table turned and looked at me. "My God!" he yelled, "I watch you every week in San Francisco." He brought us a bottle of wine, I toasted him and thanked the table, and then toasted my driver, Mr. Lee. He sat there most confused.

The wine that Eric, my new-found friend, brought to us was quite good. It was a white much like a Semillion, from the Great Wall Wine Company. The bottle explained that the beverage came from a grape called Great Dragon's Eye. Isn't that a wonderful name and image?

Wine making has been common in China for thousands of years, though the beverage was generally made from grains, usually millet but often wheat. During the Han dynasty grapes were brought in by Western exporters and a genuine grape wine has been prized ever since. That means that grape wine in China began a little more than two thousand years ago.

Beverages made from grains, "chiu," have always been used in cooking. While I have tasted several varieties of such wine I really prefer to use a dry cocktail sherry in my Chinese cooking. Other Chinese chefs say that Chinese chiu makes all the difference. I think it too strong. You will enjoy the following recipes simply with sherry.

THE CHINESE KITCHEN

Choose and blend among these dishes. All seem to match each other in the Chinese method. It is perfectly all right to serve one course at a time. That is the way the Chinese do it and it also means that you can spend time with your guests. For information on special ingredients, please see Glossary at the beginning of the book.

Wine Suggestion: With Chinese foods I like to serve a dry Riesling, dry Gewürztraminer, dry Muscat, or dry Chenin Blanc.

Slow-Cooked Pork with Wine Sauce

(China)

This recipe was given to me during my days as a university chaplain. A student from Taiwan cooked this dish for me while the whole school was out on a peace march, and she was with us. The wonderful thing about this pork is that you put it in the oven and leave it there for several hours.

- **2 pounds boneless pork, shoulder or butt**
- **½ tablespoon sugar**
- **½ cup light soy sauce**
- **¼ cup water**
- **½ teaspoon black pepper**
- **¼ cup dry sherry**
- **½ teaspoon freshly grated ginger**
- **½ tablespoon mein see (page 37)**
- **2 green onions, chopped**
- **1 star anise**
- **2 garlic cloves, crushed**

Mix all the ingredients, except the pork. Place the pork in an ovenproof casserole that is just large enough to hold the meat. It should not have too much room. Pour the sauce over the meat and bake, covered, for 6 hours at 275°. I know this sounds too simple but the slow cooking will do a great job of blending these unusual flavors.

SERVES 6 AS PART OF A CHINESE MEAL.

◆

Ants Climbing Up a Tree

(China)

This dish will simply delight your children. There are no ants in the dish, of course. You were rude to ask! However, this dish from the northern regions of China does give the appearance of little creatures climbing on thin branches. (The little creatures are chopped black mushrooms. The branches are fried glass noodles.)

- 1 pound pork shoulder steak, boned and finely chopped, not ground
- 2 tablespoons light soy sauce
- 2 tablespoons Chinese rice wine or dry sherry
- 1 teaspoon grated fresh ginger
- 6 green onions, sliced thin
- 1 cup finely chopped cabbage or Napa (celery cabbage)
- 1 ounce Chinese dried mushrooms, soaked in water for 2 hours, drained, and finely chopped (reserve the water)
- 4 cups peanut oil for deep-frying
- 1 package (4 ounce) glass noodles (sai fun)
- 3 garlic cloves, chopped
- 1 tablespoon hot bean sauce (page 35)
- Pinch of sugar
- Freshly ground black pepper to taste
- 2 tablespoons cornstarch dissolved in 2 tablespoons water
- 1 tablespoon toasted sesame oil (page 40)
- Iceberg lettuce leaves, 2 or 3 for each person

Bone and finely chop the pork. Do not grind this as you want very small pieces to "climb" on the branches of the noodles. Marinate the pork in the soy, wine and ginger for about 15 minutes.

Slice the green onions. Finely chop the cabbage and mushrooms, reserving the soaking water from the mushrooms.

Heat the oil in a wok until it is just beginning to smoke. Use good ventilation in your kitchen for this one! Open the noodle package and undo them a bit. Drop into the hot fat in small batches. They will immediately puff up into wonderful white crunchy noodles. Turn quickly to be sure that all of them are cooked. Remove from the pan and drain on paper towels. Be very careful with this. You could burn yourself. Set the noodles aside.

Heat another wok or frying pan and add 1 tablespoon of the peanut oil. Add the chopped garlic and toss for a moment. Add the meat and marinade and stir-fry, mixing it about, until the meat is tender but not dry, about 3 minutes on high heat. Remove the meat mixture and add the vegetables to the wok. Stir-fry over high heat for 3 more minutes. Return the meat to the pan and add the hot bean sauce, sugar, and black pepper. Stir-fry for 1 minute and then add the cornstarch dissolved in the water. Stir until the sauce thickens. If you have too little sauce, add a bit of the water in which you soaked the mushrooms. Add the sesame oil and stir.

Place the fried noodles on a large platter and pour the meat and vegetable mixture over the noodles. Do this carefully so that the little pieces of pork and mushroom will cling to the "branches." Toss at the table in front of your guests. Each person then takes a bit of noodle and meat sauce and places it in the center of a lettuce leaf. Roll it up like a burrito and enjoy.

SERVES 6–8 AS PART OF CHINESE MEAL.

HINT: **How to Use Your Chinese Wok**
See page 22 for a discussion of what kind of wok you should purchase.

Cure the wok by washing it once with soap and water . . . and then never put soap in it again. Heat the wok on the burner until it is very hot; then add 2 tablespoons peanut oil to it. Swish the oil around, and allow it to cool. Remove and discard the oil, and heat the wok to smoking. Add oil, and continue this routine until you have done it three times. Now wash the wok. It will then be ready to use. Never again wash with soap, even if things stick at first. Soak the wok in water, and then brush out the remaining food particles. Always hang your wok on its side so that it will not rust.

Onion Chicken in Casserole

(China)

The Chinese cook has been using clay casseroles on the top of the stove for hundreds of years. If you do have one you use a covered metal casserole. In either case you will love the sweet flavor that the chicken receives from the onions. Remember onions contain a great deal of sugar.

1 frying chicken, hacked into 2-inch-square pieces
2 tablespoons light soy sauce
3 tablespoons Chinese rice wine or dry sherry
1 teaspoon grated fresh ginger
¼ teaspoon five-spice powder (page 35)
2 large yellow onions, peeled
1 head iceberg lettuce
4 green onions or scallions
4 tablespoons peanut oil
1 garlic clove, sliced thin

Using your cleaver, hack up the chicken. Cooking chicken with the bone in prevents the meat from drying out. Marinate the chicken pieces in the soy, wine, ginger, and five-spice for about 15 minutes.

Cut the peeled onions into wedges and separate the leaves of the onions.

Tear the lettuce into saladlike chunks.

Clean the green onions or scallions and slice lengthwise, once, then into 2-inch pieces.

Heat the wok or large frying pan until quite hot. Add the oil and the garlic. Toss for a moment. Add the chicken pieces drained of the marinade. Reserve the marinade. Stir-fry the chicken pieces until they are well browned on all sides. You may have to do this in two batches if you are using a small frying pan. Remove the chicken and set aside.

Add the onion leaves, along with 1 tablespoon of peanut oil, to the pan and stir-fry until they turn a bit brown. Do this slowly so that the sugar in the onion will caramelize a bit. When the onions are soft and brown return the chicken to the pan, along with any juice that has accumulated around the chicken. If the mixture appears to be too dry, add a few tablespoons of the meat marinade. There should be about ¼ cup of juice in the bottom of the pan. Toss for a moment and remove from the heat.

Place the lettuce in the bottom of a 2-quart metal casserole with lid. Top with the chicken and onion mixture and then with the sliced green onion. Cover and place on a medium-high burner for a few minutes until the lettuce has cooked and become tender but still has some body. Serve from the casserole.

SERVES 4.

Mongolian Lamb with Lamb's Wool

(China)

This is another dish that is great fun to serve and not at all complicated to prepare. The fried noodles really do look like lamb's wool and in this case you have the whole lamb on the plate. Only the Chinese could be so clever!

1 package (4 ounce) glass noodles (sai fun)
4 cups peanut oil for deep-frying
1½ pounds lean lamb, leg or shoulder
1 tablespoon light soy sauce
½ tablespoon freshly grated ginger
1 tablespoon Chinese rice wine or dry sherry
3 garlic cloves, sliced thin
6 green onions, sliced lengthwise once, then into 2-inch pieces
½ teaspoon freshly ground black pepper
1 teaspoon red chili and garlic paste (page 39)
1 teaspoon sugar
2 tablespoons cornstarch mixed with 3 tablespoons water
1 tablespoon toasted sesame oil (page 40)

Fry the glass noodles in the oil according to the instructions in the recipe for Ants Climbing Up a Tree (page 320). Set aside.

Remove as much of the lamb fat as possible. Slice thin and then into shreds about ⅛ inch wide. Marinate in the soy, ginger, and wine for about 15 minutes.

Heat a wok or frying pan until quite hot and add 2 tablespoons of the peanut oil and the garlic slices. Stir-fry until the garlic begins to change color and then add the lamb, drained of the marinade. Reserve the marinade. Stir-fry for 3 or 4 minutes over high heat and then add the green onions. Toss well and then add the black pepper, the chili paste, and sugar. Add more marinade if needed. Stir-fry for a moment more and then add the cornstarch mixed with the water, along with 2 tablespoons of the reserved marinade. Toss until the sauce thickens. Add the sesame oil and remove from the burner.

Serve over the lamb's wool noodles. It can be eaten this way or wrapped in lettuce leaves as in the recipe for Ants Climbing Up a Tree.

SERVES 6.

◆

Spinach with Wine and Sesame

(China)

Please understand the reason why Chinese vegetables taste so good. It is simple. The Chinese do not cook them, they just threaten them! I do not care for cooked spinach, but this dish is done so quickly that you will enjoy the fresh taste. Don't bother trying this with frozen spinach. It will not be the same. You can try this with any other leaf vegetable such as Swiss chard, kale, mustard greens, or even lettuce.

- 2 tablespoons toasted sesame seeds
- 2 tablespoons peanut oil
- ½ teaspoon salt
- 2 bunches fresh spinach (about a pound), washed and stems removed
- 2 tablespoons Chinese rice wine or dry sherry
- 1 tablespoon toasted sesame oil

Toast the sesame seeds by simply placing them in a hot frying pan or wok and stirring them about until they are a light brown. I generally make a cup at a time and use them in additional dishes.

Heat a wok or large frying pan and add the oil and salt. Stir for a moment. Shake the excess water off the cleaned spinach and toss into the pan. Stir-fry over high heat, very quickly, until the spinach wilts a bit and is hot. Add the rice wine and sesame oil. Garnish with the sesame seeds and serve.

SERVES 4.

Chicken with Peas and Wine

(China)

This dish is great for that night when you think that you have no time to cook. This takes very little time and you have a meat and vegetable in one dish. If you wish to cut down on the fat content, remember to remove the skin from the chicken before you cut it up.

- 1 pound fryer chicken thighs
- 2 tablespoons light soy sauce
- 1 teaspoon grated fresh ginger
- 4 tablespoons Chinese rice wine or dry sherry
- 2 tablespoons peanut oil
- 2 garlic cloves, crushed
- Freshly ground black pepper to taste
- 1 box (10 ounce) frozen peas

Using your cleaver, hack each thigh in half. Marinate in the soy, fresh ginger, and 2 tablespoons of the wine for 15 minutes.

Heat a frying pan or wok and then add the oil and garlic. Stir for a few seconds and add the chicken, drained of the marinade. Reserve the marinade. Brown the chicken over high heat, stirring often. When all is brown, add the pepper and remaining 2 tablespoons wine. Cover and cook for a few minutes, then toss again. When the chicken is almost tender, add the peas along with 2 tablespoons of the reserved marinade. Toss and cover. Cook until the peas are just hot, not cooked and mushy!

SERVES 4.

HINT: Potato Ricer for Squeezing

When you wish to get rid of the excess moisture in chopped vegetables such as cabbage or spinach, try your potato ricer. It will do the job without effort.

Beef with Radish Sticks

(China)

When I found out that the young fellow seated next to me was from the Chinese ship anchored in the harbor, I immediately introduced myself and asked him if I could meet the cook on board the ship. Yes, I really do have that kind of gall. Just think of all the neat people that you have never met (and all of the great meals that you have missed) just because you did not want to appear forward. I received an invitation to lunch . . . from the captain, yet. I was told to come early so that I could watch the cook at work. I discovered that they have two galleys, one for the crew and one for the officers. I was escorted to the officers' chef and he showed me this dish.

- **1 pound large white Oriental radishes (daikon)**
- **½ pound boneless beef roast, sliced thin and cut into sticks**
- **2 tablespoons Chinese rice wine or dry sherry**
- **1 tablespoon hot bean sauce (page 35)**
- **1 tablespoon hoisin sauce (page 35)**
- **1 teaspoon sugar**
- **3 tablespoons peanut oil**
- **½ teaspoon salt**
- **1 tablespoon sesame oil**

Wash the radishes and cut them into matchstick size or julienne (page 257). I use a special grater for this. It cuts them into thin sticks. Do not grate with a box grater or you will have mush.

Marinate the beef sticks in the wine, hot bean sauce, hoisin, and sugar; 15 minutes will be ample time. Heat the wok and add half the peanut oil and half the salt. When very hot, stir-fry the beef sticks until done to taste, no more than 3 minutes. Remove the meat from the wok.

Heat the wok and add half the peanut oil and half the salt. When the pan begins to smoke a bit, count to 5 and then throw in the radish sticks. Toss in the oil and stir-fry just until hot. Add the cooked meat to the pan. Toss and then add the sesame oil. Toss once more and serve.

SERVES 4 AS PART OF A CHINESE MEAL.

Glass Noodles with Pork and Shrimp

(China)

This is actually a peasant dish. So what else is new? I still contend that the peasants have taught the aristocrats how to eat. You can prove it to yourself by trying this one. It is delicious and inexpensive.

- 1 package (4 ounce) glass noodles (sai fun)
- ⅓ pound boneless pork, shoulder or butt
- 1 teaspoon grated fresh ginger
- 2 tablespoons Chinese rice wine or dry sherry
- 2 tablespoons light soy sauce
- 2 tablespoons peanut oil
- 1 ounce dried shrimp (found in the Oriental grocery), soaked in water for 1 hour
- 1 yellow onion, peeled and sliced thin
- 6 green onions, chopped
- 4 ounces cooked ham, diced
- 6 Chinese dried mushrooms, soaked for 1 hour, sliced
- 2 cups Chicken Soup Stock (page 101) or used canned
- 2 eggs, beaten

Soak the noodles in tepid (barely warm) water for ½ hour.

Dice the pork and marinate in the ginger, wine, and soy for about 15 minutes. Heat the wok or frying pan and then add the oil. Add the meat, drained of the marinade. Reserve the marinade. Add the shrimp, drained. Discard the water. Stir-fry the pork and shrimp for 3 to 4 minutes, or until just tender. Remove to a bowl.

Add the yellow onions to the pan, along with a bit of peanut oil. Stir-fry over high heat until they are clear. Add the green onions, ham, and mushrooms. Stir-fry until all is hot. Return pork to the pan. Drain the noodles and add to the pan. Add the chicken stock and toss. Cover and simmer for a moment. Toss again and cook until the noodles absorb the broth, about 3 minutes. Stir in the beaten eggs. Remove from the heat.

SERVES 4 AS PART OF A CHINESE MEAL.

Scallops and Garlic

(China)

Scallops are generally easily available and one of the most delicious treats from the sea. Most often, however, when ordering them in a restaurant, they are overcooked. No, I do not mean deep-fried. That is a sin to a scallop. I mean they are simply overcooked. You will avoid that problem if you stir-fry them in a hurry. This recipe works well.

- 4 **green onions**
- 1 **tablespoon soy sauce**
- 1 **tablespoon dry sherry**
- ½ **teaspoon grated fresh ginger**
- 1 **pound scallops**
- 3 **tablespoons peanut oil**
- 2 **garlic cloves, peeled and sliced thin**

Slice the green onions lengthwise once, then into 1-inch pieces.

Prepare the sauce by mixing the soy, sherry, and ginger together. Have this ready before you cook the scallops.

Be sure that the scallops are well drained. The excess moisture will cool the pan and toughen the mollusk. Heat the wok or frying pan to almost smoking and add the oil and garlic. Add the drained scallops (I drain mine on paper towels prior to cooking) and stir-fry for a moment. Add the green onions and continue over high heat until the scallops are cooked to taste. This should take very little time. Add the sauce, toss, and serve. Your pan should be hot enough so that the sauce immediately begins to reduce when it hits the pan.

SERVES 3–4.

◆

Pork Dumplings with Hot Sauce

(China)

In the northern regions of China, wheat is a major food staple. Noodles of every form are relished in the winter, along with enough pepper sauce to keep you warm. These are fun to prepare and make for a most hearty meal.

¾ pound ground lean pork
½ tablespoon cornstarch
1 tablespoon Chinese rice wine or dry sherry
2 tablespoons light soy sauce
1 teaspoon grated fresh ginger
2 garlic cloves, crushed
4 green onions or scallions, chopped
1 tablespoon sesame oil
1 egg, beaten
1 teaspoon freshly ground black pepper
½ teaspoon salt
4 cups cabbage chopped fine and drained well
1 package wonton wrappers

SAUCE:

2 tablespoons soy sauce (Kikkoman)
1 tablespoon Japanese rice wine vinegar
1 teaspoon red chili and garlic paste (page 39)
1 teaspoon sesame oil
1 tablespoon chopped green onion

Mix the sauce ingredients together and set aside. Mix all the other ingredients, with the exception of the cabbage and the wrappers. Mix in a bowl by hand, stirring the mixture until it holds together well. Using a towel, squeeze as much moisture as possible out of the cabbage. (I use a potato ricer, see page 326. Works great!) Stir the cabbage into the meat mixture.

Place ½ tablespoon of the filling in the center of a wonton noodle. With your finger, wet two adjoining sides of the noodle with a bit of tap water. Keep a cup of water handy for this. Fold the opposite sides over on top of the two moistened edges, thus giving you a triangle. Seal carefully. Be sure and press out all the air bubble or the noodle will explode.

To cook, drop the noodles into boiling water and stir very gently with a wooden spoon so that they do not stick together. After a few minutes, they will float to the top. Cook them 1 more minute and then remove them with a slotted spoon.

Serve several in a bowl for each guest. Allow the guest to put on his own sauce.

SERVES 8 AS PART OF A CHINESE MEAL.

THE FRENCH KITCHEN

France has three religions and three hundred sauces. The Anglo-Saxons have three sauces and three hundred religions.

—Talleyrand

• The French Kitchen and Wine •

Surely French cuisine is one of the most highly respected in the world, second, I suppose, only to that of China. But we must be fair and give the Italians due credit for greatly influencing French cooking. In 1533 Catherine de Medici (1519–1589) came to France to become the bride of Henri II. She brought with her the Florentine cooks that had cared for her . . . and France was never the same. A culinary renaissance began in France and it has not ceased. It is interesting today to see that France is influencing Italy. It should be so.

France remains the center of the wine world. Each region offers wines so varied and wonderful that it stands to reason that the food of the regions would be varied as well. If you were to take wine from the French kitchen you would lose the chef as well, I am sure.

•

Pork and Sausage with Sauerkraut

Choucroute

(France)

Many people are surprised that sauerkraut is so very common in France. One thinks of Germany, surely, but seldom France. But the cabbage is basic to the diet of several regions in France, and in the Alsace-Lorraine region, in the northeast portion of France, this dish is very popular.

You will also be surprised at the flavor of the sauerkraut when cooked with wine. It becomes delicious and light in flavor. This dish is the ancestor of what Americans call "sauerkraut and wieners," a dish I dislike. This one is popular at our home, however, and Channing would just as soon have it weekly.

6 slices bacon, diced
3 yellow onions
3 garlic cloves, peeled and sliced thin

2 apples, cored and sliced
3 pounds sauerkraut (1½ quarts) lightly rinsed and drained (Buy kraut that is fresh or in glass; avoid cans.)
2 cups white wine
15 juniper berries
8 peppercorns
2 bay leaves
1 tablespoon brown sugar
2 pounds pork spareribs, cut into 3-inch pieces
½ pound smoked ham, cut into 2-inch cubes
2 pounds sausages (garlic sausage, Polish sausage, German smoked sausage, knackwurst, or any combination)

Heat a 6- to 8-quart enameled cast-iron casserole (do not use aluminum or black iron) and sauté the bacon until clear. Add the onions and garlic and brown lightly. Add the apples, sauerkraut, and wine. Tie the juniper berries, peppercorns, and bay leaves in a bit of cheesecloth, if you wish. I often just leave them to run about the pot. Place juniper, peppercorns, bay leaves, and brown sugar in the pot and stir. Top the mixture with the cut spareribs and cover. Cook for 2 hours on medium-low heat, keeping the pot just at a simmer. (This could be done the day ahead and then refrigerated at this point.) Stir the ham cubes into the kraut and top everything off with the sausages. Do not cut them. Cover and cook until all is hot, about ½ hour. Cut the sausages into smaller pieces just before serving.

I put this whole dish on a single giant platter and we all cheer when it comes to the table. Wonderful!

Boiled potatoes with parsley and butter would be a traditional accompaniment to this meal, or serve with a green salad with White Wine Vinaigrette (page 128), rolls, and Carrots in Vermouth (page 261).

Wine Suggestion: Alsatian Gewürztraminer.

SERVES 8–10.

Spinach Crepes with Salmon

(France)

I had this dish the first time in the city of Bordeaux. The restaurant was ostentatious, the wine flamboyantly served, when it could have simply been poured, and the city itself must be the filthiest in Europe. But this dish was good. And very simple!

- 6 spinach crepes (page 95)
- ¼ pound lox or lightly smoked salmon, sliced
- 1 cup Basic White Sauce (page 287)
- 6 slices Swiss cheese

Place a bit of the salmon in each crepe and roll up like a burrito or blintz, ends open. Arrange in a baking dish and top with the sauce and the cheese slices. Bake in a 400° oven until all is hot and bubbly, about 20 minutes.

This is a great first course.

Wine Suggestion: White Burgundy or white Bordeaux.

SERVES 6 AS A FIRST COURSE.

Snails with Celery and Cream

(France)

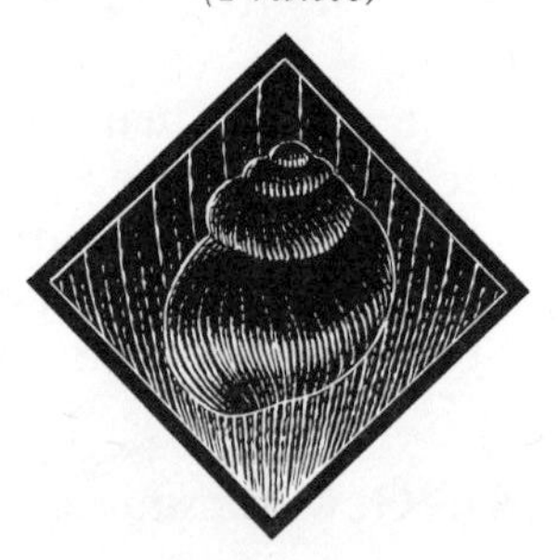

Yes, this is flamboyant. But now and then you need a dish that is rather special so that special people know that you appreciate them.

- 1 tin (7½ ounce) medium snails, (contains 3 dozen)

- 1 celery root, about 1 pound, peeled and cut julienne (page 257)
- 2 tablespoons olive oil
- ½ cup dry white wine
- ½ cup cream or half-and-half or Mock Cream (page 289)
- ¼ teaspoon cumin, ground
- Salt and black pepper, freshly ground, to taste

Drain the snails and discard the juice. Peel and julienne the celery root. Heat a medium frying pan and add the oil. Sauté the celery root until barely tender, about 5 minutes. Do not brown the vegetable. Remove the celery and keep warm on a plate. Add the remaining ingredients, except the snails, and bring to a boil, then turn down to a simmer. Reduce the sauce by half. Add the drained snails and simmer until they are hot, about 3 minutes. Serve the snails over a bed of the celery root, with the sauce on top.

Variation: You might want to try this with mushrooms instead of snails. Sauté the whole mushrooms first and then go on with the recipe.
Serve as a first course.

Wine Suggestion: Vouvray.

SERVES 6 AS A FIRST COURSE.

◆

Mushrooms with Garlic and Parsley

Bordelaise
(France)

Whenever you see the term "bordelaise" on the menu it generally means that the dish has been prepared with a wine sauce loaded with garlic and parsley. What would French cooking be without wine, garlic, and parsley? Don't answer that!

- 1 pound fresh mushrooms
- 5 tablespoons olive oil
- 3 garlic cloves, crushed
- 4 tablespoons dry red wine

Salt and black pepper, freshly ground, to taste
2 tablespoons chopped parsley, for garnish

Remove the stems from the mushrooms. No, do not wash them. Wipe them with a damp towel if it will make you feel better. Heat a large frying pan and add half the oil. Sauté the caps on high heat, tossing them about so that they cook evenly. Very lightly brown them. Set aside on a warm plate.

Chop the mushroom stems to a coarse mince. Sauté this in the remaining oil, along with the garlic, for 3 to 4 minutes. Add the wine and cook until the wine is almost gone. Salt and pepper to taste. Place the chopped mushroom and garlic mixture on top of the mushroom caps. Garnish with the parsley and serve.

Serve as a side dish or vegetable.

SERVES 4.

◆

Pork with Grapes and Wine Sauce

(France)

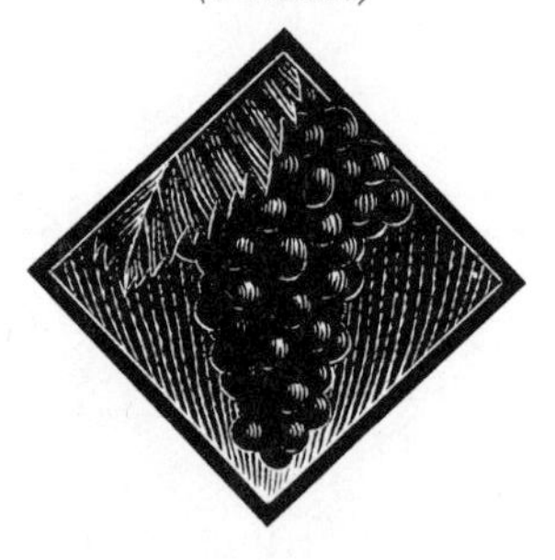

Some things are so attractive on the plate that it is hard to eat them . . . or hard not to. This is one of those dishes. You will be surprised how good cooked grapes are with the meat.

3 pounds pork butt roast, boned and tied

MARINADE:

- 1 onion, peeled and sliced
- 2 garlic cloves, peeled and sliced
- 1 teaspoon thyme, whole
- ¼ teaspoon rosemary, whole
- 1 bay leaf
- ¼ teaspoon black pepper, freshly ground
- 2 tablespoons olive oil
- ¼ cup brandy

SAUCE:

- 2 tablespoons butter
- 2 tablespoons olive oil
- 1 cup dry white wine
- 2 pounds white seedless grapes, removed from the stems
- ½ cup whipping cream or half-and-half or Mock Cream (page 289)
- Salt to taste

Have your butcher bone and tie the roast.

Prepare the marinade and, using a large glass or stainless steel bowl, marinate the meat for 2 to 3 hours, turning several times.

Remove the meat, reserving the marinade. Pat the meat dry with paper towels. Heat a stovetop casserole or covered Dutch oven large enough to take the meat. Melt the butter for the sauce, add 2 tablespoons oil, and brown the roast, turning several times. Strain the reserved marinade into the pot, discarding the solids. Add the wine, cover, bring to a boil, reduce the heat, and simmer very gently for 1½ to 2 hours, or until the meat is tender. You may need to add a bit more white wine. Add three quarters of the grapes to the pot, cover, and cook 5 more minutes. Remove the meat.

Stir the cream into the pan juices and cook for 2 minutes, stirring. Taste for the need for a slight amount of salt. Slice the meat and place it on a large platter. Pour the grapes and sauce over the top. Use the remaining grapes for garnish.

If you prefer a thicker sauce, stir in a roux (page 288) made of 1 tablespoon each butter and flour.

I love this with Baked Polenta (page 161) and a green salad with Garlic Dressing (page 129).

Wine Suggestion: Red Burgundy.

SERVES 6.

Swiss Cheese Soufflé

(France)

There is no great secret to making a good soufflé. Remember that the eggs need to be at room temperature and the cheese sauce must not be too hot when you gently fold it into the whipped egg whites. This dish must be prepared just as your guests are about to arrive. You want it to come from the oven at the right moment as it will fall in a few minutes after being removed from the oven.

3½ tablespoons butter
4½ tablespoons flour
1½ cups hot milk
½ teaspoon salt
Pinch of cayenne
Speck of nutmeg
6 egg yolks
1 cup coarsely grated Swiss cheese
8 egg whites
½ teaspoon cream of tartar

In a saucepan, melt the butter and stir in the flour. Cook for just a few minutes. Remove from the heat. Stir in the hot milk, using a whisk, and return to the heat. Stir until thickened. Add the salt, cayenne, and the nutmeg.

Stir in the egg yolks. Add cheese and set aside to cool for a few moments.

Beat the egg whites, along with the cream of tartar, until stiff and forms nice peaks. Very gently, fold the cheese sauce into the egg whites. Place in a 1½- to 2-quart soufflé dish and bake for 25–30 minutes at 375°. Serve immediately.

Serve as a luncheon dish or as a first course.

Wine Suggestion: Light red Bordeaux or white Burgundy.

SERVES 4–6 AS A SIDE DISH.

THE ITALIAN KITCHEN

Eggs of an hour, bread of a day, wine of a year, a friend of thirty years.

—Italian Proverb

• The Italian Kitchen and Wine •

I don't think that Italy has been given proper credit for the influence of its cuisine. Well over two thousand years ago we find an understanding of food, a sophistication, that was not equaled in any other part of the Western world. Notice I did not eliminate China. They were still far ahead, but Italy was next. I am pleased that the influence has not ceased.

Today there are so many northern Italian restaurants that is hard to find a place that serves pasta with tomato sauce. Northern Italy has never been much for tomato sauces of any sort, preferring instead a lighter sauce, generally made with wine. The popularity of northern Italian cuisine, which I dearly love, and the simultaneous rise of French nouvelle cuisine was to be expected. We seem to be into lighter food, better presentation, and menu costs that are just absurd. This time I have included a cheap and creative Italian gravy. The idea came from a viewer who explained that in her region of Italy, the South, this kind of heavy cooking is expected and enjoyed.

I returned to Venice last fall after an absence of twenty-five years. I was just delighted with the quality of the food and I assumed that things had improved. The improvement is of less import than the fact that when I was there in 1960 I was a student on a motorbike and I could afford only the cheapest eating stalls. This time we ate where we would, and I had a wonderful time. You must spend time on the island of Torcello, just outside Venice. The main restaurant there is superb, and not expensive. You can take a cab to get there, or a public bus. (Both are boats!)

If you were to list the three most important ingredients in Italian cuisine of all the regions you would have to list olive oil, garlic, and wine. Tomatoes come later. Pasta is important in every form, of course, but what would pasta be without garlic, olive oil, and wine?

Between this section and the pasta section you should find ample dishes for full Italian meals. I have included more legitimate peasant food in this Italian section than I did in the previous book since these dishes are much quicker to prepare at the last minute. Remember that a full Italian meal generally begins with an antipasto or appetizer course, and then moves on to pasta, and then a main course of meat. Salad may be served with the meat course or at the end of the meal. Consult the Index for more Italian dishes. And the wines of Italy are marvelous and just a terrific buy!

Real Garlic Toast

Bruschetta
(Italy)

Let's get down to basics. Garlic! Yes, wine and garlic were meant for each other, always have been. In Italy one makes a wonderful meal out of nothing but wine, salad, olives, and garlic bread, or bruschetta. It will provide you with a great deal of fun if you will make this bread in the backyard, using your charcoal grill.

I prefer a bread that is a bit heavy. When I make my own bread, I add a bit of rye flour to the loaf. It should be heavy and crusty. A good heavy French bread will do almost as well. Slice it almost an inch thick so that it will be crusty on the outside and soft on the inside.

Bread, crusty and rich
Garlic cloves, peeled, with the tops cut off
Olive oil, Italian, extra virgin

So simple. Toast the bread on both sides, preferably over a fire. Or use your charcoal cooker. When the bread is toasted, immediately pass it to your guests and let them rub an entire clove of garlic into the bread. Rub until the garlic clove disappears. Drizzle oil on the bread and enjoy. Keep the wine, olives, and light salad coming!

◆

Italian Gravy

Tomato Sauce
(Italy)

In southern Italy one can find a thousand variations of this gravy. It is not used in classic cooking in the northern regions. Make a batch and keep it sealed and refrigerated. It will keep for a good week and one can prepare dozens of dishes with this basic "gravy."

2 **large cans (28 ounce) tomato purée**
1 **can (6 ounce) tomato paste**

- 1 quart Chicken Soup Stock (page 101) or Basic Brown Soup Stock (page 100) or use chicken bouillon
- 2 cups dry red wine
- ¼ cup olive oil
- 2 yellow onions, peeled and minced
- 6 large garlic cloves, chopped
- 2 celery stalks, with leaves, minced
- 1 carrot, grated
- ½ cup chopped parsley
- ½ pound fresh mushrooms, chopped (optional)
- ½ teaspoon crushed red pepper flakes
- 1 tablespoon oregano, crushed
- 1 teaspoon dried rosemary
- 2 bay leaves
- 1 tablespoon dried basil or 2 tablespoons fresh
- 2 whole cloves (optional)
- ½ tablespoon black pepper, freshly ground
- 2 tablespoons salt, or to taste
- 1 teaspoon sugar
- 1 pound pork neck bones or chicken backs and necks

In a large pot, place the tomato purée, tomato paste, chicken or beef stock and the wine. Heat a large frying pan and add the olive oil. Sauté the onions, garlic, celery, and carrot until they just begin to brown a bit. Add to the pot along with all remaining ingredients. Bring to a light boil and then turn to a simmer. Simmer for 2 hours, partly covered, stirring often. Remove the bones and discard, or make a private lunch of them. Skim the fat from the top and discard. Store in the refrigerator, covered, in either glass, plastic, or stainless steel. It will keep for a week. Use for a pasta topping or for any other dish calling for Italian tomato sauce or "gravy."

This freezes very well.

MAKES 3 QUARTS.

Italian Sausages in Gravy

This is one of those dishes that you can prepare at the last minute and really enjoy, providing you have made preparations earlier in the week.

Italian sausages (pages 245 and 249) or buy from the market
Olive oil, very little for frying
Italian Gravy (page 341)

Prick the sausages so that they will not pop when cooking. Heat a covered frying pan and add the oil. Add the sausages and lightly brown. Add Italian gravy and simmer, covered, for about 20 minutes. Serve with pasta or as a main meat course, or serve with Vegetables North Beach (page 258) and a plain pasta.

Wine Suggestion: Hearty Italian red such as Barbera.

Italian Pork Chops with Gravy

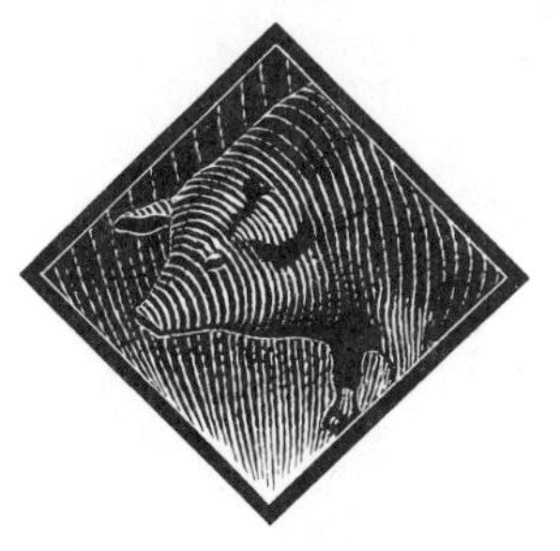

Another dish that is a quickie. Pork chops are generally too dry for my taste. If you will cook them just like the Italian Sausages in Gravy, however, you will have a fine dish. You might add a few fennel seeds to the gravy when you are cooking the chops. Serve along with pasta. Add plenty of freshly grated Parmesan or Romano cheese to the top.

Serve as above.

Wine Suggestion: Hearty Italian red such as Barbera.

Spareribs in Italian Gravy

You are going to think that I want to eat nothing but Italian gravy for a week straight. Well, I could do it! The sauce keeps fine in the freezer, so don't avoid trying this one.

3 tablespoons olive oil
3 pounds pork spareribs, cut into 2-inch pieces
1 cup dry red wine
1 cup Italian Gravy (page 341)
1 piece of lemon peel, 1 x ½ inch

Heat a large frying pan and add the olive oil. Brown the spareribs lightly in the oil. You will probably have to do this in two batches. Remove them from the frying pan and drain the excess fat and discard. Place the ribs in a heavy saucepan. Deglaze the frying pan with a bit of the wine and add to the ribs. Add the remaining ingredients and cover. Simmer until the ribs are very tender, about 1 hour. Check seasoning for salt and pepper.

Serve with pasta and salad.

Wine Suggestion: Hearty Italian red such as Barbera.

SERVES 4.

Chicken Gizzards with Marsala

(Italy)

This dish is just wonderful and rich. If you have not had chicken gizzards cooked properly then you are probably not interested. Your memory is burdened with thoughts of tough and dry little things that were impossible to chew. Please try this. It will change your mind.

3 tablespoons olive oil
2 pounds chicken gizzards, cleaned and cut in half
2 garlic cloves, peeled and sliced thin
1 cup dry Marsala
1 cup Italian Gravy (page 341)

1 piece of lemon peel, ½ inch square
Salt and black pepper, freshly ground, to taste
Parmesan or Romano cheese, freshly grated, for topping

Heat a frying pan and add the oil and garlic. Sauté the gizzards until lightly browned. You will probably have to do this in two batches. Place the gizzards in a heavy covered saucepan. Deglaze the frying pan with a bit of the wine and add to the gizzards. Add the Marsala along with ½ cup water. Cover and simmer for 1 hour. Add the Italian gravy, the lemon peel, and black pepper to taste. I enjoy quite a bit of pepper. Cover and cook for ½ hour longer, or until very tender. Check to be sure the liquid does not evaporate. If so, add more wine and water. Serve with cheese on top.

Serve with Ravioli with Vegetable Sauce (page 152), green salad, and rolls.

Wine Suggestion: Italian Dolcetto.

SERVES 4.

Lentils and Italian Sausages

Lentils remain one of my favorite legumes. They are very rich and satisfying, either in a soup, in a casserole, or in this dish. It is quick to make and will store well in the refrigerator for three or four days.

2 tablespoons olive oil
6 to 8 Italian sausages (pages 245 and 249) or from the market (about 1½ pounds)
1 large yellow onion, peeled and chopped
2 garlic cloves, crushed
2 cups lentils, rinsed
3 cups water
2 cups Italian Gravy (page 341)
Tabasco to taste (optional)
¾ cup dry red wine

½ cup chopped parsley for garnish
½ cup freshly grated Romano or Parmesan cheese, for topping

Heat a heavy metal 2-quart covered casserole. Add the oil and the sausages. Prick the skins first. Lightly brown the sausages and remove to a plate. Add the onion and garlic and sauté until clear. Cut the sausages in half, lengthwise, and add to the pan. Add the lentils and water. Cover and simmer for ½ hour. Add the Italian gravy, Tabasco, and wine. Cover and simmer for 45 minutes, or until the lentils are tender but not mushy. Stir in half the chopped parsley and place all in a serving bowl. Top with the remaining parsley and cheese.

If the dish is too wet, remove the lid during the last 15 minutes of cooking.

I like this with Green Rice (page 158) and Tuna and Potato Salad (page 136).

Wine Suggestion: Italian Barbera or Dolcetto.

SERVES 4 AS A MAIN DISH, OR 8 AS A VEGETABLE DISH.

◆

Spinach with Italian Sausages

Try this for a quick and very flavorful dinner. Along with a nice pasta dish, it makes a great main course and completes the meal.

I love spinach . . . but most often it is cooked far too long. Spinach is delicate, and I much prefer to fry mine quickly rather than steam it to death.

6 to 8 Italian sausages (pages 245 and 249) or from the market (about 1½ pounds)
1 tablespoon olive oil for the sausage
3 tablespoons olive oil for the spinach
2 tablespoons peeled and chopped yellow onion
2 garlic cloves, crushed

3 **bunches fresh spinach (about a pound and one half), stemmed, washed, and drained**
½ **cup dry white wine**
Salt and black pepper, freshly ground, to taste

Slice the sausages in half, lengthwise.

Heat a large frying pan. (Actually, I prefer my larger wok for this dish.) Add the 1 tablespoon of olive oil and brown the sausages on both sides. Add ¼ cup water to the pan and cover. Cook the sausages for another 10 minutes. Remove to a plate and drain the pan.

Heat a wok or frying pan again and add the 3 tablespoons olive oil, onion, and garlic. Do this on high heat. When the garlic is light brown, throw in the spinach and toss it in the hot oil. Add the wine. Cover the pan and allow the spinach to collapse. Stir often. This should take only a few minutes. Do not overcook. Return the sausages to the pan and toss with the spinach. Season with salt and pepper. Serve the sausages on little beds of spinach.

This is great with Baked Polenta (page 161), along with Zucchini, Rolled and Marinated (page 348).

Wine Suggestion: White Italian Orvieto.

SERVES 4.

◆

Dried Cod in Cream Sauce

Baccala in Cream Sauce
(Italy)

My wife, Patty, and I recently took the Venice Simplon Orient Express from London to Venice. What a joy and a delight. The food and wines were wonderful, the service outstanding, and the train fascinating. We also enjoyed the ride! When we hit Venice we heard about a restaurant that serves dried cod in cream sauce. Doesn't that sound disgusting? I tasted the dish and have since learned to make something that is close to this treasure of Venice. Do try this. You can find the fish in an Italian grocery and at many fish markets. It is worth the search. It is peasant food from Italy. Cod is salted and dried for the sake of preservation, much in the same way that Norwegians make lutefish, another peasant dish.

2 pounds boneless baccala (dried cod)
1½ to 2 cups half-and-half or Mock Cream (page 289)

Simple ingredients but astounding results! Have the fish man help you pick out the fish. You want a boneless piece of about 2 pounds. Find one that is thick in the center so that you have a great deal of meat when this process is finished. Soak the baccala in a very large plastic tub or plastic bucket, the bigger, the better. A 5-gallon tub is perfect. Fill the tub with water and soak the fish for two days. Change the water after about 2 hours and continue to soak, changing the water again four or five times. Drain the fish and cut it into 4 or 5 pieces. Place it in a heavy saucepan just big enough to hold it, and add the cream. Simmer, covered, for about 1 hour. Watch it carefully; you want the fish to absorb the moisture of the cream, leaving you with something that looks like fish chunks in light cream cheese.

Serve this warm over Baked Polenta (page 161) or simply on pieces of toast. It is great with Real Garlic Toast (Bruschetta) (page 341). Add raw green vegetables to nibble on, a good dry white wine, and you have raised the whole concept of peasant food to new glory.

Wine Suggestion: Very dry white.

SERVES 4–6, DEPENDING ON ROLE IN THE MEAL.

Zucchini, Rolled and Marinated

(Italy)

It is not fair! At my favorite Italian restaurant in New York City they make me walk past the antipasto table before I am seated.

And you should see this antipasto table. It is a work of culinary art.

The restaurant is called Felidia's. Felix and Lidia own the place and have a dish similar to this one on their table. You must try this for your next Italian meal. I serve it right along with the meal in place of another vegetable or salad.

4 zucchini
2 eggs, beaten
½ cup milk
2 tablespoons flour
3 tablespoons olive oil

MARINADE:
½ cup olive oil
2 tablespoons fresh lemon juice
Salt and pepper to taste

Slice fresh zucchini the long way, very thin (⅛ inch thick). I use an Oriental vegetable cutter for this step. (See mandoline, page 25.)

Prepare a batter of the eggs, milk, and flour. Dip the slices in the egg wash and fry in a bit of olive oil over medium-high heat. Brown lightly on both sides. Remove and place on a tray to cool.

When the slices reach room temperature, roll each up like a little jelly roll and secure with a toothpick. If the rolls appear to be too wide, they may be sliced into two rolls, each being secured with a toothpick.

Place the rolls on a serving plate. Mix the marinade and drizzle some on each. Serve as a vegetable or in place of a salad, or you might serve it as an appetizer.

SERVES 6.

THE JAPANESE KITCHEN

Food should feast the eyes as well as the stomach.

—Japanese Proverb

• *Japanese Recipes* •

Many Americans think that there is some connection between the cuisines of Japan and China. Both cultures deny such affinity. As a matter of fact each thinks that the other does not know how to eat. The only similarity that I can see is the use of beans and bean products in ingenious ways.

The Japanese proverb "Food should feast the eyes as well as the stomach" clearly marks a major feature of Japanese cuisine. A great deal of time is spent cutting and preparing things so that they appear in beautiful and artistic forms. The Japanese have been so skilled at this, and for so long, that I am sure they must be credited with the creative and colorful food presentations now going on in nouvelle cuisine. Who else is to be given credit? When the Japanese were arranging things beautifully the Western world was simply throwing things on a plate, preferably in neat but ill-shaped piles.

My friend Mary, who runs Family Cleaners in Tacoma, takes care of me in two ways. She watches my schedule and has my shirts ready for the next trip, always. Secondly, she invites me to be at her table on New Year's Day. Her Japanese background and her own skill in cooking offer a table of the most beautiful, delicious, and varied dishes that one can imagine. None of these recipes is hers, and I know that when she reads this section she is going to call me and tell me about some better ideas. I will share them with you next time.

There is one strange thing about Japanese eating habits that bothers Patty, my wife. She has been very active in the women's movement for years and was surprised when a sukiyaki set arrived from Japan with only five place settings. When I told her it was because the Japanese traditionally did not expect the women or wives to be at a formal table she frowned severely. This custom is not followed in this country, thank goodness. But now you understand why some of these recipes are for five persons. It is only tradition. Add a bit more and go from there.

Wine is used regularly in Japanese cooking, though it is made from rice rather than grapes. Sake has been popular in Japan for hundreds of years. It is light in flavor but strong in alcohol.

The Japanese have found that sake does a great job of tenderizing meats because it contains amino acids. It also helps extract saltiness and fish flavors from foods. From it is also made a wonderful rice wine vinegar that is just superb in salads as well as cooking. You can find the vinegar in both regular and sweetened form.

The following two spinach dishes will help you become familiar with some Japanese seasonings and ingredients. Most of these items are readily available at Japanese markets. See the ingredients list in the Glossary for a full explanation of these food products.

Spinach with Sesame and Bean Paste

(Japan)

2½ tablespoons sesame seeds
2 tablespoons light miso (page 37)
½ teaspoon sugar
10 ounces fresh spinach
1 tablespoon peanut oil

Heat a wok and add the sesame seeds. Stir over medium-high heat until they are lightly toasted. Cool and crush the seeds with a mortar and pestle or food blender. Mix with the miso and sugar.

Wash the spinach and drain well. Heat a wok or frying pan and add the oil. Stir-fry the spinach just until it collapses. Remove from the wok. Stir the miso and sesame paste into the spinach.

Serve hot or cold.

SERVES 5 AS AN APPETIZER OR PICKLE DISH.

Spinach with Sesame Seeds

(Japan)

3 tablespoons sesame seeds
3 tablespoons soy sauce
1 pound spinach
1 tablespoon peanut oil

Toast the seeds as in the above recipe. Grind and blend with the soy sauce.

Wash the spinach and cook as in the above recipe. Mix with the sesame and soy mixture and chill.

SERVES 6 AS AN APPETIZER OR PICKLE DISH.

Sukiyaki

(Japan)

In Western cultures this dish has come to represent the most loved and understood ways of Japan. It is served in fancy Japanese restaurants and cooked at the table by lovely Japanese women dressed in full kimono. Such a sight and such a meal! The Japanese have been cooking at table for a long time, since the whole family would crowd around the cooking source due to the lack of central heating. Beef, however, was not introduced to Japan until the 1850s, so we can hardly call this an ancient dish. It is delicious and very easy to prepare. You do not need a fancy cooker for your table. Use your electric frying pan. Our family has been doing that for years.

- 1 cup soy sauce
- ½ cup sake (page 39)
- 1 cup Basic Brown Soup Stock (page 100) or Chicken Soup Stock (page 101) (beef is more traditional) or bouillon cubes in a pinch
- Sugar to taste
- 2 tablespoons peanut oil
- 1½ pounds round steak, sliced diagonally in very thin slices
- 2 bunches green onions, sliced once lengthwise and then into 2-inch pieces
- 2 yellow onions, peeled and sliced thin
- 1 block tofu (bean curd), cut into ¾-inch cubes
- 1 bunch fresh spinach, washed well and drained
- 3 ounces dried Chinese mushrooms, soaked for 2 hours and sliced into sticks
- 3 celery stalks, sliced diagonally
- ½ pound fresh mushrooms, sliced
- 4 ounces glass noodles (sai fun), soaked in water for ½ hour and drained
- Raw eggs (optional)

The preparation of this dish takes some time, but it is not complicated. Prepare all the vegetables and noodles as instructed above. Arrange all in attractive patterns on large food platters. Have the soy, sake, stock, and sugar in small containers near your cooker or electric frying pan. When all are seated you are ready to begin.

This dish is cooked in shifts. Use one third of the ingredients the first time around, and then cook a second batch after you have emptied the pan. Finally, a third batch can be prepared.

Heat the frying pan. Add the oil and the beef and cook for a few moments. Add the yellow onion and celery and one third of the soy, sake, stock, and sugar to taste. Some people make this dish so very sweet. I think it is best with just a hint of sugar. Continue adding things to the pan in neat little piles. Next, the Chinese mushrooms and the bean curd. Follow with the green onions, the fresh mushrooms, and the glass noodles. Finally, add the spinach. Cook until all is done to your taste. This should only take a few minutes.

Raw eggs are placed in a bowl on the table. Serious sukiyaki eaters will crack an egg into their small eating bowl, whip it with their chopsticks, and then place bits of the sukiyaki in the raw egg. This is truly delicious.

Serve with individual bowls for eating the sukiyaki and additional individual small bowls for rice.

SERVES 6.

◆

Chicken Teriyaki

(Japan)

My wife and I argue over this one. I like it a little bit sweet, broiled, and she likes it less sweet, cooked in a frying pan. So I am going to give you both versions. (I have to! Otherwise, she will let you all know by some other means.)

CHICKEN TERIYAKI #1

- **1 fryer, cut up and drained**
- **½ cup soy sauce**
- **⅛ cup sugar**
- **1 garlic clove, crushed**
- **½ teaspoon grated fresh ginger**
- **3 tablespoons sake (page 39)**

Place everything but the chicken in a frying pan or electric frying pan. When it begins to boil, add the chicken pieces. Cover and turn down the heat to medium. Turn the chicken every 5 minutes or so. Cook until tender, about 25 minutes.

CHICKEN TERIYAKI #2

This is one of my favorites. It was given to me by the Reverend Mr. Niwa, a friend since my college days.

- **1 frying chicken, cut up and drained, or 3 pounds chicken thighs**
- **½ cup soy sauce**
- **⅔ cup Karo white corn syrup**
- **2 garlic cloves**
- **½ teaspoon grated fresh ginger**
- **3 tablespoons sake (page 39)**

In a large stainless steel or glass bowl, mix all ingredients together except the chicken. Blend well and add the chicken. Marinate for about 2 hours. Arrange on a broiling rack and broil, turning once, for 30 to 40 minutes total time.

SERVES 4.

◆

Bean Paste Soup

Miso Soup
(Japan)

This delightful soup is flavored with miso, a fermented cheeselike substance made from soybean. You will find many kinds in the Oriental market, the most common simply being called dark miso, red miso, or light miso. For soups we will use the light.

- **3 cups Dashi soup stock (I buy little envelopes of prepared seaweed and dried fish. Called Dashi-No-Moto, it takes all the pain out of making this soup. Use one little tea bag type of package for each 3 cups of stock or follow directions on the package.) or 3 cups Chicken Soup Stock (page 101)**
- **½ cup light miso (page 37)**

½ teaspoon sugar
2 pieces deep-fried bean curd (Oriental market)
½ cake fresh bean curd, cut into small cubes
2 green onions or scallions, chopped

Prepare the stock according to instructions on the package or make chicken stock. Bring to a simmer and stir in the miso, using a wire whip. Add the sugar, fried bean curd, and fresh bean curd. Divide into 5 bowls and garnish with the green onions.

SERVES 5.

Chicken Thighs Yaki

(Japan)

2 pounds chicken thighs
¼ cup mochiko (page 15)
¼ cup cornstarch
⅛ cup sugar
5 tablespoons soy sauce
¼ cup chopped green onions
2 eggs, beaten
1 garlic clove, crushed
½ teaspoon salt
3 tablespoons peanut oil

Make a slice down the side of each thigh, cutting to the bone. In a large bowl, mix all the remaining ingredients except the oil and let marinate for 2 hours. Pan-fry, uncovered, in the oil, turning once. Cook for about ½ hour on medium heat.

SERVES 3–4.

Miso Chicken in Bean Paste

(Japan)

This is delicious and just about the easiest recipe I can offer you.

- 3 tablespoons dark or red miso (page 37)
- 1 tablespoon soy sauce
- 1 tablespoon sugar
- ¼ cup sake (page 39)
- 2 tablespoons mirin (page 37)
- 4 tablespoons Chicken Soup Stock (page 101)
- 4 green onions, chopped, for garnish
- 8 chicken thighs
- 2 tablespoons peanut oil
- ½ cup dry white wine

Combine all ingredients except the chicken, oil, and white wine. Marinate the chicken in this mixture in the refrigerator overnight. Remove the thighs and pat dry with paper towels, reserving the marinade.

Heat a frying pan and add the oil. Lightly brown chicken on one side and turn. Mix the marinade and wine and pour over the chicken. Cover and cook until done to taste, about 35 minutes.

SERVES 4.

◆

Jade Chicken

(China/Japan)

This is actually a Chinese approach to a Japanese method of flavoring. I find it delicious. I doubt that many people have ever seen the dish, so you and I are in on a first.

- 2 tablespoons light miso (page 37)
- 3 green onions or scallions, chopped
- ¼ teaspoon grated fresh ginger
- 1 tablespoon brown sugar
- 1 tablespoon soy sauce
- 12 chicken thighs

½ cup dry white wine
3 tablespoons peanut oil
1 pound green seedless grapes, removed from the stems

Mix the miso, green onions, ginger, sugar, and soy. Simmer for 5 minutes and allow to cool. Marinate the chicken thighs overnight in this mixture, covered and in the refrigerator. Next day add the wine to the marinating chicken. Mix well.

Drain the chicken pieces, reserving the marinade, and wipe dry with paper towels. Heat a large frying pan or wok and add the oil. Sauté the chicken pieces until lightly browned. Add the marinade and turn the heat to medium. Cover and continue to cook for an additional 20 minutes, or until tender. Add the grapes to the dish. Continue to stir-fry gently until the grapes are hot.

SERVES 4–6.

◆

Dip Sauces

These can be used for dipping almost anything. While meat is normally dipped into these sauces, I find that they are very delightful with vegetables as well.

GINGER DIP: Mix to your taste:
Soy sauce
Ginger, fresh, grated
Rice wine vinegar
Sugar

PEPPER SAUCE: Mix to your taste:
Soy sauce
Rice wine vinegar
Chinese red chili and garlic paste (page 39) or Tabasco

VERMOUTH SAUCE: Mix to your taste:
Soy sauce
Sesame oil
Sweet vermouth
Rice wine vinegar (just a touch)

Pork Tenkatsu

(Japan)

Jason loves this dish and orders it every time we go to our favorite Japanese restaurant in Tacoma. It is a fine place run by a dear friend, Endo. It is called, romantically enough, Fujiya.

4 slices pork fillet or pork steak, deboned
4 tablespoons soy sauce
4 tablespoons sake (page 39)
1 garlic clove, crushed
Pinch of freshly ground black pepper
1 egg, beaten
1 green onion or scallion, chopped
1 cup panko (page 38)
4 cups peanut oil for frying

Debone and slice the pork thin. Pound between two pieces of plastic, using a wooden food mallet (page 175). Marinate the pork slices for ½ hour in a mixture of the soy, sake, garlic, and black pepper.

Mix the beaten egg with the green onion and dip each slice into the egg/onion mixture. Place the bread crumbs on a plate and coat each pork slice by pressing the crumbs into the pork slice. Place on trays covered with wax paper and chill in the refrigerator for 1 hour.

Heat the oil in a large frying pan. The temperature should be at about 375°. Fry the slices, a few at a time, in the oil until they are golden brown, and then turn. Brown on both sides. Remove and drain on paper towels.

Serve with Tenkatsu-sosu sauce (page 41).

SERVES 4.

Omelet on Rice

Donburi

(Japan)

The principle behind this dish is simple: You make a wonderful omelet and serve it on top of a bowl of rice. The variations are almost endless, and I offer this Chicken and Shrimp Donburi only as one possibility.

- 1 tablespoon peanut oil
- ¼ cup boneless chicken cut into bite-size pieces
- 4 large fresh shrimp or prawns, peeled and deveined
- 1 green onion, sliced once lengthwise and then into 1-inch pieces
- 3 Chinese dried mushrooms, soaked for 1 hour, drained and sliced
- 3 tablespoons chicken broth
- 1 tablespoon mirin (page 37) or cream sherry
- 1 tablespoon soy sauce
- ¼ teaspoon grated fresh ginger
- 1 egg, beaten
- Green onions, sliced, for garnish
- Rice, cooked, one bowl for each omelet

Heat a small frying pan. I prefer one lined with Silverstone. Add the oil and the chicken and shrimp. Cook for a few minutes and then add the green onion and mushrooms. Mix the broth, mirin, soy, and ginger. Pour into the pan and continue cooking for a moment as the sauce reduces down by half. Pour in the beaten egg and cover the pan. As soon as the egg sets up, the dish is ready to serve. Slide the omelet out onto the top of a bowl of rice. Garnish with green onion.

Other variations would be fun. Try pork and mushroom, or scallops and green onion, ground beef with peas, or whatever you happen to have left in your refrigerator.

SERVES 1.

THE SPANISH KITCHEN

Reading and eating should both be done slowly.

—Spanish Proverb

• The Spanish Kitchen and Wine •

Please understand that Spanish cuisine and Mexican cuisine have almost nothing in common. The cultures share a few dishes due to the Spanish influence in Mexico, but that was hundreds of years ago and the cuisine of beans and tortillas is not known in Spain. It never was.

The Spanish view the evening meal as a very important time of the day. Dinner is eaten very late in the evening after chatting with friends over a glass of dry sherry and tapas (pages 88 to 92). The dinner goes late into the night. They do not see the meal as a "before event" such as we do before the theater or before the evening gets along. The meal is the event. The evening is spent dining with your friends and family.

Americans find it hard to believe that Spaniards begin dinner about 10 P.M. But please remember, they have several meals during the day, not the ordinary three that we celebrate. So by the time the last meal of the day arrives it is time to sit back, relax, and enjoy the presence of those that you love. The American dinner is eaten in a hurry, and very early in terms of Mediterranean standards, so that we "can get on with the evening." At this point the Spanish find us very strange and difficult to understand. Why do we want to hurry anything? I think it is because we feel guilty eating when we feel we should be accomplishing something more puritanical and worklike. I'm with the Spanish.

The wines of Spain are world famous, and they should be. The great Rioja region produces first-class reds and whites, and remember that the Spanish invented sherry, a wine left in barrels to "burn" in the sun until it is nutty and rich in flavor. All of these wines are used in cooking in this wonderful cuisine.

Soups, fish, and main dishes are all here. I would also add a green salad with Garlic Dressing (page 129).

Cold Tomato Soup

Gazpacho
(Spain)

The argument over this soup is a great deal of fun. It is actually a ground-up salad . . . dressing included. The argument centers not on whether it is a soup or a salad but on whether or not it is Spanish at all. I have located recipes for thirty variations of this stuff, and each maintains that it is the genuine article, and that the dish is a very old tradition in Spain. Other experts maintain that the dish is very new in the culture. One of the first cookbooks to be published in America, *The Virginia Housewife,* lists the dish and says the recipe is from Spain, and that book was published in 1824. Who cares! This is a delicious first course or appetizer . . . or maybe liquid salad. In any case, it will get a Spanish dinner off to the right start because you can serve it in glasses and allow your guests to walk about while they are drinking their salad, or eating their first course . . . having soup.

1 garlic clove, peeled
½ green sweet bell pepper, seeded and cored
½ yellow onion, peeled
5 very ripe tomatoes, cored and quartered
1 medium cucumber, peeled and sliced
1 tablespoon tomato paste
6 tablespoons olive oil
3 tablespoons wine vinegar, red or white
½ teaspoon cumin, ground
1 tablespoon Tabasco, or to taste
Salt and black pepper, freshly ground, to taste
1 cup ice water
2 cups tomato juice
2 eggs, hard-boiled, grated for garnish

Blend all the ingredients, except the grated egg, in a food blender or food processor. You will have to do this in several batches. Chill well before serving. Pour in wineglasses or cups and garnish with the grated egg. Leave the wine vinegar and black pepper grinder out so that your guests or family might add a bit to their glass.

Wine Suggestion: Light dry white.

SERVES 6–8.

Garlic and Egg Soup

(Spain)

I have served this many times. My guests always seem impressed by the soup and assume it is complex. Actually, it is a very simple peasant dish. It makes a great soup course on a cold winter night.

4 garlic cloves, sliced
⅓ cup olive oil
6 thin slices whole wheat or rye bread
6 cups Chicken Soup Stock (page 101) or use canned, not bouillon
1 tablespoon paprika
Salt and black pepper, freshly ground, to taste
5 eggs, beaten
Parsley, chopped, for garnish

Choose a soup pan or casserole that can go into a very hot oven.

Heat a large frying pan and add the garlic and oil. (If you use a large sauteuse for this you can do everything in the same pan.) Lightly brown the garlic and remove the slices from the pan and reserve. Fry the bread slices in the oil. Do not get them too brown. Cool them and break them up into 1-inch pieces. Add the stock to the soup pot, along with the bread pieces, paprika, and the salt and pepper. Cover and simmer the soup for 20 minutes. Whip the eggs with a fork until they are frothy and light. Pour them over the surface of the soup. Place the soup pot in a 450° oven until the eggs have cooked, about 10 minutes. Garnish with the parsley.

Wine Suggestion: Try a Riesling with this.

SERVES 6.

◆

Chicken and Chick-Pea Stew

(Spain)

The Italians call them ceci, the technical name is garbanzo bean, and many people call them chick-peas. They are very popular in all the Mediterranean regions. Most often they are purchased dry and then soaked and cooked. I have done that in this recipe, though you may want to use canned, drained garbanzos. Simply add them to the pot when you add the chicken stock and chicken. However, I prefer the texture and flavor of the dried chick-pea.

- 1 pound dried chick-peas
- 1 teaspoon baking soda
- 3 tablespoons olive oil
- 1 2½-pound frying chicken, cut up, the back and neck reserved for soup stock, or 2 pounds chicken legs and thighs
- 1 slice whole wheat bread
- 1 large yellow onion, peeled and sliced
- 2 large ripe tomatoes, diced
- 1 slice bacon
- 2 cups Chicken Soup Stock (page 101) or canned, not bouillon
- 1 bay leaf, whole
- Salt and black pepper, freshly ground, to taste
- 2 garlic cloves, crushed
- 2 eggs, hard-boiled and peeled
- ½ cup dry sherry

Pick over the chick-peas carefully, discarding discolored peas, small rocks, etc. Soak these overnight in ample water to cover, along with the baking soda. Next day, drain and rinse the peas. Cover with water and bring to a boil. Simmer for 1½ hours. Drain the peas and discard the water. Set aside.

Heat a large frying pan and add the oil. Brown the chicken pieces on all sides and remove from the pan. Fry the bread in the remaining oil. Remove and set aside. In the same pan, sauté the onion, tomatoes, and bacon. Cook until the onions are clear. Place the vegetable mixture in a 6-quart lidded Dutch oven and add the chicken pieces and the chick-peas. Deglaze (page 282) the frying pan with a bit of the broth. Add the pan drippings and the stock to the pot, along with the bay leaf and salt and pepper. Cover and bring to a simmer. Simmer until the chicken is tender, about 45 minutes.

In the meantime, crush the garlic into a small bowl. Break up the fried bread and add to the garlic, along with the yolks of the hard-boiled eggs. Mash the mixture along with 1 tablespoon of the sherry. You want to create a garlic/egg yolk paste. Chop the white of the eggs. When the chicken has been simmering for 45 minutes, add the garlic paste, the chopped egg whites, and the remaining sherry. Stir the pot carefully and simmer for another 10 minutes.

Wine Suggestion: Light red Rioja.

SERVES 5–6.

Paella

(Spain)

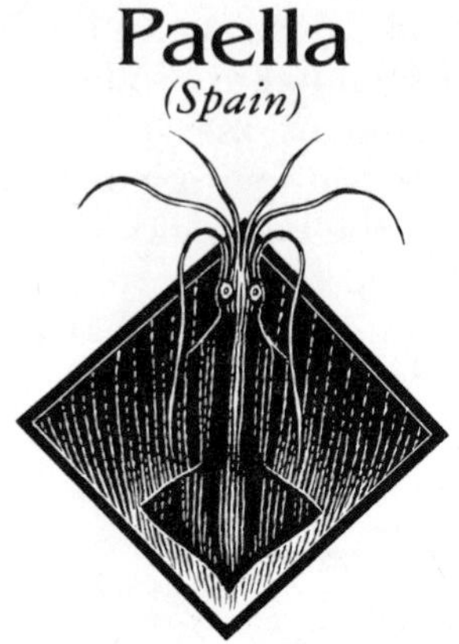

This is probably the most famous dish of Spain, at least for those outside Spain. The reputation is well deserved and the dish is not half as complicated as it sounds.

Rice is common in the diet of Spain, and we assume that the rice came from Italy at least three hundred years ago. We Americans got rice from Italy as well. It is cooked with many other ingredients; I have never seen a menu that called for plain cooked rice.

The term *paella* comes from the name of the metal pan in which the dish is cooked. It is a large round shallow pan, without a lid. Cooking rice uncovered sounds complex in terms of our understanding, but it works very well. The rice is not sticky and gooey, but lovely and light. It is one of the great entertaining dishes that I know.

- ½ cup olive oil
- 1 fryer chicken, around 2 pounds, cut up
- ½ pound Mexican Sausage (Chorizo) (page 250) or from the market
- 2 yellow onions, peeled and sliced
- 3 garlic cloves, crushed
- ¼ pound smoked ham, cut julienne (page 257)
- 2 ripe tomatoes, diced
- 2 cups long-grain converted rice (I like Uncle Ben's)
- 3 cups Chicken Soup Stock (page 101) or canned, or bouillon (this needs to be *boiling*)
- Pinch of saffron or turmeric (optional)
- 1 tablespoon paprika

¼ teaspoon crushed red pepper flakes
¼ teaspoon thyme, whole
Salt and black pepper, freshly ground, to taste
1 box (10 ounce) frozen peas, defrosted
2 red sweet bell peppers, cut into rings
1 box (10 ounce) frozen artichoke hearts, defrosted
1 pound squid, cleaned and cut into circles (page 123)
½ pound large shrimp or prawns, peeled and deveined
1½ pounds clams, in the shell, rinsed
1 cup dry white wine

Heat a large paella pan or a large frying pan. If you do not have a paella pan, plan on doing the sautéing in a regular frying pan and then placing the ingredients in a large, but shallow, Dutch oven. Add ¼ cup of the oil and brown the chicken pieces. Remove them from the pan. Add the chorizo, without the casing, the onions, garlic, and ham. Sauté until the onions are clear and then add the tomatoes. Sauté for 5 minutes more and remove all from the pan.

Add remaining oil to the pan and add the rice, stirring over the heat until the rice begins to brown lightly.

In the meantime, prepare and heat the stock. Add the saffron or turmeric, the paprika, crushed red pepper flakes, thyme, salt, and black pepper to the stock. Bring to a boil.

Pour the rice into the paella pan or Dutch oven. Pour on the peas and top with the red bell pepper slices and the defrosted artichokes. Add the chorizo mixture along with the chicken. Top with the squid and shrimp. Push the seafood down into the rice a bit and then pour on the boiling stock. Cook, uncovered, for about 10 minutes, or until the rice begins to absorb the liquid. You must be careful that this does not burn. Turn the pan often on the burner so that everything cooks evenly. Now add the clams, sticking them into the rice, hinge side down. Pour the wine over the whole works and continue cooking until the clams are open and the rice is light and tender.

Serve your guests from the buffet, allowing them to choose their own dinner from the paella.

Wine Suggestion: Light red Rioja or Chianti.

SERVES 6–8.

WINE SPECIALTIES

WINE JELLIES • WINE VINEGARS

One barrel of wine can work more miracles than a church full of saints.

—Italian Proverb

• *Wine Specialties* •

If you accept the tenet of this book, that wine is really a food, then you will appreciate the following recipes. Wine, as a food, offers us so many possibilities, and some of them are simply great fun. Don't laugh at some of these until you try them.

Garlic Wine

Wouldn't you know that I would come up with this one sooner or later! The two most wonderful flavors combined for your kitchen and creative pleasure.

Peel 8 cloves of garlic and stuff them into a bottle of light red wine, a Burgundy type. Cork the bottle and let it sit for 3 weeks, and you are ready to put a shot of flavor into soups, gravies, sauces, and meat dishes. Deglaze (page 282) the pan with this mixture, after frying chicken, pork, or beef, and have a sauce that you will not believe. What could be more simple? You might also try this with a dry white wine.

Wine Jellies

Cutting down on salt and fat is not an easy task. But since we should all do it I offer the following suggestion. Do away with the eggs and bacon for breakfast. What? Such pain!

We all know now that we will feel better and be much healthier if we eat more grains for breakfast. I love a good dark whole wheat toast with wine jelly. What a great beginning for a wonderful day, and the wine jelly has no fat or salt, of course. It is easy to make so you should try some soon. Don't worry about the alcohol because it cooks out right away.

2 cups wine
3 cups sugar
3 ounces liquid pectin (1 pouch)

I like to use a flavorful wine. You can use port or sherry for a sweeter jelly, but I prefer a Zinfandel, Gamay Beaujolais, or perhaps a Chardonnay. A Fumé Blanc is nice as well.

Stir the sugar into the wine and warm, in a stainless steel pan, until the sugar is dissolved. Do not overheat. It must not quite come to the simmer. Remove from the heat and stir in the pectin, being very careful to dissolve the pectin completely in the wine and sugar mixture.

Pour into small jars. I use 8-ounce jelly jars.

Keep refrigerated. It will keep about 2 months.

MAKES 4 CUPS.

◆

Wine Gelatin

(England)

This is very English. And it is the perfect ending of a nice meal. The dish is light and easy on the palate, but it contains enough joy to satisfy those sugar buffs at your table who must always have something sweet at the end of the meal.

- **2 envelopes unflavored gelatin**
- **¼ cup cold water**
- **Peel of ¼ lemon, yellow part only (remove with a potato peeler)**
- **3 cups red wine**
- **½ cup Madeira**
- **⅓ cup sugar**
- **Whipped cream flavored with sugar and brandy to taste (optional)**

Soften the gelatin in the water, using a 1-quart stainless steel or enamelware saucepan. Add the lemon peel and the wines and stir over very low heat until warm. Add the sugar and stir until dissolved. Remove the lemon peel and discard. Do not let this even come to a simmer. Pour into a glass bowl or wineglasses and refrigerate until firm. Top with whipped cream, if desired.

SERVES 6–8.

Rolled Grape Leaves

Sarma

(Armenia)

I have included this recipe for two reasons. First, I want you to taste this. It is served cold and is absolutely delicious. Second, I want you to know that in cultures where the vine has been important for thousands of years, nothing from the grape plant is wasted. In Greece, for instance, the cuttings from the vines each fall are dried and saved. When Easter comes, the Pascal lamb is roasted in the front yard, over coals of grapevines. Do you not see the theological significance of the wine and the lamb, blended together in the smoke of the outdoor kitchen? Besides, the vine wood gives a wonderful flavor to the lamb. I was very lucky to get Channing to continue with us on our journey through Greece just an Easter or two ago. He had been invited to turn the lamb over the grapevine coals on Easter Sunday in Delphi. He was so taken by the event, and the old Greek ladies in charge were so taken by him, that I thought he was going to stay forever.

This dish happens to be of Armenian origin. They maintain they invented wine, too. No matter. It is the gift of dear friends and musicians in Tacoma. Maestro Edward Seferian expects his wife, Jan, to prepare this for him between her appearances on the opera stage. Now, that is serious cooking!

	1	jar (16 ounce) grape leaves
FILLING:	1	cup long-grain rice, raw
	3	cups chopped yellow onion
	½	cup olive oil
	¼	cup finely chopped parsley
	¼	cup fresh dill weed, finely chopped, or 1 tablespoon dried dill weed
		Juice of 1 lemon
		Salt and black pepper, freshly ground, to taste
	¼	cup pine nuts
	¼	cup currants or ¼ cup raisins, chopped
COOKING BROTH:	1½	cups water
	½	cup Basic Brown Soup Stock (page 100)
		Juice of 1 lemon
	1	tablespoon tomato paste

Mix all ingredients for the filling.

Cut the stems off the grape leaves. Spread a leaf on a counter, bottom side up, the stem side toward you. Place 1 teaspoon of the filling in the center of the leaf. Fold the stem end over the filling, then fold the sides over to secure the filling, then roll from you toward the tip of the leaf, forming a small cigar or cylinder. Size is approximately 2½ inches long and ¾ inch wide.

Do not wrap these too tight as the rice needs room for expansion when it cooks.

Pick out the smallest of the leaves in the jar and set aside. Use these leaves for separating the layers in the bottom of a 2-quart heavy lidded kettle. Place a layer of filled or rolled grape leaves fairly tight up against one another so that they will not come apart while cooking. Place another layer of unrolled leaves on top and then a layer of rolled leaves. Continue until all rolled leaves are in the pot. Top with the remaining unrolled leaves.

Place a medium plate over the top of the leaves, as a weight. Mix the ingredients for the broth and pour over the rolled leaves. Cover and bring to a light simmer. I use a heat diffuser (page 24) for this. Cook for 1 hour. Remove the pan from the heat and allow it to cool for 1 more hour. DO NOT REMOVE THE LID or they will darken.

These may be served cold or at room temperature.

MAKES 36 SARMA.

Brunch Eggnog

This is a gift to us from the Wine Institute in San Francisco. Brian St. Pierre and the bunch there have been most kind to me . . . and I do love California wines. So here is a knockout for a brunch with friends. No, Patty and I do *not* have this each morning for breakfast, although we do share a breakfast cocktail of half champagne and half orange juice now and then.

1 bottle (750 ml) California cream sherry
4 eggs
1 can (6 ounce) frozen orange juice concentrate
2 cups crushed ice

Whip the ingredients smooth in a blender, using half amounts each time. Serve in chilled wineglasses.

SERVES 6–8.

HINT: **Cure for the Common Cold?**
One of our viewers maintains this works. I tried it and liked it, although I didn't have a cold to start with and this drink didn't give me one. So who knows? Mix equal parts orange juice and tawny port together. It looks terrible but it is supposed to help that old cold.

WINE VINEGARS—MAKE YOUR OWN

It is not true that wine will turn to vinegar if it is left open and allowed to sit. Wine is alive. It will simply die. The creation of vinegar needs a special bacterium called a "mother." She alone will give birth to the wonderful flavors and acids that mark a fine wine vinegar. You can make these at home. All you need to do is to find the "mother."

THE CULTURE OF "MOTHER"

You can purchase a starter for your wine vinegar from:

Napa Grape and Equipment Co.
948 Third Street
Napa, California, 94559

Milan Lab
57 Spring Street
New York, New York, 10012

Beer and Wine Making Supplies
154 King Street
Northampton, Maine, 01060

It is not expensive and if you can keep it alive you will have your own wine vinegars for years.

THE MAKING OF THE VINEGAR

This must be done in a very clean gallon-size glass bottle, wooden barrel, or porcelain crock with a small opening. It must be at least a gallon size because air is needed for the sake of the culture, and the container must not be more than one-third full at any time.

Choose something that has a small opening at the top, one that you can lightly stop up with cotton. The starter will be in a 6- to 8-ounce bottle. Place it in the clean container and add 2 cups wine and 1 cup water. Put in the light cotton plug and keep it in a warm place, 80° to 90° being ideal. I keep mine on the top of the hot water tank. It's perfect. In anywhere from 3 to 6 months, depending on the temperature and the health of your starter, you should have wine vinegar. From then on you draw off a bit of vinegar and replace it with some leftover wine. (No, I don't have much leftover wine at my house, either. I just add the wine!) The culture will begin to form on the top of the wine and it will resemble a thick slime. Lord, do not throw it out. You have made it! Draw the wanted vinegar from beneath the mother using a plastic tube. If you have this in a little barrel you can simply draw it off.

That is all there is to it. You can buy mothers for white and red vinegars. I have three going at the moment. One red, one white, and one that I am trying using a white starter in dry sherry. I love sherry wine vinegar for salads.

HOW TO USE THE VINEGAR:

Vinaigrette Dressing

The classic is simply olive oil, wine vinegar, and herbs of your choice. Salt and pepper are generally added as well. I prefer a pinch of dry mustard, such as Colman's. The secret is to use more oil than vinegar . . . and to use good-quality olive oil. Try any blends that sound good to you. The possibilities are endless.

♦

Tomato and Basil Salad

Elegance is sometimes just a matter of placement and simplicity. I think this is a very elegant salad.

3 ripe tomatoes, sliced thin
1 red onion, peeled and sliced very thin
4 large lettuce leaves

BASIL VINAIGRETTE:	1/4	cup olive oil
	3	tablespoons red wine vinegar
		Salt and black pepper, freshly ground, to taste
	1/4	teaspoon dry mustard (Colman's is fine)
	1/8	teaspoon sugar to taste (just a pinch)
	2	tablespoons chopped parsley
	2	tablespoons chopped basil, fresh

Blend the oil, vinegar, salt, pepper, and mustard together in a jar. Shake to blend. Check to see if you wish sugar. Gently stir in the parsley and basil.

Place a leaf of lettuce on each of four plates. Arrange the tomato and onion slices on top of one another, like roof tiles, in a circle, on the lettuce. Top with the dressing.

SERVES 4.

Little Joe's Vinaigrette

One of my favorite eating places in San Francisco is a place on Broadway called Little Joe's. It is not a tourist joint but rather a haven for hungry San Franciscans. The quality of the food is high, the amounts served gigantic, and the bill reasonable. Franco Montarello, *the* Little Joe, has a wonderful way with sauces and pastas. Here is his green vinaigrette that he serves with boiled brisket of beef. You can use it on any meat you wish. This comes from his new *Little Joe's Italian Cookbook.*

You may wish to cut down on the portions. This is simply the way the man cooks.

- 1 cup finely minced celery
- 1 cup finely minced parsley
- 1 cup olive oil
- 2 cups red wine vinegar
- 1 teaspoon minced garlic
- 1 tablespoon salt

1 teaspoon black pepper, freshly ground
1 teaspoon chopped anchovies (optional)
1 tablespoon capers, minced (optional)

Combine the celery and parsley in a large bowl. Add the oil, vinegar, garlic, salt, and pepper. Whip vigorously. If one prefers a more exotic mixture, add the anchovies and/or the minced capers. This will keep for 1 week in the refrigerator.

MAKES 4 CUPS.

Raspberry Vinegar

A very popular flavor with the nouvelle cuisine bunch. It is nice on salad and I have seen it served on everything from chicken and rabbit to fish. I prefer to stick to the salads.

This is easily made with fresh or even frozen berries. Use 3 cups of berries and place them in a large glass jar with a quart of white wine vinegar. Allow it to sit, covered, for 3 days in a cool place. Strain out the berries and add another 3 cups of berries to the vinegar. Allow to sit for 3 more days. Stir in ½ cup sugar and strain through a double thickness of cheesecloth placed in a colander. Keep refrigerated.

Herb-Flavored Vinegars

Try putting herbs into your wine vinegars. Simply put whole herbs into a small bottle of vinegar and then use it for flavoring. These are some of the possibilities:

Garlic vinegar
Basil vinegar
Tarragon vinegar
Rosemary vinegar
Oregano vinegar
Dill vinegar
Thyme vinegar

It is best if you use fresh herbs for these vinegars. If you use dry, you must strain them out after a few weeks.

COFFEE FOR ENTERTAINING

You are responsible for the comfort of your guests all of the time that they are under your roof.

—Brillat-Savarin

Coffee for Entertaining

The history of coffee is filled with wonderful and doubtful stories. The discovery of coffee is attributed to a Moslem priest or Mullah, Chadely by name. He lived during the first part of the ninth century and could not stay awake during his prayers. In an act of mercy, The Holy One led the priest to a goat herdsman. The herdsman told him that there was a plant nearby that attracted his goats. When they ate from the plant they stayed up all night jumping about and playing around. The Mullah made a brew from the berries of the shrub and was delighted to find that he could stay up all night in prayer and not suffer any side effects. To this day it is common for a pilgrim in Mecca to be offered coffee before his prayers.

Coffee probably originated in Ethiopia and spread throughout the Middle East. One of the first promises that Turks must make to their wives is that they will never run out of coffee. And "coffee should be black as Hell, strong as death, and sweet as love."

The beverage came to Europe, and by the end of the sixteenth century coffee had become so important that the Roman church banned it as the wine of Islam. It was only to be drunk by infidels. Pope Clement VIII somehow tasted it, however, and decided that "this Satan's drink is too delicious to let the heathens have it all to themselves. We will baptize it and make a Christian beverage of it." He did, and we have been sitting up all night ever since.

Chicken Coffee Paprika

Try this dish simply so that you can understand that coffee flavor is very good in many foods.

- 2 pounds chicken breasts, pounded thin
- 1 cup fresh lemon juice
- ¼ cup flour
- Salt to taste (about ½ teaspoon)
- Freshly ground black pepper
- 1 cup peeled and sliced yellow onions
- Olive oil for sautéing
- ½ cup strong brewed coffee
- 1½ tablespoons paprika
- 2 tablespoons cornstarch
- 1 cup half-and-half
- Paprika and fresh parsley for garnish

Pound the chicken breasts thin using a wooden mallet and plastic sheeting (page 175). Marinate in the lemon juice for 5 minutes. Drain and pat dry, reserving the lemon juice for later use in the sauce.

Mix flour, salt, and black pepper. Place on a large plate and flour each of the breasts. Shake off excess flour.

Sauté onions in oil until soft but not discolored. Remove from pan. Add a bit more olive oil to the frying pan and brown the chicken pieces.

Add coffee to the pan, along with the paprika and the onions. Bring to a boil. Remove from heat. Stir the cornstarch into the cream and add to the frying pan. Mix well and then return to the heat. Stir until thickened. Add the leftover lemon juice. Stir well and pour over the chicken breasts. Garnish with more paprika and parsley. Serve immediately.

SERVES 4.

Kahlúa-Style Coffee Liqueur

We have made this stuff in our home for years. I offered this recipe during our very first show in 1974. I cannot believe that people are still asking for the recipe.

4 cups sugar
4 cups water
1 bottle (2 ounce) Spice Island Instant Antiqua Espresso
1 fifth bourbon whiskey
1 whole vanilla bean

Bring the sugar and water to a boil, stirring. Remove from the heat and whisk in the instant coffee. Allow to cool. Pour into a gallon jug and add the bourbon and the vanilla bean. Seal and let sit 1 month before serving.

◆

Crème au Café

This is just great. A perfect ending for a nice dinner.

2 cups milk
4 ounces coarsely ground espresso coffee
¾ cup sugar
Pinch of salt
3 tablespoons brandy
5 egg yolks

In a small sauce pan, place the milk and the coarsely ground coffee beans. Bring to a simmer and remove from the heat. Let sit for 10 minutes. Strain out the grounds. Stir in the sugar, salt, and brandy. Whip the egg yolks and quickly whip the hot milk into the yolks. Return to very low heat and stir until thickened. You may wish to use a double boiler for this step.

Chill the custard and serve with small cookies for dessert.

SERVES 6.

Sambuca and Coffee Ice Cream

1 quart vanilla ice cream
3 tablespoons instant espresso coffee
¼ cup Sambuca liqueur or Ouzo (Greek anise liqueur)
Whole coffee beans for garnish

Allow the ice cream to defrost until it is soft enough for mixing. Mix the coffee with 2 tablespoons very hot water and dissolve. Mix coffee and liqueur into the ice cream. Place the ice cream mixture in a mold or steel bowl and refreeze. Serve for dessert with 1 coffee bean sitting on top of each serving.

Mr. Stewart's Favorite Sundae

The Stewart family has been roasting and selling excellent coffee in Chicago for several generations. One of the sons told me that his favorite ice cream sundae consists of very high-quality vanilla ice cream on which you sprinkle dark roasted ground coffee. I have tried it and it is unusually good.

◆

Coffee Ice

Prepare a very dark coffee, extra-heavy brew. I prefer espresso. Freeze in ice-cube trays. When ready for a smashing dessert, place coffee ice cubes in the food processor. Add a few tablespoons of additional coffee and process to an ice or sherbet. Serve with a little whipped cream on top. This is very Italian!

DESSERTS

Never serve wine with dessert.

—Out-of-Date Home Economist

• Dessert and Wine •

You do not think wine is appropriate with dessert? I even like a dry white with a piece of pumpkin pie. It is a lovely contrast and each flavor feeds the other.

SAUTERNES AND BARSAC

These are the most wonderful of desserts. The wine is rich and sweet, with a bouquet so bright that everyone in the neighborhood will know what you have done.

The richness of the wine is due to a wonderful quirk in nature . . . no, a blessing from God. There is a fungus or mold that attacks grapes and in certain areas the grape develops gray rot and spoils, while in other areas, particularly in France, the grapes wither a bit, due to the fungus drawing out much of the moisture, and the wine produced from these grapes is a great concentration of sugar and flavor and delight. The fungus is called *Boytrytis cinerea.* The French have become so expert at using this mold that they call it *pourriture noble,* literally meaning "noble rot"! What a wonderful gift it is. It helps us produce these very sweet wines in France, as well as in Germany, and the famous Tokay Aszu of Hungary.

The history of the discovery of this method of wine production is hidden somewhere in the midst of many stories. My favorite holds that a bishop of the Church, and owner of a fine vineyard, not an unusual combination in Church history, was called to Rome. It was just before harvest time and it was the bishop's custom to bless the pickers and the grapes, before they were picked. He became delayed by some ecclesiastical matter and did not appear when the grapes began to ripen. Knowing how urgent proper timing is in harvesting wine grapes, the pickers went to the edge of the fields each day and waited for the bishop to arrive. Finally, the grapes began to wither on the vine. Noble rot had set in. Just as the pickers were about to give up, down the road came the Holy Father, his coachman whipping the horse in his quest for speed. The coach reached the pickers on the edge of the field, the bishop jumped from the coach, threw on his stole, and raised his hand in the sign of the cross. "In the name of the Father, the Son, and the Holy Ghost. Now pick!" he shouted. They thought the crop was gone, it had so dried out. They pressed the grapes nevertheless . . . and Sauternes was born.

The birth of this wine must have occurred in a situation very close to the one above. You now understand why these wines are so very expensive. They are dear because a whole bushel of grapes will not even yield enough juice for a single bottle. It is a very delicate and costly process, this dessert wine. But it is a process I adore. Talk to your wine merchant about a Sauternes or Barsac that is not quite so expensive. It is the best of all desserts. Serve after everything else is gone. Everything! It will stand on its own without the need of any other flavor or influence.

PORT AND CHOCOLATES

Sounds strange to you? You have only to try. Serve good, fresh chocolates with wonderfully gooey and rich centers. Either light or dark chocolate. It will not matter. Serve with a tawny port, one that is not too sweet.

Port is actually a fortified wine, that is, it has extra alcohol added in the form of brandy. Brandy is made from distilling wine, so we are still dealing with natural alcohols and sugars. The grapes are pressed and allowed to ferment. At the proper time the wine master adds brandy to the vat, thus stopping the fermentation. Yeast can work in only so much alcohol and then it dies. In the case of port the yeast dies with the injection of the brandy, which is about 20 percent of the total volume of the port. The wine is then aged and bottled. The sweetness is controlled by timing the addition of the brandy. Sweeter wines are stopped in their natural fermentation process earlier than dryer wines.

CHEESE AND WINE

These two just belong together. It is one of few marriages that has lasted hundreds of years. Remember that cheese makes a wine taste better, sometimes better than it should. Cheese is so supportive of wine that wine merchants always serve cheese at a formal tasting so that the wine will come off at its best. Without the cheese you might not think so much of the wine. No matter, eat them together. The cheese tastes better for it as well.

Wine and cheese make a great dessert. In France, following a meal, the cheese cart is brought to your table, even in blue-collar establishments. The cart is elaborate and the cheeses fully and properly ripened. I think such a cheese, along with a good wine, makes the very best dessert of all. I am not particularly fond of sweet things, and I certainly do not need the sugar or the calories. That is why I have so few sweet desserts in my cookbooks. Cheese makes a better dessert. There is one restaurant in Paris that serves nothing but cheese. You order a wine and then have cheese as an appetizer, dinner, and dessert. That's it! And it is wonderful. The place is so busy that you can't even get into it most of the time. Maybe we Americans will learn.

JUST PORT

Port has the most wonderful effect on everyone. An evening of good eating and celebrating with friends comes to a proper and calming end when the port is offered. Or you can just serve port to a friend in the evening. Great conversations will ensue.

Port has color, sweetness, depth, flavor, warmth, body, and history. Port has history. I cannot drink port without thinking of people like Sir Winston Churchill, who refused to go to bed without his port, even during the London blitz of World War II. During that war, Churchill was a source of great inspiration to the people of the Commonwealth, and to the Americans and Allies. At one particularly tense time during the war, Eisenhower told his officers that they had to get Churchill off the streets or he was going to be killed by a bomb. Colonel James Stack, one of Eisenhower's right-hand men, took the Prime Minister underground in the City of London. Winnie, it seems, was in the habit of simply wandering the streets during the day, his hand held high in the air with the sign of "V" for victory. While cheering on the troops and townspeople, he placed himself in grave danger. So underground he went, and he was not pleased with the thought of being away from his people. Colonel Stack set up a room beneath the city and he kept Sir Winston there and in his sights for several days. The bombs were falling on the city, right over their heads, as they sat down under old London town. I asked the colonel what they did during that frightening time. "Oh," he said, "we talked and drank port. We talked a lot and drank a lot of port. A lot, indeed."

So, here's to port. It will heal your anxieties and calm you to the point where you might just reconsider what it is that you are doing in the world. God save Jolly England!

◆

Wine Pudding

You will not believe how simple this is . . . and how delicious. Use a 4¾-ounce package of vanilla pudding and pie filling. Substitute 2½ cups of ruby or tawny port for the milk. Cook according to the instructions, being careful not to boil it long. Just bring it to the boil and remove from the heat.

This pudding may separate a bit on you if you save it until the next day. Best to serve it on the same evening that it is prepared. Whip with an electric mixer if it should separate.

SERVES 6.

Pears Poached in Port

This dish is easy and dramatic. It draws upon the wonderful flavor and depth of the port and the fruitiness and sweetness of the pear. Have everything done ahead of time and you can turn this on to cook as you are clearing the table for dessert.

- **1 cup sugar**
- **1 pint water**
- **1 cinnamon stick**
- **4 cloves**
- **1 piece fresh orange peel, 1 inch long**
- **6 pears, ripe but firm**
- **1 cup port, tawny or ruby**

In a saucepan just large enough to take the pears comfortably, mix the sugar, water, cinnamon stick, cloves, and orange peel. Bring to a simmer and then cool.

Peel the pears, leaving the stem intact, if you were lucky enough to find pears that still had their stems. Cut a bit off the bottom of the pear so that it will stand upright in the port and in the serving dish. Leave them set in a stainless or glass bowl covered with mild salt water until ready to cook.

When ready to cook, drain the pears and place them in the sugar syrup pan, upright. Add the port and bring the whole to a gentle boil. Turn to a simmer and cover. Cook until the pears are tender but still a bit firm, about 15 minutes.

Serve each pear upright in a small glass bowl or dish. You might put a puddle of the port broth in the bottom of the dish.

SERVES 6.

Wine Custard

Zabaglione
(Italy)

People always tell me that they have trouble with desserts from Europe. "Too much trouble. And besides, it won't turn out well anyway." This one will. It is a classic from Italy and the restaurants charge a fortune for it. You can make it at home and enjoy it. You don't even need a fancy copper zabaglione pot.

4 egg yolks
¼ cup sugar
½ cup sweet Marsala wine

Traditionally this is done with a wire whip in a copper zabaglione pan. However, you will have great results, perhaps even better than the old method, if you will use an electric mixer and a double boiler.

Place the egg yolks and the sugar in the double boiler. Blend until creamy, using an electric mixer. Place the lower pot, filled with water, over the heat. When it begins to boil, place the upper pot, now containing the yolks and sugar, in place. Add the wine and continue beating as it cooks. It will swell up and form soft peaks. Remove from the heat and spoon into wineglasses or sherbet cups. Serve immediately.

Wine Suggestion: Asti Spumante.

SERVES 4.

Pears and Gorgonzola

A glass of wine, a pear, and Italian bleu cheese? Yes, this makes a most unusual spread for ripe pears. It has become a favorite at our dinner parties.

¼ pound Gorgonzola
¼ pound butter, softened or at room temperature
Pears, ripe and sliced

Cream the cheese and the butter together. Serve alongside the pear slices. Butter the pear slices with this mixture and enjoy.

Wine Suggestion: Sauternes.

Champagne Cream

- 1 large bunch white seedless grapes
- ⅓ cup sugar
- 5 egg yolks
- ¾ cup brut champagne
- 2 tablespoons whipping cream

Wash the grapes and remove them from their stems. Divide them among four stemmed dessert or large wineglasses.

In a double boiler, place the sugar and egg yolks. With a wire whip or an electric mixer, blend until creamy. Add the champagne and cream and blend well. Place over boiling water and continue to whip as it cooks. It will form soft peaks and cook in about 5 minutes.

Remove from heat and pour over the grapes. Serve immediately.

Wine Suggestion: Champagne, of course!

SERVES 4.

SHERBETS AND ICE CREAMS

To as great a degree as sexuality, food is inseparable from imagination.

—Jean-François Revel

• *Sherbets and Ice Cream* •

The difference between ice creams, sherbets, and ices is primarily one of butterfat. Ice cream is anywhere from 10 percent to 14 percent butterfat, but there is no law about how much air you can whip into the stuff. Sherbets have very little milk or egg white in them. Ices are primarily juices and have little or no butterfat.

In Europe, it is not uncommon to serve a sherbet or ice right in the middle of the meal. I like the practice because it cleanses your palate and allows you to continue to enjoy the dinner.

The following recipes work very well with a Donvier Ice Cream Freezer (page 25). You can find one of these in almost any gourmet shop or large department store. This machine is inexpensive and works better than anything else on the market.

•

Lemon and Champagne Sherbet

This is just great right in the middle of the meal. It also works well for dessert.

1 cup sugar
1 cup water
Juice of 1 orange
Juice of 2 lemons
2 cups dry Sauternes, or dry white wine*
½ cup whipping cream

Boil the sugar in the water for 5 minutes. Allow to cool completely. Add the juices and the wine. Chill. Freeze. When just about frozen, whip the cream and fold in. Freeze a bit more. Great between courses at formal dinners.

SERVES 8.

*Just lie about the champagne. The bubbles will be gone anyhow and the Sauternes will do just fine.

Lemon Champagne Ice

This is a very refreshing bath for the tongue in the midst of a rich meal. Serve this about halfway through the dinner and you will liven up appetites again!

- **1 cup water**
- **1/4 cup sugar**
- **Juice of 2 lemons**
- **2 cups champagne, medium to dry**

Heat the water and dissolve the sugar. Add the juice and wine and chill. Freeze in a Donvier hand freezer, according to instructions. Please note that it is best to do this just before you sit down, so that the ice will be a bit soft and very smooth.

SERVES 6 AS A MID-MEAL ICE.

◆

Peach Sherbet

This is just as simple as it looks and it tastes as fresh as you hope.

- **1/4 cup sugar**
- **1 cup water**
- **3 large ripe peaches, peeled and pitted**
- **Juice of 1/2 lemon**
- **1 teaspoon brandy**

Dissolve sugar in water. Purée the peaches in a food blender or processor. Add the sugar water, lemon juice, and brandy. Chill. Then freeze in an ice cream machine.

MAKES 1 PINT.

Raspberry Ice

This one came out of an old American cookbook. They had to go to a great deal of work to get something that you and I can do in very little time.

1/4 cup sugar, or to taste
1 cup water
3 cups raspberry juice or crushed frozen berries, defrosted
2 egg whites, beaten

Mix sugar, water, and juice. Place in freezer. When about frozen, fold in the beaten egg whites. Freeze in an ice cream machine.

MAKES 2 PINTS.

◆

Watermelon Ice

I did this one morning at my studio, WTTW, Chicago, and the crew could not believe this dish. It is best to make this during the summer when the melons are very ripe.

Remove the rind and all the seeds from an entire watermelon. Purée the pulp in a food processor or food blender. Sweeten to taste and freeze in the Donvier. You may wish to add 2 beaten egg whites. Proceed as above.

Ginger Ice Cream

This is so rich and good that it will start a fight among your children. You scoop it out and divide it. Don't let them even try!

1 pint light cream
1/8 teaspoon salt
1/2 cup sugar
1 tablespoon candied ginger diced very fine

Warm the cream along with the ginger. Do not allow it even to come to a simmer. Stir in the salt and sugar. Allow to cool slowly. Chill. Freeze in Donvier.

MAKES 1 PINT.

ON ENJOYING WINE

MATCHING WINE WITH FOOD • ON BUYING WINE • STOCKING THE FRUGAL WINE CELLAR • ON TASTING WINE AND WINE TASTINGS • SURVIVING THE SOMMELIER • SERVING WINE • WINEGLASSES FROM THE FRUGAL GOURMET'S KITCHEN • WINE BOTTLES • CORKSCREWS

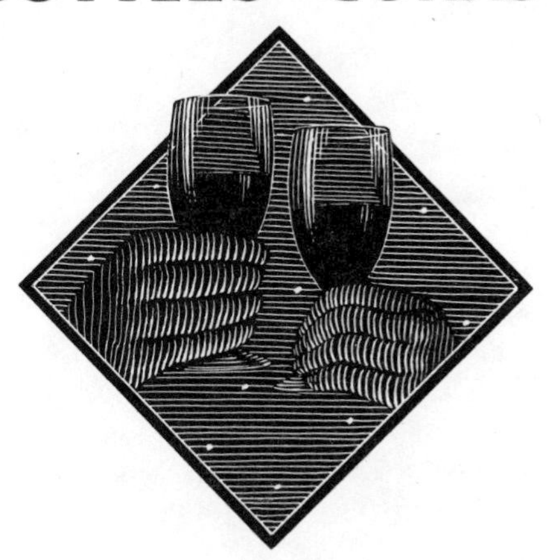

• Matching Wine with Food •

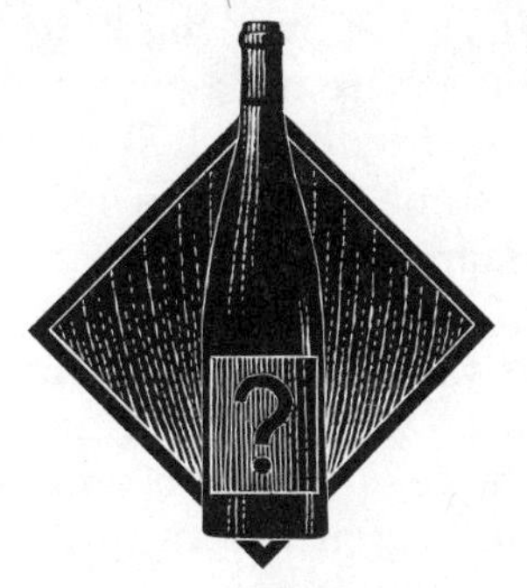

Meet my priest and friend, Father Corbet Clark. He loves wine and has offered us the following articles.

Fr. Clark is an unusual young man. He has a brilliant mind, a quick but dry wit, and a knowledge of wine that makes me jealous. His interest in wine has been with him since he was a child, as his father was fascinated with wine and bid his sons share the joys. I still contend that that is the best way to introduce your children to wine. There is nothing mysterious about it. Wine is a food, and it should be treated very matter-of-factly, as you would any good food. So it is with Corbet.

We first met when he came to our parish in Tacoma, the "new young priest." I was on his doorstep with a bottle of welcoming wine a few hours after he arrived in town. I did not even suspect that our mutual appreciation of theology and wine would bring about such a relationship as this.

So, there you have it. The cooking is done by a United Methodist cleric—myself. The instruction in wine, and joyful instruction it is, is offered by an Episcopalian priest, Fr. Clark. We both expect you to enjoy these articles, instructions, biases, recipes, and, in the end, your own relationship with your fellows.

by Father Corbet Clark

1. Drink the wines you enjoy with the foods you enjoy. You have a thirst for Riesling and a hunger for steak? So be it. You will not be zapped with lightning for putting the two together. And in truth, the flavors that your palate prefers will probably go together just fine.

2. Experiment. You might make some ghastly choices (perhaps Zinfandel is not the best wine for clam linguine after all). But you will stimulate your own thinking about food flavors, as different wines accent different flavors in a dish (gee, that Chardonnay sure brings out the dill in this). And you may, perhaps by dumb luck, hit upon some wonderful marriage of food and wine that will win you acclaim in your kitchen.

3. Third principle is really a choice you need to make: Do you want to show off the food, or the wine? This is especially an issue when you're entertaining. If you are preparing a tricky and special dish that you hope your guests will ooh and ahh over, don't distract them with an expensive twenty-year-old wine. Hungry people eating and drinking can concentrate on only so much at a time. Serve a good wine that will complement the meal but will not be too assertive.

Likewise, if you are dusting off a fine old bottle or have invested a small fortune in the hottest new wine, make sure you get the hoped-for reaction by preparing simple food that will provide a tasty background for the wine.

4. The fourth principle also involves a choice: You can match for similarity or for contrast. For example, if you are serving fish with a rich, buttery sauce, you might want to pick a Chardonnay or white Burgundy that has very buttery characteristics, as many do. In other words, you find food and wine with similar flavors (not always an easy task). But sometimes you may use wine as a counterbalance, to cut through or set off aggressive flavors in a dish. A good example here are oily types of fish, which often do best with tart, crisp white wines like Pouilly-Fumé or Italian Chardonnay, both of which refresh the palate.

This principle also gives you a wonderful out when, in your experimenting, you make a real blooper. As your family grimaces over a nasty battle between food and wine you can observe to them that you hope that the contrast between food and wine flavors has worked out to their satisfaction.

5. Match strength to strength. If you're serving a delicate cod dish, don't attack it with a full-flavored California Chardonnay. If you're serving a rich, spicy, tomatoey pasta dish, don't let it overwhelm a pale red Burgundy. Light flavors deserve light wine; heavy flavors, or spicy ones, need heavy wine.

6. The sixth principle is one that slightly complicates your task—The Secret is the Sauce. In many cases you want to match a wine not to the main ingredient in a dish but to the sauce. Why do you use a sauce? Because it changes the flavors of the food you're preparing. Salmon with creamy dill sauce is rather different from salmon with lobster sauce—a wine that is good with one might not complement the other. So consider the balance of sweetness

and tartness, the creaminess, the herbs in the sauce when thinking of a wine.

7. This principle involves the one bit of wine chemistry that is significant for wine and food. It is the acid in a wine that makes it taste tart (or sour), but acid is the backbone of any wine, and the best food wines are nearly always those with healthy acid levels. The hazard of trying to evaluate a wine without food is that a wine that tastes overly tart by itself may be delightfully refreshing and stimulating with a meal. Likewise, a wine low in acid (often called "soft") that tastes lush and flavorful by itself may simply have its flavors disappear when served with food. All the other flavors in wine "hang" on the acid—so consider the acid of a wine when matching with food.

Just because a wine is sweet doesn't mean it is low in acid. German Rieslings are usually slightly sweet, but they have good balancing acid—more, in fact, than many other white wines. This makes them, despite what you've heard, actually rather good food wines, particularly with rich foods.

8. Let the last principle be . . . tradition. American food and wine lovers have devoted a decade or so to the serious business of matching food and wine, and in typically American fashion, have come up with a variety of technically sophisticated and well-organized approaches. Meanwhile, Europeans have for the better part of two millennia been happily sating their appetites with local wines made to suit the local cuisine—and have so mastered this art that they needn't think about it.

So the marvelous sweet beef of Burgundy matches beautifully with Pinot Noir, while the fat fowls, freshwater crawfish, and delicate cheeses of the region make one crave Chardonnay (which, fortunately, is what they produce). The rich, spicy dishes of Germany suit Riesling just fine, thank you very much, while Italian Chianti does very nicely with the prosciutto, minestrone, and grilled meats and game of the Tuscan hills. The easiest way to deal with the vexing question of matching wine to food is simply to follow the lead of our forebears. It's difficult to go wrong serving a lovely Italian wine with an Italian dinner. (Yes, there is such a thing as "spaghetti wine.") When serving seafood, look for wines made by those close enough to the sea to smell it.

• On Buying Wine •

If you are just starting out and are feeling intimidated you need to strike up an acquaintance with your local wine merchant. He or she can make recommendations on specific wines, and possibly even let you sample some wines (depending on state laws). Be careful, though; in areas where wine is peddled alongside hard liquor, you may have to look hard for a merchant who really knows wine.

Look for a merchant with a good selection of wines from all over the world—not just a few dozen of the best-known labels. A good merchant will carry a healthy selection of moderately priced ($5–$10) bottles, including wines from Italy, Spain, the Pacific Northwest, lesser-known Bordeaux estates, small but not-quite-fashionable California wineries. Check to see that the shop has recent vintages of wines, which would indicate a pretty good turnover. If all the whites, for example, are four or five years old, you should be suspicious that a) no one shops there and b) the merchant is peddling wines that are probably not very good.

Once you've found a good shop, there are a few clues you can derive from the appearance of the bottle you're interested in. Don't buy bottles that have the cork sticking out past the end of the glass, or that have wine oozing out. If the cork does not make a firm seal the wine may easily have been damaged. Be careful about buying wines with stained labels. If the stain comes from the wine in that bottle, again, it suggests a poorly sealed bottle. On the other hand, sometimes labels are stained by something outside the bottle, and sometimes wineshops discount these at good prices.

Look at the level of wine in the bottle. It should be within no more than an inch of the cork. If there is more airspace in the bottle, the wine may be suffering from oxidation. Some white wines have small white crystals floating about in them, which detracts from their appearance. These crystals, which are tartrates, do not affect the flavor at all, and if the wines are reduced in price because of this problem, they may be good buys.

Wine prices are being affected by the move to discount merchandising and by the global wine glut. In many parts of the country wine is being sold at some shops, supermarkets, and "warehouse" dealers for not much more than cost. And producers and distributors are dumping unwanted wines on the market at low prices just to make room for the next vintage. So a bottle that costs $7.95 in one shop may be selling for $5.99 somewhere close by. It pays to shop around. At many supermarkets, liquor stores, and warehouses, however, the storage conditions may be less than ideal—so the quality cannot be guaranteed. A reliable local wine merchant, especially if he offers case discounts (on 12 or more bottles) of 10 to 15 percent, is still often the best place to shop. Even though the prices may be a bit higher overall, a good wine merchant can steer you to good-value wines you might not find at the supermarket or liquor store, which want to carry only the most popular brands. (Moreover, most good merchants will take back an obviously rotten bottle of wine, which a liquor store or warehouse may not.)

How much should you pay for a nice bottle of wine? That you have to decide for yourself. I can tell you that it is possible to spend $20 and buy a very mediocre wine, and it is possible to spend $5 and buy a truly fine one. If you are accustomed to paying $2 or $3 a bottle for basically jug wine, I would encourage you to spring for another $1 or $2 to get a vastly superior product—it makes a lot of difference to a nice meal. For entertaining and special occasions, $10–$15 is reasonable for a special bottle of wine. Such a wine makes an evening's entertainment, for about the same price as a night at the movies for two.

WINE LABELS

The most basic information a wine label should provide is what kind of wine is in the bottle, where it comes from, who made it, and when. Unfortunately, the laws governing the labeling of wine vary from country to country, so unless you know how each country does things, you may find it confusing.

In the United States wines are labeled according to the grape variety they are made from. If a wine says "Chenin Blanc," it must be at least 75 percent Chenin Blanc, but the rest can be anything. Many wines today are labeled "100 percent varietal," which may be a guarantee of quality, but remember that traditionally many of the best wines in the world (Bordeaux is a good example) are blends of several different grape varieties. Many American wine producers are blending grapes now, too, and either making up a name for the wine (the Mondavi-Rothschild "Opus One" is a famous, and expensive, example), or else labeling the wine with all the grape varietals included ("Cabernet Sauvignon–Merlot"). Many of the "Reserve White" or "Vin Blanc" or "Claret" names, which look as if they might belong on jug wines, actually mask very high-quality, sometimes high-value, wines.

On the other hand, there are the jug wines with pretentious names. For some reason American table wines have long since appropriated famous European names and debased them by putting them on dull and inferior wine. California "Chablis" has no consistent standard and bears no resemblance whatever (except that it's white) to the high-class French wine with the same name. Ditto for "Rhine" wine, "Burgundy," "Champagne," "Chianti," etc. If you think that because it has a name like this on the bottle you can have some idea of what it should taste like, you will often be sadly disappointed. Any wine maker in California can put any name like this he wants to on any product—it is just not regulated. So, buyer beware.

More and more, premium wines in this country have an area designation: "Napa Valley" or "Monterey" or "Willamette Valley." This may provide some clues about the quality if you know which areas have the best reputation for which grapes. In general terms, the wines from more specific areas are higher quality. Thus, "Napa Valley" is generally superior to "North Coast," which in turn is generally superior to simple "California" wine. But this doesn't always hold true.

If a wine has a vintage date on it it must be at least 90 percent from that year—be cautious about buying older wines or nonvintage bottles that look as if they have been around for a while. But the whole business about "vintage" wine is probably overrated. There are variations in vintages, but improved techniques today allow wine makers to produce very acceptable wine even from the worst vintages. And a "good" vintage is not a guarantee of a good wine. There are always those who, because they picked at the wrong time, or made mistakes in fermentation, or whatever, manage to make lousy wine in great vintages. Likewise, there are those talented wine makers whose wines are consistently good, year in and year out, no matter what the weather. I recommend trusting a reliable producer or broker instead of relying on vintage charts.

In foreign countries, wine labeling laws tend to be more complicated than in the United States, which is compounded for us because the label is in a strange tongue. The primary difference is that, with a few exceptions, European wine names are based on the *region* the wine is from, not the *grape* from which it is made. Thus, German Riesling will be labeled "Kiedricher Graefenberg" or "Schloss Johannisberg"—the estate from which the wine hails. If "Riesling" appears on the label at all, it is likely to be in small print. You just have to know that it's Riesling. Likewise, Bordeaux red wine, which is always some combination of the Cabernet Sauvignon, Merlot, Cabernet Franc, and Malbec grapes, will not tell you what it's blended from, but will be labeled "Château Chasse-Spleen" or "Bordeaux Supérieur," etc.

That, for the wine novice, is the bad news. The good news is that the most important European wine countries—France, Germany, and Italy—place very strict controls over what kind of wine can be made in each region. So white Burgundy is always going to be mostly Chardonnay, Chianti is always mostly Sangiovese. I say mostly because, again, Europeans traditionally blend their grapes—not to dilute the product but because they think the resulting wine is better.

In each country, the top wines are designated by certain words. In France, the "Appellation Contrôlée" is your guarantee that the wine is what it says it is. In Italy, it's "DOC"—"Denominazione di Origine Controllata." And in Germany look for "QbA," or "Qualitätswein mit Prädikat." You still may not like the wine, but at least you're not getting ripped off.

In addition to this, some foreign areas have classification systems that rate the wines. Bordeaux is probably the best-known example: The "best growths," the "Cru Classés," are rated from 1 (the best) to 5, while slightly lesser growths are marked "Cru Bourgeois." With a system like this, once you understand the terminology, it can be very helpful. But sometimes the (foreign) language can be misleading: "Bordeaux Supérieur" does not necessarily mean that the wine is "superior," merely that it has a higher alcohol level than ordinary "Bordeaux." The Germans have a similar system, with premium wines rated according to level of ripeness of the grapes, by words such as "Kabinett" and "Spätlese." You have to know the words to make sense of the system, but once you've got it down, it's very helpful.

The tradition in Europe has been for a long time that the company that puts wine in the bottle and labels it is not necessarily the winery that produced the wine, and this is beginning to happen in the United States as well. It can work very well if the middle man, or *négociant* as the French call him, has a good reputation. In many parts of Europe, the individual holdings are too small for the wine makers to market their own wines, and the only way foreigners can get them is through the services of a négociant. On the other hand, it is not unknown for large wine firms to buy cheap wine, slap a fancy label on it, and sell it dearly. There have even been instances of false labeling of wine.

If you don't want to take any chances, there are key words

to look for on the label. "Bottled by" and "cellared by" are usually indications that the firm whose name is on the bottle did not make the wine, whereas "produced by" means maker and bottler are one and the same. The French phrase "Mis en bouteille à la propriété" or "au château" means the maker bottled his own wine. "Erzeugerabfüllung" means the same in German, and "Imbottigliato all'origine" in Italian. (You don't really need to be a linguist to enjoy wines, but it sure doesn't hurt.)

But for imported wines, perhaps your best guarantee is the reputation of the importing firm. The importer's name is usually somewhere on the label. Reliable names to look for include Robert Chadderdon, Kermit Lynch, Frank Schoonmaker, Frederick Wildman, Wine Imports. There are also European firms that select and represent wines to importers who consistently pick top-quality wines—like Canaan and Wasserman for French wines and Neil Empson for Italian. And especially for imported wines your local merchant is a guarantee of quality. Many of them make regular visits to European vineyards (it's a rough life), sample the wines, and make their selections of the best wines to sell. You benefit from their direct experience.

• *Stocking the Frugal Wine Cellar* •

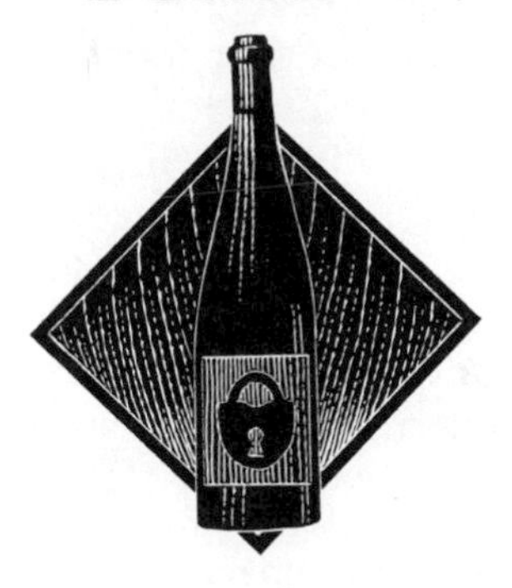

A "wine cellar" is not a snobbish luxury for the elite—it is as essential for the value-minded cook as a well-stocked larder. A varied wine collection allows you to have the right wine on hand for any occasion; it gives you the opportunity to buy wines when they are on sale for future use; it lets you educate your palate and expand your wine knowledge as you sample different wines.

The requirements for a place to keep your stash of wine are simple—a dark, dry environment of stable temperature. It is true that wine seems to keep and age best at a cool temperature (55° is traditional), but a warmer temperature is OK, so long as it doesn't get too hot or fluctuate a whole lot. A closet is fine. The wines should be laid on their sides, mainly so that the cork stays in contact with the wine and doesn't dry out and allow air to enter the bottle. If you can't lay the bottles on their sides and are planning to keep them for a while, then put them in a wine case upside down (this is how they're shipped), and they should last well.

AGING WINE

Today the vast majority of wines, even those like Italian Barolo or French Châteauneuf-du-Pape (which used to be almost undrinkable under ten years of age) are made for relatively young consumption, made in a lighter, fruitier, less tannic and alcoholic style. I suppose this is all to the good, since few of us have the patience or the wealth to accumulate a lot of wines for aging. Still, it is a pleasure to be able to lay down an occasional bottle, and one that can be very rewarding.

There are few white wines that will age well. Almost all domestic whites, from Riesling to Chardonnay, are best drunk within three or four years of the vintage—after this they begin to lose their fruit and become oxidized. French whites do rather better, but, except for dessert wines like Sauternes or the great whites of Burgundy, are also best within five years of their birth. Even vintage champagne should not be left much past ten years after vintage. Italian whites are best enjoyed in their fresh youth. Fine, sweet German Rieslings will age well, gradually losing their fruit but gaining a sort of nutty, oily elegance. But lesser wines are for drinking now.

The story is slightly different for red wines. In these the natural acid and tannin content acts as preservative and allows longer life. (It seems a general rule that the tarter a wine, red or white, in its youth, the better it will age.) But again, even red wine is increasingly made in a style that demands prompt drinking. Light, grapey wines like French Beaujolais or California Gamay, Zinfandel, Italian Dolcetto, Barbera, young Chianti—these wines, full of delicious strawberry, raspberry, or cherry flavors, sometimes (in the case of the Italians) with a slight spritz, are candidates for present enjoyment. Age robs them of their zest.

For wines to age, look to the traditional deep-colored, full-flavored reds. French Bordeaux, expensive Burgundy, northern Rhône wine, California Cabernet, Merlot, heavy Zinfandel, Italian Barolo, Barbaresco, Chianti Riserva, Spanish Rioja Reserva—these are the bottles that will reward careful storage for five to ten years (or more) and be transformed into softer, more elegant, more complex wines.

Port, of course, is the ultimate aging wine—but only true vintage port (an increasing rarity), which will age very nicely for fifty years or so and is really only decent after fifteen. (If you want to follow an English tradition, buy a bottle of the vintage of a child's birth and give it to her or him at the twenty-first birthday.)

Part of the pleasure in aging wine is the individual personality that each bottle develops. Wines do not age uniformly, and often a charming youth is followed by an awkward and even bitter adolescence (after the wine loses its fresh fruitiness but before it acquires any bottle elegance), finally redeemed by a vigorous but well-rounded maturity and gracious old age. A full-bodied, peppery Côtes du Rhône I well recall, which was splendid when young, turned suddenly hard and unforthcoming. I had abandoned my remaining couple of bottles, but a year or so later was persuaded by a friend to open one up—lo and behold the flavors had reemerged in a softer style. And I recently sampled a ten-year-old inexpensive California Cabernet that I figured was long gone—but no, though faded, its fruit and slight oakiness were still there to be enjoyed. It's this sort of unforeseen pleasure that makes a modest wine cellar a delight.

WINE CATEGORIES

Very Dry, Light Whites: Alsatian Riesling, Frascati, Italian Chardonnay, Muscadet, Pinot Blanc, Soave, Verdicchio, Vernaccia. These wines are characterized by their fresh, tart, subtle flavors. They go very well with lightly flavored dishes, especially many seafoods, light pasta dishes, vegetables, and soups.

The value-oriented wine lover will do well to explore the world of Italian wines. Italian reds have had a high reputation for years, but not so Italian whites, which were traditionally made in a heavy, oxidized style with much too much wood flavoring. But the Italians have taken a page from California's book and have started using modern wine-making techniques emphasizing the fresh fruit flavors of their grapes, and the results are impressive.

For many Americans, Italian white means Soave, a simple, inexpensive white that is a best seller in the United States. Soave has an unremarkable flavor—a neutral, slightly earthy quality—but it is a wine that slips down easily and goes nicely with a variety of light foods. A wine similar in character is Frascati, a Roman wine that is light, just off-dry, and has a pleasant aroma. Great with fettuccine. Verdicchio is another one—crisp, light, slightly flowery. This latter wine comes in fish-shaped bottles that suggest, correctly, that it is nice with light seafoods. Vernaccia di San Gimignano is yet another one, and perhaps the best of the lot, with lovely wildflower aromas. All these wines are in the under-$5 category, so it's hard to go wrong with them.

More interesting yet are the many new Italian Chardonnays. Chardonnay lovers who expect a full-bodied, oaky wine will be surprised—these wines are fairly light, tart, with lovely wildflower scents and little or no wood flavor. They, too, are great seafood wines, but also go nicely with many light foods. The Chardonnays of the giant Casarsa cooperative are quite pleasant, but the best come from small producers in the Italian northeast, like Plozner, Zeni, Pojer e Sandri, EnoFriulia. None of these should cost much more than $5, which makes them about the best bargain in Chardonnay available.

Dry, Full-Flavored Whites: Aligote, Alsatian Gewürztraminer, Chablis, Chardonnay, Graves, Macon, Orvieto, Pinot Gris (Tokay d'Alsace), Pouilly-Fuissé, Pouilly-Fumé, Sancerre, Sauvignon Blanc, Semillon, white Burgundy. Also dry, these wines often have more fruit and more body, with accompanying complexity. They will go nicely with a wide range of full-flavored but not sweet or spicy dishes, from rich fish to poultry and game, to light meats and quiche. A few (like Gewürztraminer) work nicely with Chinese cuisine as well.

Let me put in a plug here for the neglected wines of Alsace. It's a poorly understood region, probably because its wines are not quite French and not quite German. The grape varieties grown here are much the same as in Germany—Riesling, Gewürztraminer, Sylvaner—but the style is very different—completely dry, strong-flavored, often rather alcoholic. The best wines usually come from Gewürztraminer or Pinot Gris (also called Tokay d'Alsace), both with rich, rather spicy flavors. They can be real heavyweights and are a nice alternative to a rich white Burgundy, at a fraction of the cost—usually $5–$10.

Gewürztraminer in particular is a wine that works well with foods that other wines can't deal with. A spicy paella, duck with ginger, garlic chicken—any dish with strong, unusual flavors is a candidate for Gewürz. It is also excellent with rich fish, like salmon. And it has a special affinity for sausage and spicy meats. It has the staying power to match up to these. But remember, we're talking about French Gewürztraminer—the California version is a very different wine, sweet and rather flowery. Names to look for include Hugel, Trimbach, Leon Beyer, Lorentz, and Koenig, as well as a number of smaller producers. These wines age well, too.

Pouilly-Fuissé caught the American imagination a decade or so ago. It's hard to know why, unless it was the lovely name, because the wine, though quite pleasant, is nothing special and is now usually overpriced. But the other wines of the Maconnais, made from the Chardonnay grape (and sometimes labeled as Pinot Chardonnay), are often fine value. Unlike California Chardonnays or the big, expensive white Burgundies, Macon whites are medium-bodied, crisp, fruity, with soft flowery flavors. Versatile in use, from oysters to chicken to many vegetable dishes, they range in price from $5 to $8. There are many producers—Louis Latour and Georges Duboeuf are two large and consistent ones.

Slightly Sweet, Fruity Whites: Chenin Blanc, German whites, Johannisberg Riesling, Vouvray. Fresh fruit flavors mark these wines, the best of which also have good acidity. Despite their reputation as "sipping" wines, they can accompany a number of foods—those with somewhat rich or spicy ingredients.

This is a category full of wonderful values. Why? Because the fashion in the last decade has been "dry" wines, which are supposed to be more sophisticated. When the smart set talks wine, they talk Chardonnay. When was the last time you overheard a chic conversation about German Rieslings? But the truth is that many fruity, slightly sweet whites are just what people love to drink.

Vouvray is a deliciously versatile wine. It is both slightly sweet and quite tart at the same time, with an underlying honey flavor, and it works well with anything with a rich sauce—dishes cooked with Marsala, for example. With Vouvray, as with so many wines, it's worth it to spend a dollar or so more to get the good stuff—Monmousseau and Wildman are consistently good, right around $5. The American equivalent is Chenin Blanc, which is the name of the grape. California Chenin Blanc has never had much to recommend it, being often heavy and dull. But Chenin Blanc from Washington State is making its mark—with a fresh liveliness that begins to approach the French standard. Look for names like Hogue Cellars, Quail Run, Worden's, and Château Ste. Michelle, all in the $5 range.

German Rieslings remain some of the best bargains on the wine market. Forget all the wines with animals and religious figures on the label—the premium wines, beginning at the "Qualitätswein" level are so much better. Mosel and Rheingau wines are the best, but many producers from Rheinpfalz and Nahe are also making good wine these days. It's difficult to single out particular wines—there are so many villages and producers, but the level of consistency is high. If you don't like the sweetness of the regular bottlings, look for "Trocken" (meaning "dry") or "Halbtrocken" wines. In any case, the fruit of these Rieslings is balanced with crisp acidity, so they go nicely with foods that combine some sweetness and tartness—they can cut right through a confit or mustard flavors or garlic.

Sweet, Full-Bodied Whites: German Spätlese or Auslese, Late Harvest Riesling or Gewürztraminer, Muscat, Sauternes, St. Croix du Mont. These wines are sweet, with lots of flavor, but not so heavy as many full-blown dessert wines. Fruit and cheese are the best accompaniment for these wines, though you can do some unusual pairings with some very rich foods as well.

Muscat suffers from guilt by association—its name is too close to Muscatel, the horrible, cheap California stuff. Real Muscat comes in several varieties (Canelli, Alexandria, Ottonel), is extremely aromatic, and makes a lovely sweet, pungent wine, which can serve for dessert or accompany fruit and cheese. Good California examples include Quady "Elysium," Mondavi, and Sutter Home. The Northwest is also making some nice examples: Château Ste. Michelle, Paul Thomas, Arbor Crest. Most of these are good values in the $5–$10 range. The Australians make excellent fortified Muscats (really a different beast)—strong, rich, exotic fruit-flavored wines meant for sipping.

Fruity, Light Reds: Bardolino, Beaujolais, Gamay, Chianti, Italian Merlot, light Pinot Noir or red Burgundy, Valpolicella, light Zinfandel. It is the style, not necessarily the grape, that makes this category—an emphasis on very fresh, berrylike flavors, light tannin, good acidity. These wines can be served chilled and work well with flavorful, somewhat spicy, but perhaps not too serious dishes—sausage, pasta, ham, meatballs.

The technique called carbonic maceration, which is used to make the fruity red wines of the Beaujolais, is now being used by wine makers in other parts of the world. In this technique, the grapes are fermented whole and uncrushed in an oxygen-free environment, which somehow accents the fresh and fruity quality of the wine. The wines are wonderfully grapey, light and refreshing, and rarely age very well. They make terrific picnic wines, with cured meats and sandwiches. They are also splendid sausage wines, standing up nicely to all but the very spiciest of sausage (for which you'll want a heavier red).

Beaujolais is not as cheap as it used to be, but good Villages wine is still available at not much more than $5. Some good names to look for are Georges Duboeuf, Latour, and Bedin. (The Nouveaus or Primeurs that come out in November have shot up in price and are rarely worth it.) In California, Gamay or Gamay Beaujolais is usually made in this same style, though not quite as tart. The aforenamed Georges Duboeuf, Robert Pecota, Charles Shaw, and Parducci are among the nice examples, all around $5. But Zinfandel is now being made in the same way, too—Joseph Phelps being a good example. Even the Italians are getting into the act—Gaja makes a fruity wine called Vinòt using this same technique.

Medium-Body Reds: "Cru Bourgeois" Bordeaux, red Burgundy, Dolcetto, Nebbiolo, Pinot Noir, Rioja or Torres red, Rosso Toscano, South American Cabernet or Merlot, Spanna. The differences between the wines in this category and the next is often not the grape but the style. The wines in this group are made from many of the classic red wine grapes (Cabernet Sauvignon, Pinot Noir, Nebbiolo, etc.) but have less tannin, less body, often less alcohol than their "heftier" cousins. But they often have very nice complexity and richness of fruit, usually some oak aging. They are excellent wines for short-term drinking and accompany a whole range of foods, from poultry to soufflés to red meats to casseroles. Many people are perfectly content with these reds and don't much care for the heavyweights.

Bordeaux is for many red-wine lovers the standard wine. It is certainly the most plentiful, high-quality red wine in France—and for some that means the world. Unfortunately, the best Bordeaux are ridiculously expensive now. A top "cru" or growth that cost $10 twenty years ago is now $50 or $100. Talk about inflation! So forget Château Lafite or Mouton—there are lots of good "cru bourgeois" from the Médoc (the heart of the area) or good-quality wines from surrounding districts (Fronsac, Bourg, Blaye), all made from the same grapes in varying combinations: Cabernet Sauvignon, Merlot, Cabernet Franc.

The best cru bourgeois will be plenty good for most people and have the advantage that they are ready to drink more quickly. Châteaux like Gloria, Chasse-Spleen, Greysac, Latour de By, Latour St. Bonnet, and Larose-Trintaudon, all in the $8–$10 range, have plenty of the complex berry-herbal-oaky flavors and the delicate Bordeaux bouquet that develop over time. These are classic meat wines, serving lamb, beef, and pork equally well.

The red wines of the enormous Torres firm in Spain, as well as many red wines of the Rioja region, provide even less expensive alternatives to Bordeaux. The Torres Coronas line, from the simple Coronas at about $3 to the marvelous Black Label Reserve at about $12, are well-made, elegant wines. Riojas have the advantage over Bordeaux that many older reserve bottlings are readily available, and wines from firms like Berberana, La Rioja Alta, Tondonia, and Olarra in the $5–$10 range can be exceptionally good.

Full-Body, Tannic Reds: Amarone, Australian Cabernet Sauvignon or Shiraz, Barbera, Barolo, Barbaresco, California Cabernet Sauvignon and Merlot, Châteauneuf-du-Pape, Chianti Riserva, classed-growth Bordeaux, Côtes du Rhône, Côte Rotie, Hermitage, Petite Sirah, Zinfandel. These are the big boys, the red wines deep and dark in color, dense with flavor and tannin, requiring aging in wood cask and bottle to develop their marvelous bouquets and smooth complexities. Game, roast or barbecued meats, full-flavored cheeses, spicy casseroles—all cry out for one of these wines. With the proper accompaniment they become very gentle giants indeed. They are quintessential food wines—not for sipping.

Zinfandel is the workhorse red grape of California, but most of it is going into fairly insipid "white Zinfandel." Try the real stuff; dark purple, alcoholic, intensely fruity Zinfandel is a treat. There are lots of good producers of low-cost Zin, from $4 to $6, like Parducci, Fetzer, Sebastiani, Pedroncelli, Sutter Home, Santino, and even a few producers of "serious" Zinfandel, like Storybook Mountain, Lytton Springs, Château Montelena, Ridge, whose wines will match up well to Cabernet, at two-thirds the cost.

The Rhône Valley of France is a wonderful source of full-bodied red wines at reasonable prices. Côtes du Rhône, especially from one of the top firms like Guigal or Jaboulet, has deep, peppery flavors that can match up to spicy, hearty dishes. Even the best of these is no more than $6 or so.

Rosés and "Blush" Wines: Rosé of Cabernet or Grenache or Merlot, Rosé d'Anjou, Pinot Noir Blanc, Tavel, Vin Gris, White Zinfandel. These wines, though quite varied in appearance and style, share the common characteristic of being lightly colored wines made from red grapes. They vary from light and dry to rather dark-colored and quite sweet, but in any case are fresh, fruity, simple. Usually served chilled, they are ideal picnic wines and accompany smoked or spicy meats like ham, salami, etc. better than just about anything else. *Not* wines for every occasion, they nevertheless have their place.

White Zinfandel is not one of my favorite wines—it is so often dull. But there are good producers of the stuff, like Ridge, Santino, Marietta. A more interesting wine for my money is Rosé of Cabernet, which has fruit flavors and good body—Simi, Field Stone, Château Ste. Michelle have nice examples, all around $5. In the same league is Pinot Noir Blanc (also called Vin Gris), with good ones coming both from California, e.g., Edna Valley, and Oregon, e.g., Tualatin.

Sparkling: California "Champagne," French Champagne, German Sekt, Italian Spumante, Spanish Cava. These vary dramatically in taste and quality, but all have bubbles, and all get served on fancy or festive occasions. It is not true that champagne goes with everything—it is not that great with delicately flavored foods, for example. But at the beginning or end of a meal, with zesty flavored appetizers or not-too-heavy desserts, it does very nicely. (See champagne article.)

Aperitif: Sherry—Fino, Amontillado, Olorosa; Sercial Madeira, Marsala. These dark-colored, strong-flavored wines, which can be anything from perfectly dry and rather light to sweet and heavy, have been famous for centuries for stimulating the appetite and preparing the palate. As such, they are really meant to be drunk by themselves, though a dry sherry is the perfect accompaniment to very salty appetizers that other wines can't deal with. Sherry is not much served anymore (the ubiquitous and often atrocious "glass of white wine" is the pallid substitute), but an experienced host or hostess knows that a small glass of sherry placed in the hand of a hungry guest has an almost immediate relaxing and vivifying effect. The best wines for this purpose are the driest—Fino or Amontillado—but some will swear by cream sherry, too.

Good sherry is not expensive—it is worth getting the real, Spanish stuff. Sandeman, Don Tomás, Gonzalez Byass, Domecq, Harvey are good names to look for, and expect to pay $7 to $8 for top-quality wine. Remember, the bottle will last awhile.

Strong-Flavored Dessert: Commandaria, Malmsey Madeira, sweet Muscat, Port—Ruby, Tawny, Vintage, Setubal, Tokaj Aszu, Vin Santo. Sweet, fortified wines can be either from red or white grapes. In either case, the flavors are dense, strong, rich, at best complex as well. All pack an alcoholic punch. They are probably best sipped by themselves at the end of a meal, as they definitely dominate the palate. But cheese, nuts, even chocolate may prove sturdy enough partners to enjoy them with.

I confess to being a port nut—but only the real stuff. There is lots of cheap, sweet California wine that calls itself port and has as much resemblance to the drink from Portugal as Madonna does to Marlene Dietrich. But there are some good California ports from small firms, often using the Zinfandel grape. Most are in the $5 to $10 range. Reliable producers are Ficklin, Quady, and J. W. Morris.

Portuguese port comes in several different styles—all of them sweet, but with the sweetness balanced by a spicy, peppery quality. Fruitiest (and least expensive at $5 to $7) is ruby port. Tawny port, which is aged in wood for years, is lighter, smoother, nuttier. And vintage port, which is expensive but worth it, is a marvelous, fiery drink that requires years to mellow out. Like Bordeaux, this is a wine made popular by the English, and most of the great port houses have English names: Sandeman, Dow, Taylor-Fladgate, Warre, Graham, and Fonseca are among the ones to look for.

BEGINNING A CELLAR

When you're beginning your modest wine collection, what you put in it will depend on a variety of factors: the wines you prefer, the foods you eat, availability of wine in your area, how much you want to spend, how long you're planning to live (my mother, whose cellar I supply, is not interested in wines that will be "ready" in 1997). So the following guidelines are necessarily general, trying to cover a broad range of tastes, and emphasizing, as always, good value.

Let's suppose you have space or money for only twelve bottles of wine—what should they be? The possibilities are numerous, but let me suggest a broadly representative list—one bottle of each.

German Mosel or Rheingau, Kabinett level (Riesling)
French Vouvray or Northwest Chenin Blanc
Italian Soave or Verdicchio or Vernaccia or Frascati
California Sauvignon Blanc (Fumé Blanc) or French Graves
California or Northwest Chardonnay or French Macon
French Beaujolais or California Gamay

French red Bordeaux, Cru Bourgeois or California Cabernet Sauvignon
French red Burgundy or Oregon Pinot Noir
California Zinfandel or Petite Sirah
Italian Chianti or Spanish red Rioja
Spanish Dry Fino Sherry
French Champagne, Spanish Cava, or premium California sparkling wine

With this list you should be ready for just about any eventuality, whether you're serving fresh halibut (Sauvignon Blanc) or pasta (Chianti) or barbecued beef (Pinot Noir) or fruit and cheese (Mosel). (If you want a dessert wine, substitute a port or sweet Muscat for something on this list.) Good examples of all these wines are available for less than $10, though better ones may cost a good deal more. And all of these should be pretty readily available. You can see that you have an option in some cases between a foreign and domestic wine—as they are roughly equivalent, what you choose may depend on price or availability in your area.

Now let's suppose you want to expand a bit, lay down a few more bottles. We will make our intermediate cellar thirty-six bottles, three cases, an arbitrary number, but one that most people should be able to manage and that will afford a good measure of variety.

If you should go out and buy the three cases all at once, at an average price of, say, $7 a bottle (which is quite generous), we're talking about $250 for your wine. The price of a new TV or compact disc player—but easier to maintain and unlikely to be stolen. If you are just developing an interest in wines, however, I encourage you *not* to go out and buy caseloads of wine right away. As your tastes develop they will change and you will be stuck with wines you don't really want. Build your cellar slowly: Remember, wine is not like gold or diamonds—they make more of it every year.

Let's start with the basic whites. In my cellar I probably keep about a tenth the number of white wines that I do reds. And not just because I am a red-wine lover. Most whites are meant to be drunk young and expire after four or five years—there is simply no point in keeping them around. So, in our beginning cellar I would suggest perhaps a dozen whites, depending on your tastes.

For sipping wines you will want a couple of bottles of good German Riesling, Northwest Riesling, or Chenin Blanc. From the better German vintages (like 1983) it is worth investing in a bottle or two of Kabinett, Spätlese, or Auslese level wines, because they will age rather nicely and develop some complexity. A bottle or two of Vouvray (or good Chenin Blanc) is also a wise investment.

For drier whites, a bottle or two of Muscadet, Verdicchio, or Frascati should cover the light seafood requirements. Then you should have several bottles of good-quality Chardonnay or Sauvignon Blanc (French Macon, Chablis, or Burgundy, or Graves) for stronger flavored seafood and a whole variety of other foods. Be careful with these. Many California white wines are wonderful when quite young, but fall apart in a year or two because of their lack of acid. The French and Italian wines hold up much better, and their natural tartness makes them excellent with seafood.

I also urge a bottle of Gewürztraminer (preferably Alsatian) to be kept on hand, because it goes so nicely with many spicy dishes that other wines won't work with.

On to the reds. Let's deal first with some wines to buy and sock away, wines for the future. The classics are the best for this purpose—Cru Bourgeois Bordeaux, California Cabernet or Merlot, red Burgundy, Italian Barolo or Barbaresco. Find several bottles of a good vintage and plan to keep them for five to ten years—you will be amazed at how they reward you. I find it's most fun if I have at least several bottles of the same wine that I want to age. That way I can open a bottle every couple of years and see how it is progressing and enjoy it from youth to old age (not mine, the wine's). It is, of course, possible to buy older wines in a wineshop, but the prices are generally exorbitant—the time to buy a wine like this is when it's first released (usually two to four years after vintage) and therefore more abundant.

Now for the wines for current or near-term drinking. There are loads of light, fresh, fruity reds on the market—everything from inexpensive California Cabernets to Beaujolais to Italian Dolcetto or Merlot. You don't really need more than a couple of wines in this category, since they are best when young and fresh.

But you may want a good supply of medium-body reds with some character, because they go so well with so many different foods, including pasta, meat, poultry, even soup. Inexpensive Bordeaux or Burgundy, Italian Chianti, Spanish Rioja will meet your needs here. You can afford to stock up on these, as they are not expensive, and while they may not develop a lot in bottle, they will hold their own. I would say at least six bottles here, in a nice variety.

The heartier reds should also be represented—wines like Zinfandel, Côtes du Rhône, Australian reds, Barbera. These spicy wines will go nicely with your lasagne, or bean casserole, or even pizza. These, too, will age reasonably well, though many people prefer them in their youth when the fruity, berry flavors are strongest. I would suggest four to six bottles.

In addition to these reds and whites, there are some special-purpose wines to have on hand. (I do not include rosé among these, unless you're a real rosé fan. I find that I serve rosé not very often—better to go out and get a bottle when you need it.) A bottle of sherry is a necessity—actually, I keep cheap sherry to cook with and a nice, dry sherry to serve before a meal. You might prefer a sweeter style. Sherry, like many strong wines, will last pretty much forever unopened and even when uncorked deteriorates very slowly. A bottle or two of some kind of dessert wine—Late Harvest Riesling, Sauternes, port, Madeira, Muscat, etc. should also find a place in your cellar. Many of these (Sauternes, Late Harvest Riesling) will benefit from aging and allow you to enjoy a treat you can't buy in a store. But many dessert wines, like ruby or tawny port, are made to be drunk when they are released—no aging is necessary.

Last, but perhaps most, there is champagne. You never know when you may need a good bottle of bubbly—a promotion, winning the lottery, having friends drop by—and one bottle often leads to another, so I always keep at least a couple. (But don't keep them too long.)

Keep reviewing your cellar—watch what tends to get used most often, and what seems to keep sitting there. And if you find there's some wine you're just not drinking, remember—there's always Christmas. It's bound to be someone's favorite.

CHAMPAGNE: ALL THAT SPARKLES IS NOT "CHAMPAGNE"

In customary usage in this country, the term "champagne" has come to mean any sparkling white wine. This makes French blood boil, because to them champagne is a national treasure—a high-quality sparkling wine made in a very limited area of northern France from Chardonnay and Pinot Noir grapes. The best sparkling wine is always "méthode champenoise" or "champagne method," a labor-intensive process that uses a secondary fermentation after the wine has been bottled to produce the bubbles. These bubbles, very fine and long-lasting, burst from the wine when it is sipped and do wonderful things with one's nose and taste buds.

Most of the sparkling wine made in this country is made using the "bulk" or "charmat" process, which makes the bubbles in large, pressurized tanks before the wine is bottled. The wine produced is perfectly drinkable, but the bubbles are not the same. The French, with typical haughtiness, call these bubbles "toad's eyes" because they are so large. The effect is not the same, but bulk sparkling wine is much cheaper to produce. Cheap "champagne" also uses lesser grapes than Chardonnay and Pinot Noir, so the flavors are often pretty dull.

There are good sparkling wines being made in this country,

by traditional champagne methods, often called "Blanc de Blanc" or "Blanc de Noir." Domaine Chandon, Schramsberg, Korbel, Hanns Kornell, Shadow Creek are some of the top producers, at prices ranging from $10 to $15. But the best values in "champagne method" wines come from Spain and are called "Cavas." They don't have the same flavor as the French ones, but the bubbles are just as prolific and the price compares favorably with many cheap California sparklers, often as low as $4. Names to look for include Codorniu, Freixenet (the two biggies), Segura Viudas, Monistrol.

Other countries also produce sparkling wines. We occasionally see a little German Sekt, made from Riesling grapes. And we see a lot of Italian spumante. Spumante just means "sparkling," so an Italian spumante may be made from anything. But the most popular ones, Asti Spumante, from the Italian northwest, are from the Muscat grape. Made in the bulk method, they can nevertheless be very fine, with rich, slightly sweet, applelike flavors.

Champagne terminology can be confusing. There are varying grades of sweetness, from "Very Dry," which is the *sweetest* grade we usually see in this country, to "Brut," to "Naturel," which is the very driest. When most people talk about "dry" champagne, they're talking about brut. Vintage champagne is very fine but very expensive—a better value is the nonvintage blend that most firms produce, which at holiday times gets down to around $15. And true rosé champagne, not that common, is delicious.

A JUG OF WINE

"Jug" wine has probably done more to promote the idea of wine as an everyday drink for the table than anything else in this country. We are indeed blessed in having an enormous wine-producing area in the hot valleys of California that can deliver to us a cornucopia of grapes for making into inexpensive table wines. And in fact, the quality level of this American "vin ordinaire" is generally superior to that of most European countries.

On the other hand, much of the "Chablis," "Burgundy," and "Rhine" wine sold is pretty dull stuff. Not awful, just dull. A good jug wine should be fresh and fruity, "cleanly" made, with no peculiar or chemical odors. It should be balanced in sweetness and tartness. It should not be too heavy or harsh but should not taste like water either. It should be able to accompany food, and it should be pleasant enough that you can drink more than one glass.

Sadly, there are a number of California jug wines that do not meet these criteria. Some are possessed of a ghastly sweetness that will cloy the least discriminating of palates. Some are so earthy and vegetal that you wonder who put the cabbage and dill in them.

Some taste unripe, some like cleanser. It's sad, especially because for some people this is their only experience of wine, and having tried one of these they decide that wine is not for them.

But there are some decent jugs out there, put out by California's enormous wineries. "Chablis" usually designates a fairly (though not totally) dry white wine—some nice examples are Gallo Chablis Blanc, a reliable old-timer, and Colony Classic Chablis. "Rhine" wine is almost always sweeter, sometimes quite sweet, with varying degrees of fruit. Almadén Mountain Rhine and Carlo Rossi Rhine are decent examples for those who like that style. "Burgundy" is red wine that can be in any of a wide variety of styles, from rather sweet and dull to dry and herbal. Colony Classic Burgundy is reliable, as is Almadén Mountain Burgundy, with Gallo's Hearty Burgundy a good example in the sweeter, softer style.

One would think that varietal jugs, named after single grape types, would be superior wines, but that isn't necessarily the case. Much French Colombard is quite dull, and much Cabernet Sauvignon is quite vegetal. The blends are often superior and less expensive.

There are also some "premium" jug wines—in the same large-bottle format, but selling for a dollar or two more. Often these wines, made by wineries that also produce premium varietal wines, are considerably better than the standard jugs. Robert Mondavi, Parducci, and Fetzer are some good names to look for.

There is a definite role for jug wine. We don't always want, nor can we afford, to open a nice bottle of wine for every meal. Often we just want a simple glass of wine to relax with. So, sure, keep a bottle of red and white on hand if you like—it's always useful for pouring into the pot, in any case.

But you may find just as good value in the long run by experimenting with French "Zip Code" wines (blends by big French exporters identifiable only by their Zip Code number on the bottle), or lesser-known wines from countries like Italy, Spain, Argentina, Chile, Romania, Yugoslavia. Don't expect these bargain wines to be Chardonnay or Cabernet in disguise, but often they provide very good everyday drinking.

A word, too, about wines in a box. The bottle and cork are so traditional for wine that it seems very strange indeed to buy wine in a vacuum-sealed box with a spigot on the side—I'm sure people once thought the same about milk in a box. But there are some real advantages to this form of packaging. Inside the box, the wine is in a collapsible plastic bag that doesn't affect the flavor but will protect the wine from spoiling because of contact with the air. This means you can buy a large amount of wine at an inexpensive price, stick it in your refrigerator, and use it glass by glass at your convenience. There is no need to finish the bottle, so the box may promote more moderate use of wine. It is easier to store, and it is easier to carry around. So far most wine in boxes has been typical jug stuff, but if boxes prove successful, look for higher-grade wines to appear this way.

• On Tasting Wine and Wine Tastings •

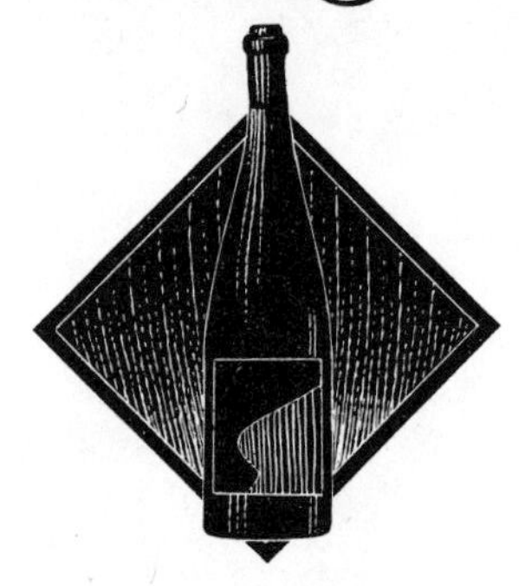

The value of the nose as an instrument is immeasurably enhanced by another tool that most of us have in good working order—the memory. Brain experts tell us that the sense of smell has a more or less direct line to the brain. Smell is our oldest sensory organ, it is most nearly connected to our instincts and involuntary reactions (ever felt your stomach beginning to work when you walk into a savory-smelling kitchen?), it is the last sense to fail us at death. Our memory for smells is very good—I don't remember much about high school chemistry, but the odors I can recall vividly, and when I smell them on occasion today, images of chemistry lab come pouring out. It is this ability to identify smells from memory—"That's the smell of the sea!" or "I smell fresh apple pie" or "That's my grandmother's perfume"—that allows us to sort out and identify the aromas of various wines. The process of tasting and comparing wines over time really involves storing our sensory memory bank with a mass of data that will help us, literally, "make sense" of what we drink.

HOW DO I DO IT?

To "taste" or evaluate an individual wine involves three basic elements: color, aroma, and taste. It is true that what the wine looks like does not affect its flavor, but color is the first clue to a wine's condition. A poorly colored wine is likely to have "off" flavors, just as a green piece of meat or a black tomato is likely to harbor essential defects. This is why wine is best poured into a crystal-clear glass—older-style colored wineglasses were often meant precisely to disguise defective wine. And make sure there is sufficient light (not fluorescent) so you can really see it. Take a good look at the wine. It should be quite clear, without any cloudiness. (Older red wines, particularly those made in traditional fashion, may be slightly cloudy without being bad, while some white wines will deposit whitish tartrate crystals that don't affect flavor.)

A young white wine should be a pale yellow or straw color, perhaps with a bit of green. If a white wine is deeply yellow or gold it has probably oxidized and may not be very appetizing (unless it's a sweet wine like Sauternes or German Auslese, in which case it's just right). A young red wine should be somewhere between bright red and purple and may be quite dark. The darker the wine, the heavier and, perhaps, rougher it will be. An older red will be more of a brick color, with brown or orange hues around the edges. If a red wine is brown all through, it, too, is probably oxidized. (Again, there are exceptions, like tawny port, which should be a sort of mahogany color.)

Having determined that the color is OK, you need to get your nose inside the glass and take a strong whiff of the stuff. To make sure that the aromas of the wine are being released, swirl it in its glass. Glasses that are tulip or bowl shaped, with a narrow opening at the top are best for this, because they concentrate the aromas at nose level—and they shouldn't be filled more than halfway, or you won't be able to swirl or get your nose in. A couple of deep whiffs will allow you really to smell the wine.

The more exotic a description you can attach to a wine, the better you will remember it. I well recall a wine I tried many years ago that smelled exactly like hamburger that had lain forgotten in the refrigerator for several weeks. Not one of my favorites. Yet another wine has, to me, such an unmistakable smell of a fresh, red rose that I cannot see a bottle of the stuff without thinking about my garden. When you can attach this kind of sensory label to a wine (and the more you sample, the easier this becomes) you will not only find it easy to recall its flavor, but you will more easily make an appropriate match with food.

Trust your own nose. If someone tells you a wine reminds him of spring wildflowers, that's fine. But if you smell moldering compost, that's how you should remember it. Don't be bashful—you have to live with your own nose.

Taking an actual sip of the wine is the last step—one that should confirm what your nose has already told you. When you sip, swirl the wine around with your tongue, and if it's appropriate (probably not at a formal dinner party), suck some air in with the wine and gurgle a bit—the more contact with air, the more the flavors come out. With your tongue you can measure the sweetness and tartness of the wine—whether dry or sweet, these should be in balance, neither cloying nor puckery. The alcohol should also be noticeable, providing a feeling of weight and perhaps some bite (though a wine that is obviously alcoholic is not so good). And if it's a red wine, the tannin will give a feeling of roughness or grittiness in the mouth—the same feeling you get when chewing on grape seeds. This, too, provides a sensation of "body" in the wine but should not be too harsh.

When you swallow, what sensation does the wine leave in your mouth? Is there a peculiar aftertaste, or perhaps none at all? Do you find yourself reaching for a glass of water? In what the experts call the "finish," there should be an overall sense of pleasure and harmony and an aftertaste that lingers and invites you to another sip.

Your overall impression of the wine is the most important point. Unless it brings a smile to your face and lets you think that perhaps the world is a fine place after all, it has not done its job. Trust your first impression—it's likely to be the right one.

THE WINE TASTING

If you taste a number of, say, white wines over a period of time, you may recall their all tasting rather alike. If you taste them all at the same time, side by side, you will readily distinguish the differences and be able, I hope, to store those away in memory. This is the point of a wine tasting. Professionals may taste and compare fifty wines a day, but most of us will be overtaxed if we have to do more than fifteen or twenty. Six to twelve is probably an ideal number.

If you're going to taste wine, you need not only the wines, but need a congenial group of fellow tasters, not only to help consume the wine but to provide the stimulus of their own sensations and flavor associations. Fortunately, I have never had any particular difficulty recruiting folk to taste wine with—it's much easier than persuading them, say, to help you move or to paint the house. A dozen or so people with even a modest interest in wine is sufficient for a very pleasant evening of sipping.

WHAT TO SERVE AT A WINE TASTING

You *cannot* have it all—not all at the same time, anyway. You cannot do justice to the evaluation of wine and enjoy wonderful, flavorful food simultaneously. The reason, of course, is that food changes the flavor of the wine, which after all it's supposed to. So what to serve at a wine tasting to sustain the body without wrecking the palate.

The traditional prescription of bread and cheese is a good one, within limits. First, the bread should be plain—a French- or Italian-style loaf is best. It should not be too salty, as salt tends to dull the palate. Chewing on a bit of bread between glasses of wine performs a valuable service—it cleans the palate of wine flavors and prepares you to taste the next wine without being prejudiced by the previous one. (Water does the same thing, but I find that, particularly with strongly flavored wines, bread is best.)

Cheese makes a wonderful accompaniment to wine—but beware. Cheese is so good with wine that it tends to deceive one about the taste of the wine itself. And a strong-flavored and aromatic cheese—sharp Cheddar, blue cheese, even Swiss cheese—may cause you to miss a lot of subtle flavors in wine altogether, rather like visiting the Louvre with your sunglasses on. If you're going to serve cheese, then stick to the very mild, creamy ones—like Havarti, or mozzarella, or fresh goat cheese. These will provide enough stimulus to your taste buds to keep them going, without overwhelming them.

Now, of course, there are some exceptions, notably with dessert wines. A number of sweet, full-flavored dessert wines cry out for flavorful cheese to serve with them, even at a tasting. Sauternes and blue cheese is not only a combination created in heaven, but the cheese seems to draw out the flavors of the wine, which by themselves might be overwhelming. Something similar happens with vintage port, which softens and opens up with a nice, smelly cheese like stilton or very old cheddar. Here again, the wine itself can so easily stun the palate that it is helpful to have something to counterbalance it. Don't, incidentally, try to mix a tasting of dessert wines with dinner wines—your mouth will never forgive you.

WINE NOTES

If at the end of an evening of tasting, let us say, ten Chardonnays you can remember with precision the characteristics of each and how you would rank them, you are doing better than I. I find that if I don't make a few notes on each wine as I taste it, I just don't remember very well. Even an informal tasting, with lots of casual conversation and wandering around, should be able to accommodate note-taking. I do a couple of things. First, I write a few words to describe the color, aroma, and taste of each wine. For example: "dark purple, blackberries, bit of oak, tart, medium body." Second, I give it a score, using a simple five-point scale. With even a few words written down, I find it easy to recall the flavor of the wine even some time after I've tried it.

THE LANGUAGE OF WINE

There are a few terms most wine drinkers can agree on. Terms like "sweet," "tart," "fresh," "watery," "grapey," "tannic" are largely self-explanatory. There are a few more basics: "fruit" or "fruity" refers to whatever fruit the flavor may resemble, "dry" means not sweet, "soft" the absence of tartness or harshness, "body" (as in "full-bodied" or "light-bodied") refers to the feel of the wine on the tongue—is there a lot of stuff in it or not? "Big, fat, heavy" all refer to this sense of full body—"lean, thin" to the opposite. Wine with relatively high acid may be "crisp, refreshing" or "sour, biting." A high alcohol content may contribute to a wine's tasting "strong, rich, hot." Lots of tannin in red wine may make it "hard, harsh, coarse." "Balance, elegance, roundness" all refer to the wine's overall impression and how well the different parts, like sweetness and acid, fit together.

A NOTE ON "DRY" WINE

Beware the term "dry" when applied to wine. Most people these days tell me that they like their white wine "dry." I'm not sure what that means to them, but I do know that in blind tastings, most people prefer slightly sweet white wines to completely dry ones. In theory, "dry" means that all the sugar has been fermented out of the wine, so that all one tastes is the contrasting tartness, or acid. Dry does not mean better. It is simple to make a wine dry—I have tasted many wines that were indeed dry and wouldn't let me forget it. They were sharp and lip-puckering and would have been more at home in my salad dressing.

A touch of sweetness (and I'm talking about just a slight sweetness, not candylike) can be very beneficial to a white wine especially. First, in ordinary table wine, it gives a little added interest and flavor. I have rarely tasted a completely dry ordinary white table wine that didn't seem thin and watery. A little sugar plumps it up a bit. Second, in tart wines, a little sugar will give balance and harmony and make them more pleasant. Third, most of us just plain prefer a little sweetness.

• Surviving the Sommelier •

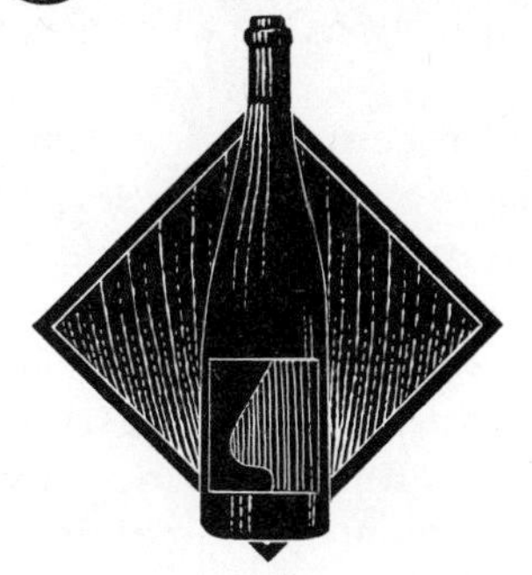

There are many fine restaurants that have experienced and knowledgeable wine stewards who are genuinely solicitous of the needs of customers and who provide welcome service in helping to select and serve wine. But the image of the imperious sommelier is too well entrenched not to have considerable truth in it. There is nothing you can do to change a fussy or know-it-all wine steward, but being prepared for the ritual of ordering wine should reduce your anxiety considerably and prevent it from being an ordeal.

The ordeal may begin with the arrival of the wine list, which is frequently too long, disorganized, and uninformative. A decent list will specify not only the type of wine but the producer and the vintage as well, since these make significant differences. I frequently annoy waiters by having them go to check the vintage of an undated wine, but I feel well within my rights. If you are feeling baffled by the list, ask the wine steward's advice—that's what he's there for. A good sommelier will inquire not only about what you are ordering for dinner but what your general tastes in wine are, and will then make several suggestions. If they are within your price range, make a selection, and you are set.

Don't be bashful about balking at the price of some bottle. I find it difficult to enjoy a wine I feel is out of my price range. You may get a sneer when you inquire about a less expensive wine, but be brave. Remember, it's your money. The sad truth is that in American restaurants wine is almost always expensive, since it's priced on the same basis as hard liquor. In European restaurants, where wine is as basic to the meal as good bread, wine is priced much more reasonably. To pay $10 for dinner and $20 for a bottle of nice wine would be considered outrageous. Then, too, even in fairly snappy restaurants on the Continent, the house wine is likely to be very decent. But in American eateries, the house wine is often pathetic stuff that the proprietor buys for a song and marks up excessively—you are probably better off with an inexpensive bottle off the list. At least you will know what you're getting. (Again, there's no harm in inquiring as to what the house wine is—it may be a good deal.)

The most hopeful recent development in restaurants is wine by the glass. Many places now offer a selection of premium wines by the glass, which allows you to sample a wine you're not sure about, or to avoid ordering a whole bottle you're not sure you can drink. (But beware—the prices may still be steep, and several glasses may end up costing as much as a whole bottle.)

If the restaurant is without a wine steward, don't expect too much help from your regular waiter or waitress. These jobs turn over so quickly there is little opportunity for them to master a wine list.

A surprising number of upscale eateries keep, in addition to the stock of regular wines on the list, a small stash of special wines. If you see nothing on the list that interests you and would like something special, ask if there is a "captain's list" or any other wines available, and frequently you will be rewarded (though at a price). Best of all, of course, is to establish a regular relationship at a local restaurant, where they will come to know you as an appreciator of fine wine and will go out of their way to make sure you enjoy the best.

When you order wine, make your preferences clear. One of the justified complaints of wine stewards about customers is that they claim to like wines that they don't really enjoy. For example, people have been taught that it's chic to prefer "dry" wines, but many in fact like wine with a bit of sweetness. If the steward is told you want a "nice dry white, like Chenin Blanc," he may feel justifiably confused. Be honest—you'll be happier. And don't just stick with the best-known wines. Less popular wines are frequently better value and often more interesting. When you travel, sample the local wines. This may not work so well in Minneapolis or Miami, but good wine is being made in many parts of the country now, from New York to Maryland to Indiana to Missouri to Texas to Washington—take the opportunity to sample.

There is actually a purpose to some of the ceremony of restaurant wine service. The bottle should always be presented for your inspection before it is opened—more than once I have had to send something back because it was not what I ordered (a Ruffino Chianti Classico once instead of a Frescobaldi Chianti Rufin*a*, for example.) Make sure it's the vintage you thought it would be. When you have given the OK, the steward will open the bottle and present you with the cork. What you do with the cork is your own business, but I cannot see any earthly reason for this odd business. There is nothing to be discovered from the cork that can't be discovered in the bottle—and the cork may be moldy and crumbling but the wine within perfectly fresh. If you sniff the cork you will smell cork—I would prefer to sample the wine. One expert advises placing the cork carefully in the ashtray in the hopes it will be carted off. Best, perhaps, to do nothing at all. But do make sure, after the cork is extracted, that the waiter wipes the rim of the bottle with a clean cloth—otherwise a little mold or dirt may spoil your wine.

Whoever ordered the wine will get a small dash of it in his or her glass for sampling. This is the key moment. The sommelier will properly wait until you have given the go-ahead to pour. A quick sniff and a sip should allow you to tell whether the wine is potable. At this point, the bottle opened, it's not really fair to try the wine and decide you just don't care for it. You are looking only for ovious defects in the wine—a bad bottle, with a really foul taste. If such occurs, refuse the bottle. I have heard of instances when the manager himself has assured skeptical diners that a bottle was just fine when indeed it was not. My experience has always been much happier—once in a small French restaurant I had the owner catch a whiff of the wine she was serving me, frown, stick her nose right into the bottle, and march the offending wine away, muttering Gallic imprecations under her breath. Most restaurateurs will gladly furnish a fresh bottle.

At this point, when glasses have been poured all around (only halfway, mind you), the wine steward will leave you alone, if you are lucky. With the bottle on the table you ought to be able to serve yourself at your leisure. Unfortunately, some waiters, determined that you should order a second bottle, will continually "top you up"—and everyone at your table. This infuriates me. I hate having my glass too full, I hate anyone interfering in my dinner, and I hate people forcing liquor down anyone's else's throat. It's abominable and should be stopped by any means short of whacking the offender's hand with your dessert spoon.

Ice buckets are worth a word of warning. There are times when you may want a wine kept thoroughly chilled, but most wines, if they have been chilled ahead, will do just fine gradually warming up as they sit on the table. An ice bucket will keep many whites just too cold for their flavors really to come out (though it does keep champagne from going flat too quickly).

Lastly, I don't know about yours, but in my state it is now legal to take an unfinished bottle of wine home with you—a law that encourages sobriety as well as conservation of precious liquid resources. I feel no embarrassment at all in hauling my bottle of wine home. I just remember: I paid for it, I can do what I want with it.

• Serving Wine •

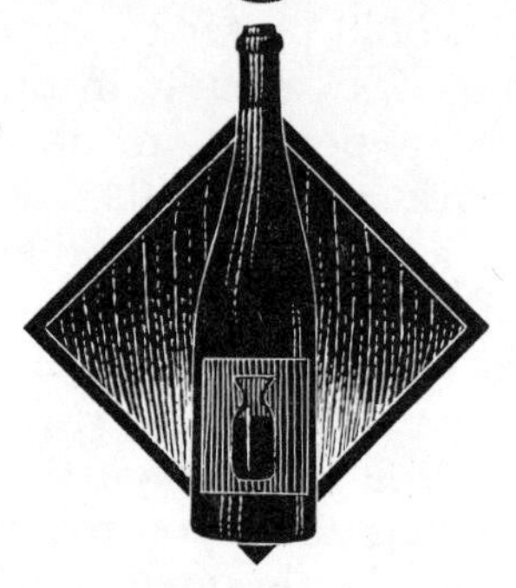

Let us assume you are putting on a small dinner party for, say, eight people. The table is set, the food, in several courses, is under preparation. Now you must deal with the wine. How many bottles will you need? Clearly that depends to some extent on who your guests will be, but I usually plan on a bottle for every two or three people—assuming there are no cocktails before dinner.

First minor crisis. Someone will appear at your door with an offering of wine. Best to thank the donor and whisk the wine away—if it seems appropriate, open it, but it's a gift and you can do with it what you want.

To chill or not to chill. Cold does two things for wine. It adds another component of taste sensation—the chill stimulates the palate just as sugar and acid do, but it also dulls the inherent flavors. Thus, inexpensive wines are often best quite cold—this adds some interest to them and serves to mask deficiencies of flavor.

White wines are traditionally chilled a bit before serving, though a common mistake is to overchill, so that the flavors are quite dead when the wine is opened. If a bottle is at room temperature, one hour in the refrigerator should get it adequately cold. The experts say never to put a bottle in the freezer, but I have done so frequently when pressed for time, with no ill effects (except when I have forgotten it was there.) In this case twenty minutes should be tops. Quicker still, as restaurants know, is a bath in a bucket of ice water (not just ice—it must be ice and water). There is no need to keep the wine cold during the meal. Place the chilled bottle on the table in a wine coaster or saucer, to catch drips, and let it warm up during the meal. This adds yet another dimension to the taste, as the flavors will open up and evolve as the temperature rises.

Red wines are traditionally served at "room" temperature. But one person's "room" is another's icebox, so if you like to keep your house very warm, you may want to consider putting a slight chill on your reds. And many reds do very nicely slightly cold, particularly young, fresh, fruity ones like Beaujolais or Gamay, or a light Zinfandel.

With the number of handy corkscrews on the market now, there's really no excuse for not being able to open a bottle of wine. (Special mention must be made of the Screwpull corkscrew, which requires not even a semblance of skill.) A note on mold: Many bottles, especially if they've been in storage for a time, will have a thin layer of mold between lead cap and cork. This means nothing either good or bad for the wine, but take care to wipe it off from the rim of the bottle before the wine is served, so it doesn't get into the wine as you pour.

Opening a bottle of champagne does require a bit of know how. Shooting a cork into the ceiling or into your mother-in-law's lap may get a dull party off the ground, but is best done with cheap wine. A far more impressive effect is achieved, I think, by removing a champagne cork in front of a crowd cowering behind their napkins with a gentle twist and soft pop—it can be done. The wine needs to be well chilled (which also ensures longer-lasting bubbles). Take a small cloth and wrap it around the neck and cork (not your neck, the bottle's). Tilt the bottle away from you and, keeping a firm hold on the cork, twist (don't pull) it gently. The natural force of the gas will ease the cork out effortlessly into the cloth—and the wine is ready to pour. (Unfortunately, this doesn't work with plastic champagne corks, which are notoriously hard to budge. A vice-grip may come in handy.)

If you are suffering from an advanced case of wine snobbery, you will be interested in decanting the wine. There are two authentic reasons for decanting, that is, pouring the wine into a decanter, which can be any clean, glass receptacle. The first occurs when the cork breaks, disintegrates, or slips into the wine instead of coming out of the bottle. There are handsome and ingenious devices for retrieving lost corks, but simpler still is merely pouring the wine into a decanter and leaving the cork to its fate. The second reason is when a red wine has thrown a sediment—deposited a muddy layer of "fallout" from the wine onto the side and bottom of the bottle. This stuff is perfectly natural but not very appetizing, and by gently pouring off the wine, you can get all but the last finger or so into a new container of clear wine. If you really must put on a show, light a candle and hold the neck of the bottle in front of it so you can see exactly when the sediment begins to reach the lip of the bottle.

The issue of decanting leads naturally to a discussion of wine's "breathing." A less charming term for this process is oxidation, which is really a process of decay brought on by the contact of wine with air. All wines oxidize, eventually to their detriment, but for some wines, especially full-bodied red wines, oxidation helps the flavors develop, especially the "bouquet" of the wine. There are a number of schools of thought on this point. Some experts say you must open a red wine hours before serving it to allow that crucial interaction of wine and air. Others argue that simply uncorking the wine does very little, and that if you want any action you had best decant the wine, which allows more mixing of air into fluid. Others warn that opening a fully matured wine, or decanting it, will allow the precious and delicate bouquet already developed to escape. And still others, born skeptics, insist none of this makes any difference—open and drink the bottle when you are ready.

All of this has the feel of eighteenth-century medicine—a lot of profound and rational theories based on very little concrete evidence. So the best advice is probably to do whatever suits you. What you will discover is that most red wines (and all of this concerns reds rather than whites) do change and develop in the glass, where they are really exposed to the elements. Often a rather hard-flavored and simple-smelling Cabernet, for example, will blossom in the glass and reveal softer and more complex scents of herbs and spices. More than once, I have tasted an unfinished bottle opened the day before, expecting it to have deteriorated badly, and discovered instead that it was now better. This is part of the wonder of wine, but whether it is enhanced by early opening of the bottle is still to be proved. (Incidentally, don't worry about any of this for jug wines, which have been heavily processed to make them stand up to prolonged exposure to air.)

Now we're ready to eat and drink. The bottles should be on the table. As host you may want to make the first pour, filling the glasses no more than halfway. This allows the bouquet of the wine to be concentrated in the glass, so that your nose can get the full effect. (How many times have I poked the end of my nose into the wine itself and come up gasping for breath.) But then invite your guests to help themselves thereafter—this way no one gets more wine than he or she really wants. For heaven's sake, don't keep the wine on the sideboard or out in the kitchen. I well remember an elegant dinner at the home of an elderly friend who poured me a small glass of wine and then left the bottle on the sideboard directly behind my head and promptly forgot all about it. I couldn't bring myself to get up and fetch it, and no amount of commenting on the wine or toying discreetly with my empty glass could attract her attention. It's unfair to make guests beg.

A quick trick on pouring: To avoid having a drop or two of wine fall on the tablecloth as you are pouring, make a slight turn of the bottle with your wrist as you finish the pour, and the wine will stay in place.

It's always difficult to know what kind of wine to serve your guests. If you are entertaining your boss or a client, it's probably best to stick to well-known, popular brands—even if he doesn't like it he can't really fault you. Large family feasts are not the time to serve your best wines. The attention won't be on the wine anyway, so stick with a fairly simple red or white. If you are inviting a known wine snob to dinner and are feeling intimidated, buy an obscure and inexpensive bottle at your wineshop—you may get points for being adventuresome.

It is with a few close friends or with just my wife that I most enjoy sharing my best bottles—they know that I appreciate good wine and make an effort to do the same.

—FATHER CORBET CLARK

WINEGLASSES FROM THE FRUGAL GOURMET'S KITCHEN

The above glasses are typical of a serious wine lover's collection, though you certainly do not need them all.

1. Bordeaux, 24 ounces
2. Burgundy, 16 ounces
3. White, 9 ounces
4. All-purpose, 8 ounces
5. Sherry, 5 ounces
6. Champagne Tulip
7. Champagne Trumpet
8. American Champagne

Start your collection with the 8-ounce all-purpose. Later, add the 9-ounce white. You can serve anything in those two glasses. The advantage of the larger glasses is that you will have room to swirl and smell the wine. The sherry glass is probably next, and then, when you are feeling smart, buy a set of champagne glasses. Avoid that silly American champagne. The glass so spreads out the champagne that the bubbles are lost and the wine spills on the floor.

WINE BOTTLES

Above are the most common shapes of wine bottles, and you can tell immediately what wine is being offered simply by looking at the shape of the bottle.

1. Bordeaux—classic Cabernet and Claret
2. Burgundy—lighter reds, such as Petite Sirah and Beaujolais, and whites such as Chablis
3. German or Alsatian whites
4. Champagne

CORKSCREWS

The corkscrews below are all from my own collection. All work, sooner or later, but some are much easier to use than others.

Please note that you need to avoid a solid "screw" such as the twin lever. If you cannot put a wooden match up into the center of the helix or core of the turned-wire corkscrew, you will be in trouble. The solid screw often just pulls itself out of the cork. The open-wire or heavy-helix corkscrews will grab onto the cork and offer a much better grip.

The twin-blade cork puller is fun to use, but it takes some practice. The Screwpull is hot on the market at the moment, but I just broke mine trying to open a simple California white. It fell apart. Stick with the wooden twin screw and you will have little trouble.

—JEFF SMITH

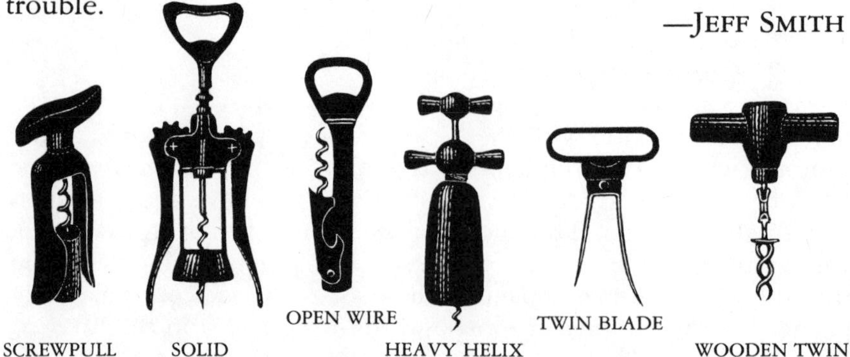

INDEX

Also available from William Morrow

THE FRUGAL GOURMET

JEFF SMITH

Jeff Smith's cookbook from his first public television series spent more than a year on the *New York Times* best-seller list and has sold more than 800,000 copies. With over 400 recipes from a rich assortment of international cuisines, including many low-salt and low-fat dishes, *The Frugal Gourmet* shows what *frugal* really means: getting the most out of your time, your money, and your kitchen.

Available at your local bookstore